SOMETHING ABOUT KIERKEGAARD

David F. Swenson

SOMETHING ABOUT
KIERKEGAARD

BY

DAVID F. SWENSON

EDITED BY
LILLIAN MARVIN SWENSON

FOREWORD TO THE
ROSE EDITION BY
MARY CARMAN ROSE

Mercer University / ROSE
Press
Macon, Ga. 31207

ISBN 0-86554-084-5

Something About Kierkegaard, by David F. Swenson,
originally was published by
Augsburg Publishing House, Minneapolis,
in 1941; revised and enlarged edition, in 1945;
and is reproduced as a ROSE edition by
permission of the original publisher.

The ROSE edition is copyright © 1983 by
Mercer University Press, Macon GA 31207.

MUP/ROSE . . . . . February 1983.

[Photomechanically reproduced from the original pages
by Omnipress of Macon, Inc., Macon GA;
with added ROSE design and text copy as composed by
Omni Composition Services, Macon GA;
Haywood Ellis, designer, MUP;
Janet Middlebrooks, assistant director, OCS.]

All Mercer University Press books are produced on acid-
free paper that exceeds the minimum standards set by the
National Historical Publications and Records Commission.

Library of Congress Cataloging in Publication Data

Swenson, David F. (David Ferdinand), 1876-1940.
    Something about Kierkegaard.

    Reprint. Originally published: Minneapolis:
Augsburg Publishing House, 1945.
    Bibliography: p. 254
    Includes index.
    1. Kierkegaard, Søren, 1813-1855.   I. Swenson,
Lillian Marvin.   II. Title.
B4377.S8   1983   198'.9   83-998
ISBN 0-86554-084-5

TABLE OF CONTENTS

I want honesty, neither more nor less. I stand neither for Christian severity nor for Christian mildness; I stand solely and simply for common human honesty.

SØREN KIERKEGAARD

DAVID F. Swenson (1878-1940), professor of philosophy at the University of Minnesota until 1939, "discovered" Kierkegaard and introduced the venerable Dane to English-speaking students of philosophy. Swenson, a Danish-reading Swede, chanced upon a copy of *Concluding Unscientific Postscript* on the shelves of a local library in the spring of 1898 while he was a graduate assistant at Minnesota. He thereupon did little else (for a Saturday night and Sunday) until he had read the entire *Postscript,* swallowing it, as he was wont to say, "at a single gulp." Swenson's discovery of Kierkegaard for himself led him to resolve to devote his career to the task of making Kierkegaard available in translation to the English-speaking world, a resolve that was curtailed only by his death.

Convinced of the genius of Kierkegaard, Swenson set about the task of learning as much as he could about the man and his works. Then in 1914, in a course on "Great Thinkers of the Nineteenth Century" (University of Minnesota), Swenson lectured on Kierkegaard, evidently the first public address on Kierkegaard in this country.

In December 1916 Swenson read a paper before the American Philosophical Association meeting in Philadelphia—"The Anti-Intellectualism of Kierkegaard," subsequently published in the *Philosophical Review* (1916), and reprinted as chapter 5 in the present volume. This paper is still one of the best general introductions to Kierkegaard.

Swenson faithfully carried out his resolve to make Kierkegaard known as widely as his influence would reach in the English-speaking world. In the foreword to this ROSE edition one of his students tells of how well he did so in the classroom. Swenson demanded such scholarly perfection of himself, however, that he had not time to translate all of Kierkegaard; yet the works that he (and his wife, Lillian) did translate remain a standard of clarity and faithfulness to the originals by which all subsequent renderings of Kierkegaard must be judged. Likewise the collection of studies about Kierkegaard written by Swenson and collected by his wife under the unpretentious title *Something About Kierkegaard* remains a standard in the field.

Editor, MUP/ROSE
January 1983

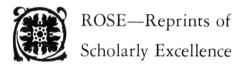 ROSE—Reprints of
Scholarly Excellence

Certain good books should be, like the rose, not only hardy perennials in their intrinsic worth and usefulness, but also perennial in their availability. The purpose of the ROSE series is to make available such choice books from the past that are not otherwise available.

ROSE is intended primarily to meet the needs of the university classroom. Volumes are included in the series upon the recommendation of professors in the classroom who indicate a need for a currently out-of-print text. When investigation indicates that a reprint is warranted and available, ROSE reprints the text in an attractive and durable, yet affordable, format—equal or even superior to the original in quality.

Roses come in many varieties. So do books in the ROSE series. ROSE is not restricted to any one subject area but will reprint classics from any and all classes—the humanities, the sciences, the arts. But each is a "rose" of a reprint—preeminent among its kind, rare, of scholarly excellence.

FOREWORD

IN his *Concluding Unscientific Postscript,* Kierkegaard has used as a heading for one of the chapters the expression, "Something about Lessing." The phrase is almost deceptive in its simplicity. It promises so little, and yet it is comprehensive enough to cover not only Kierkegaard's conception of the contribution made by Lessing to the history of philosophical thought, but also his own admiration for Lessing as a thinker. In the compilation of this small volume of interpretations of the thought of Søren Kierkegaard, I have ventured to paraphrase his own expression, and call it "Something about Kierkegaard," not because it is inclusive, but because it is unpretentious.

While Kierkegaard has long been recognized in continental Europe as one of the world's foremost thinkers, it is only recently that he is coming to be known by the English-reading public. His first work to be translated into English, the *Philosophical Fragments,* appeared only five years ago. Since then some eight or ten of his more important books have been published in English, with a prospect of more in the near future. As a result of this tardy recognition, English interpretations of Kierkegaard's thought and commentaries concerning it, have been practically non-existent, a condition which is bound to alter rapidly as he becomes better known, since his ideas are not only thought-provoking but frequently controversial in content. Meantime, the publication of this little book of interpretations, meagre though it is, seems justified, representing as it does a lifetime of devoted study on the part of its author. Four of the eight chapters have already appeared in philosophical journals; the first two chapters were used as the basis for more or less popular lectures delivered at various times. The remaining two were left in manuscript, and consequently lack the revision their writer would undoubtedly have wished to make before publishing them. One of them, the exposition of the doctrine of sin, while complete in itself, was designed as the central theme of a much longer paper, of which only the outline was finished. While I am conscious of the fact that there is a certain overlapping, particularly in the first two chapters, it seemed unwise to attempt radical alterations, even if I had been competent to make them.

As all of the papers included were written before any English translations had appeared, the references in the footnotes were of course to the Danish edition of Kierkegaard's works. As far as possible, I have adapted these to the English translations now available, and hence where the reader finds a reference to a Danish title, it means that it is not yet available in English. In the references to *The Journals,* found in the chapter on the Press, the page references are immediately followed by the number of the paragraph to which the citation refers. The first two chapters, which had been used as addresses, had not been annotated. Since they include rather copious quotations, I have attempted to indicate the source of the quotations for the benefit of the interested reader, although a few of these I have failed to locate.

I wish to express my appreciation to *The International Journal of Ethics, The Journal of Philosophy,* and *The Philosophical Review,* for courteous permission to reprint; to the Oxford University Press, for permission to use three excerpts from *The Journals of Søren Kierke-gaard,* translated by Alexander Dru; and to the Augsburg Publishing House, for kind and helpful cooperation.

LILLIAN MARVIN SWENSON.

FOREWORD TO THE SECOND EDITION

SINCE the publication of *Something About Kierke-gaard* in 1941, English translations of nearly all of Søren Kierkegaard's most important works have become available to the public. There now remain only two volumes of the *Edifying Discourses* and the *Works of Love,* and these are to be published in the near future. Consequently it is now possible to refer the reader to the English instead of the Danish versions of the individual works. In many cases where direct quotations are used in the present volume, the reader will not find them identical in form with the published translations, since they were translated by the author many years before anything of Kierkegaard was available in English, and frequently give a better idea of Kierkegaard's characteristic poetic feeling than do the later translations.

This book was first published in the hope that its interpretations of various phases of Kierkegaard's thought, which had been the outgrowth of a lifetime spent by its author in a serious and devoted effort to appropriate his teachings, might have value for those just beginning their acquaintance with Søren Kierkegaard. In this second edition two chapters are added: one, which follows Chapter II, offers a brief literary resumé of Kierkegaard's works. This was written for *Scandinavian Studies* in 1921 (by whose kind permission it is included in the present volume) , and was, if I am not mistaken, the first extended critical discussion in English of the great Danish philosopher's work. As in the case of the first two chapters, there was a certain overlapping, inevitable since they were written at different times and for different purposes, but, as far as possible, the purely biographical portions have been eliminated, and references to quotations already used in the preceding chapters have been given, instead of repeating them *in extenso*. The other chapter, now the concluding one, is made up of extracts from letters discussing translation problems, unpublished papers, and comment on questions submitted to the author by various individuals interested in Kierkegaard's thought and teaching. Characterized as these are by a certain directness and informality impossible in a set paper, those who have read them have felt that this fact gives them a certain additional pertinency. I deeply appreciate the kindness of the individual recipients of these communications in having made their inclusion possible by returning the material to me.

THE EDITOR

FOREWORD TO THE ROSE EDITION

D AVID F. Swenson, himself a graduate of the University of Minnesota, taught philosophy at that institution from 1898, when he became a teaching assistant in the Department of Philosophy, until the close of the academic year 1938-1939. My reflections on Swenson as teacher and scholar derive from my experience as his student during the last years of his teaching career. I wish, however, to begin this introduction with some observations concerning the source of this volume and the importance of Swenson's interpretations of the existentialism of Søren Kierkegaard for twentieth-century philosophy. These observations derive from my four decades of teaching, writing, and studying philosophy and my watching the tensions and dynamics of philosophical inquiry during this period.

• 1 •

In chapter 1 of *Something About Kierkegaard* Swenson tells of his discovery of Søren Kierkegaard as a major philosophical-religious thinker. He often told this story to his students, adding that upon making this discovery he resolved to devote his career to the translation of Kierkegaard's works into English. Swenson was faithful to that resolve and worked indefatigably on the translations until the spring of 1939 when, at age 61, he suffered a severe stroke from which he never recovered. Yet when he died in the spring of 1940, his translation project was far from finished; for, as I will emphasize below, being a perfectionist in his scholarship, he worked very slowly. After Swen-

son's death, his wife, Lillin Marvin Swenson, learned
Danish and saw some of the translations through publication. She also brought out two volumes of Swenson's essays
and lectures: *Something About Kierkegaard,* and *Kierkegaardian Philosophy in the Faith of a Scholar* (Westminster
Press, 1940).

A word concerning Swenson's attitude toward his role as
translator and interpretor of Kierkegaard's creativity will
be illumining here. As Swenson's commentaries on Kierkegaard are again made available it is important to emphasize
the fact that anyone who knew him could have detected the
boundless care and intended precision with which he
worked. Swenson never lost sight, moreover, of Kierkegaard's avowal that he wrote out of the depth of his own
ever developing and deepening Christian commitment; and
Swenson repeatedly told of his aspiration to make that
spiritual path his own. Thus, in his translating and commenting on the works of Kierkegaard, Swenson drew con-
tinuously and with great caution on his own existential
understanding of philosophical-religious convictions which
he had built upon Kierkegaard's thought. Since Swenson's
death, other theological and philosophical thinkers who
were less personally involved with Kierkegaard's spirituality and perhaps influenced by secular interpretations of
either Kierkegaard or Christianity or philosophical inquiry
have provided translations and commentaries on Kierkegaard different from those provided by Swenson. To be
sure, any student of Kierkegaard's creativity may find any or
all of these diverse views of Kierkegaard useful. At the very
least, even those interpretations with which we disagree
become helpful in our own work if we think through the
reasons for our disagreement with them. Nonetheless,

Swenson's commentaries on Kierkegaard like his translations are of central importance in our present-day understanding of the content of Kierkegaard's writing and of his
intention in his creativity. Swenson's interpretations and
translations are always noteworthy. Having observed at
firsthand his deep commitment to high standards of scholarship and intellectual integrity, I believe that I possess
ample evidence that his philosophical and religious reflection was never merely idiosyncratic and that he was incapable of being careless.

• 2 •

Søren Kierkegaard has been called the "first existentialist." However fruitful that perspective on Kierkegaard and
on existentialism may be, the fact is that Swenson was
drawing attention to the work of Kierkegaard at least a
decade before the term *existentialism* was widely used in
American philosophical circles. A course in contemporary
philosophy taught at the University of Minnesota during
Swenson's last year of teaching there featured the thought
of John Dewey, Henri Bergson, Samuel Alexander, C. Lloyd
Morgan, and Bertrand Russell. To be sure, during the late
1930s in the Midwestern academic milieu, there was no lack
of the logical empiricism that had its roots in selected
strains of the early thought of Ludwig Wittgenstein. Professor George P. Conger, who taught the course in contemporary philosophy did not, however, deem it necessary to
mention either logical empiricism or Wittgenstein in his
lectures. At that time, moreover, the work of Edmund
Husserl and Martin Heidegger and the term *phenomenology* were not yet central concerns in the teaching of philosophy in America.

When, some years after Swenson's death, existentialism and phenomenology became dominant in the investigation and teaching of philosophy in this country, they ushered in a family of philosophical views which were not significantly like the existentialism created by Kierkegaard and introduced into American thought by Swenson. There are now in existence two kinds of existentialism, usually known as "religious existentialism" and "atheistic existentialism." The question concerning the relations between these two types of existentialism will repay examination, and I suggest that the following is an appropriate, fruitful way of distinguishing between them.

The existentialism that became dominant in American philosophy was in large part the atheistic thought of Sartre and Camus with its roots in the existentialism of Nietzsche and in the interpretation of the nature of philosophical inquiry as proclaimed by Husserl and the highly specific type of ontologically oriented phenomenology of Heidegger. And of course the types of phenomenology which have become dominant in American philosophy likewise have their roots in the work of Husserl and Heidegger. Thus, twentieth-century French existentialism, which is aggressively opposed to Western monotheistic interpretations of man and his relation to reality, has presuppositions pertaining to ontology, the meaning of reality and truth, and the loci and source of what can possess authentic value for the individual. Thus, any phenomenological inquiry carried on within the perspective of atheistic French existentialism has a prior orientation by virtue of its presuppositions pertaining to all the most fundamental philosophical issues.

The earlier existentialism of Kierkegaard, however, had an entirely different intent and has potentially an entirely

different role within philosophical inquiry. Central to Kierkegaard's existentialism is a desire to draw attention to his
conviction that beliefs pertaining to what constitutes a good
life must be appropriated (that is, accepted as one's life
commitment) in order to be assessed or even understood.
Aside from this conviction, which of course Kierkegaard
has in connection with Nietzsche, Sartre, and Camus, Kierkegaard's existentialism has no philosophical presuppositions, and in this he differs profoundly from the foregoing
three thinkers. Rather, Kierkegaard's aim is to make clear
the existential situation generated by many types of life
commitments. He explores, for example, the existential
situation of the esthete; of the person who devotes all his
energies to the cultivation of a particular talent; of a judge
with a deep ethical, albeit not Christian, commitment; and
of the orthodox Christian.

This existentialism generates its own distinctive phenomenological activity as is seen in Kierkegaard's exploration of the dynamics, values, ideals, commitments, tensions,
doubts, satisfactions, and modes of dealing with despair
which arise from the appropriation of diverse views of the
human condition and the human spirit. Thus, unlike
twentieth-century German phenomenology which has
shaped the existentialism of Sartre and Camus, the phenomenological inquiry implicit in Kierkegaard's thought is
a true observational and analytic dimension of philosophy,
intended to discern and report the de facto dynamics and
structure of any one existential situation. Like Socrates,
Kierkegaard also articulates and to some extent assesses the
philosophical beliefs that give rise to these existential situations which he examines. In addition, of course, Kierkegaard is arguing for the superiority of the existential
content that is born only of Christian faith. He leaves to his

"poet," however, the task of providing philosophical illumi-
nation and development of Christian teachings and of the
epistemological structure of Christian faith.

The foregoing characterization of Kierkegaard's Christian existentialism is necessary here because, as I have
suggested, American philosophical thinkers learned about
French existentialism before they had carefully examined
Kierkegaard's existentialism to which Swenson called
attention before French existentialism became a dominant
theme in American philosophy. Certainly Swenson's exposition of Kierkegaard's thought has not been widely influen-
tial in the interpretation or criticism of either religious or
atheistic existentialism. Rather, there has been a tendency
to assess and even to interpret the content of Kierkegaard's
thought in terms of features drawn from atheistic existentialism. An example of this is the willingness to follow
Sartre in defining existentialism in terms of rejection of
essentialism, even though Kierkegaard is at pains to elucidate the existential import of Christian essentialism—that
is, of the import in Christian spirituality of the "universally
human," as Swenson puts it. In fact, the irreducible differences between atheistic existentialism and that of Kierkegaard
are particularly clear in respect to their views on
essentialism.

Thus, the reprinting of *Something About Kierkegaard* at
this time is important and timely. It would, indeed, be
important at any time and place because Swenson possessed
a distinctive and extraordinarily penetrating insight concerning Kierkegaard. On the other hand, during the past
thirty years American thinkers and general readers have
had an opportunity to become acquainted with existentialism. At the beginning of this period there was considerable

curiosity and some bewilderment concerning the content, intellectual roles, and value of existentialism. That time has passed; although there is not now consensus on these issues. Rather, the curiosity has been replaced by several conflicting and firmly held opinions on them. Yet, despite this diversity, many agree that existentialism with its commitment to the study of the human situation, human experiences, and human ideals is properly seen as an essential element in philosophical inquiry. Perhaps, then, the time is right for a next step in existentialist studies: an explicit comparing, contrasting, and assessment of these diverse views of existentialism. The reprinting of this volume is timely because Swenson's commentaries on Kierkegaard are a major contribution to this project.

• 3 •

If as scholar Swenson was outstanding for his intellectual integrity and clarity, as teacher and friend he was also outstanding for his unstinting sharing of his gifts for philosophical reflection as well as for his spiritual presence in the classroom. In American education in recent years we have not paid enough attention to the spirituality of the teacher, particularly that of the person who teaches undergraduates. Yet the guidance of the pliant spirituality of these students is central to their educational needs. For some are in rebellion against their spiritual and intellectual upbringing. Others are seeking reaffirmation or development of the values they espouse, while still others are seeking new, deeper ideals and commitments.

Many students at the University of Minnesota found in Swenson's teachings and in his articulation of his own religious preferences and convictions support for their own

views which, as a rule, derived from their family back-
grounds. Some students, although I think only a few, were
impatient with what they interpreted as Swenson's belabor-
ing the differences between his view of philosophical
inquiry as well as his interpretation of human life and those
expressed, for example, in Bertrand Russell's "A Free Man's
Worship" and John Dewey's *Reconstruction in Philosophy.*
Other students were able to discern his intellectual and
spiritual stature while rejecting his Christian commitment.

From my personal experience as Swenson's student,
however, I know that his teaching could elicit still another
response and, further, a response that could become the
ground of an eventual religious conversion and could provide spiritual direction for a lifetime. Having had no religious upbringing I was in rebellion against no particular set
of religious teachings and brought none of my own to my
undergraduate education. Nor did I have any religious long-
ings, although I did have a spontaneous thirst for truth and a
great preference for truth seeking in the mathematical
sciences. Through Swenson's spiritual presence in the classroom, however, I became consciously aware that in him I
had found a person whose faith involved no insult to the
intellect and which I judged to be as valuable as it was
profound. It was many years before I was enabled, through
the experiences that life brought me, to develop my own
faith. Yet my memories of what I learned from Swenson
concerning spirituality, religious commitment, and faith
were essential instruments of my religious development.
What explains this powerful influence?

Swenson's spirituality exemplified Socrates' prayer at the
end of the "Phaedrus": "... may the outward and the inward
man be one." In this respect, Swenson's view of what it

meant to be a thinker was not typical of the views on this subject widely held in philosophical circles in his day. For, unlike many in his profession, Swenson took human life in both its actuality and its ideality as not only a legitimate but as an essential area of philosophical inquiry. This was in vivid contrast with the philosophical fashion coming into vogue at the end of Swenson's career in which philosophy was charged with analysis of language and inquiry but not with questions pertaining to human spiritual potentialities or to what constitutes the good life. Again, Swenson lived his philosophical as well as his religious convictions, and in the living of them he found opportunity for testing their existential worth and for strengthening and clarifying them.

Very important in Swenson's life as well as his thought was his emphasis on what he called "otherworldliness" and its "transformative power" within the individual's spirituality and hence his desires and his powers to work in the world. Shortly after Swenson's death, of course, the term "otherworldliness" became one of opprobrium. According to logical empiricism "otherworldliness" meant a philosophically illegitimate concern with words that have no cognitive meaning. For instrumentalism it named a nonscientifically based life-orientation. For Sartrian existentialism it meant an inauthentic choice of ideals. For the several forms of metaphysical naturalism it meant—and still means—at best, the choice of a view of reality and man which can survive philosophical scrutiny only if it is demythologized and, at worst, the irresponsible indulgence of a personal "failure of nerve." Swenson was using the term "otherworldliness," however, before the above-mentioned positions became dominant themes in American philosophy. For him "otherworldliness," grounded in Judeo-Christian transcendent theism with its personalistic conception of the divine, was the high point of understanding of human spiritual potentialities.

His commitment to this metaphysically grounded life-orientation was the source of existentially significant convictions which he often articulated in class and which some of his students (I do not know how many) came to cherish. Thus, he would not have accepted the secular concept of "rational love" which has as its correlative a justified "rational hate." Rather, he talked about an ideal: "Endeavor to love the unlovable for the sake of making it lovable." In a time of widespread acceptance of determinism he pointed out one facet of the existential ground of his own aspiration: "Any one who has faced the future with moral passion knows that he is free." He often spoke of his having learned at first hand that the most difficult experiences can be so appropriated that they become opportunities for spiritual awakening and hence for deepened commitment to one's work in the world. He often accompanied this with an expression of a wish for us: "I hope that no one of you is ever so far out in life that you choose the religious as an alternative to despair." And it is clear that the expectation of eternal life was in no sense fundamentally the words of a creed or the conclusion of a philosophical argument. This expectation was for him an existential reality which leavened and gave meaning and depth to all aspects of his life. Taking note of the logical empiricist emphasis on experiential verification, he often said that eternity is the "true verification of otherworldly religion," of the significance of its ideals, and of its hope for everlasting life. Thus, otherworldliness for Swenson was not a flight from the realities of life nor an exclusive concern with one's own spiritual welfare. Rather, this Kierkegaardian otherworldliness wished for moral and spiritual development precisely for the sake of sustained service to the world. And its hope for eternal life was a source of strength undergirding and leavening that service.

The reprinting of *Something About Kierkegaard* is significant not only for philosophical inquiry but also for present-day and future work in theology and for our reflections on the goals of education. A part of its significance for theology is that it draws attention to the fact that central to any philosophical-religious position is the type of inwardness and spiritual development it fosters. Today we are faced with conflicting revisionist interpretations of Christian teachings, each of which in its own way either provides new language for the articulation of Christian beliefs or provides new meanings for traditional language—for example, "God," "faith," or "divine creativity." In this situation it is noteworthy that Kierkegaard, as Swenson reminds us, taught us to assess any interpretation of life in terms of the spirituality and commitment it produces. *Something About Kierkegaard* also has import for education. In the decades that I have taught in American institutions, I have repeatedly heard colleagues praised for the clarity and courage of their secular humanistic or atheistic stance. I have heard colleagues tell students that the "rational faith" that refuses to believe anything not clearly derived from empirical inquiry has set us free from Kierkegaard's "leap of faith" which is not so based. I wish to recall, however, the clarity, courage, and intense respect for the intellectual independence and integrity of his students with which Swenson confessed the deep roots of his own spiritual life. It was a mode of teaching and a message that have proved their great worth during the years; and as, paraphrasing Kierkegaard, Swenson often said, "The proof of the pudding is in the eating."

Finally, I wish to express my gratitude to Professor Robert L. Perkins for his sustained efforts in working for the reprinting of *Something About Kierkegaard* and to Professor Rex Stevens of Mercer University Press for making this reprinting possible.

Mary Carman Rose

I. SØREN KIERKEGAARD

AS an introduction to this paper, I wish to relieve myself of a personal feeling, a sense of gratitude and obligation. It is many years now since I first made acquaintance with the works of the remarkable man whose life and thoughts I shall seek to characterize in the present lecture. I was then a young graduate student in philosophy, earnestly wrestling with many problems far beyond my strength—a situation, I imagine, in which many young graduate students of philosophy find themselves. It was quite by accident that I one day picked up a Danish book from the shelves of a library, a book which seemed to have a philosophical content, since a hasty turning of its leaves showed me that its pages were liberally sprinkled with abstruse philosophical terms. The name of the author told me nothing, for I had never heard of Søren Kierkegaard. On a venture, I took the book home. It was Saturday evening, and I did not rise from the reading begun on reaching home, until half past two Sunday morning. By Sunday night I had finished the more than five hundred closely printed pages of the book, so impossible was it for me to lay it aside until I had finished it. It was not only a new philosophical book that accident had brought to my attention, but a new kind of philosophical book. Never before had I met with such mastery of dialectic, such superior ease in the handling of the most abstruse and difficult philosophical concepts; and never before had I met such resources of irony and wit, humor and pathos, or seen such lofty objectivity side by side with such passionate expression of enthusiasm and scorn. I did not wholly understand it at the first reading, nor indeed at the second or third, but the impression made upon my mind was none the less powerful because it was not entirely clear. Needless to say, from that time on I seized upon every book of Kierkegaard that I could lay my hands on; I read them and re-read them many times. In the years since then I have not outgrown that first indelible impression; I have found in his pages an increasing inspiration for the common tasks of life, as well as clearness and light upon a multitude of intellectual problems of the highest dignity, a matchless delineation of ideals in their ideality, as well as wonderful compass in the expression of humanly significant moods and feelings of every kind. I should even like to say more than this, but I dare not. For I seem to see Kierkegaard himself standing before me with a humorous twinkle in his eye, while he says to me in that ironical Socratic way of his: "My friend, have you really learned all this from me?" And I cannot help feeling that I should be compelled to hang my head in shame when I realized how small is the treasure I have really made my own out of all the wealth revealed in the pages of these books. Therefore I quit the dangerous ground of personal confession to pass over into the safer realm of objective narrative and characterization.

On the 5th of May, 1913, Denmark celebrated the centennial of the birth of Søren Kierkegaard. He died on the 11th of November, 1855, at the relatively early age of forty-two. Outwardly his life was quiet and uneventful; born in Copenhagen, he made that city his home and the scene of his prolific literary activities, and in Copenhagen he found his grave at the close of an exclusively literary life. Yet few personalities have lived with greater intensity, or won from their experiences a wisdom of more universal import for humanity. Kierkegaard illustrates in many ways the truth of that profound remark of Wordsworth's: "One being is elevated above another in proportion as he possesses the capacity to be excited to significant feeling without the application of gross and violent stimulants"; and he is a striking example of his oft-quoted principle that "the feeling therein developed gives importance to the action and situation, and not the action and situation to the feeling." Thus many an event in Kierkegaard's life, which in the case of another might have passed off without leaving a ripple on the surface, produced in his case storms that stirred his soul to the depths, and feelings that by the restless activity of his original mind were transmuted into the gold of an ethico-philosophical reflection of permanent significance. Some of his biographers treat this peculiarity as a mark of weakness. Wordsworth would have held it a mark of distinction, and considered its recognition tantamount to a eulogy.

Intellectually, Kierkegaard was an aristocrat of the aristocrats. He was initiated into the pleasures and refinements of a cultivated social life as that life tends to flower in the metropolis and seat of government. Yet his birth was thoroughly plebeian. His father was Michael Pederson Kierkegaard, a prosperous woolen merchant who had come to Copenhagen at the age of twelve from the heaths of Jutland, in order to seek his fortune. Already fifty-seven years old at the time of Søren's birth, the father had native traits of temperament and character, in addition to those incidental to his advanced age, which served to account for the sombre severity with which he trained his youngest child. Naturally imbued with a deep strain of melancholy, the father carried with him till his death the ruminating memory of an experience of his early childhood, while he was still herding sheep on the heath. Lonely and hungry and cold, he had one day mounted a hill and cursed God, who had given him so wretched a life. In Søren's papers for the year 1846, we find the following entry:

> The terrible fate of the man who as a small boy once mounted a hill and cursed God, because he was hungry and cold, and had to endure hardships while herding sheep . . . and that man found it impossible to forget this when he had reached the age of eighty-two.[1]

When this passage was shown to the elder brother, Bishop Peder Christian Kierkegaard, long after the death of Søren, the old man burst into tears, and said: "That is our father's history, and his sons', too." It is a testimony to the power and depth of the strain of melancholy in the Kierkegaard family that this event should have played so large a role in the relationship of father and son. Søren was twenty-five years old when he first became aware of this hidden source of his father's dark moods, and he refers to the revelation as "the great earthquake." In *Stages on the Way of Life,* we find the following imaginative rendering of this sad fellowship:

> There once lived a father and son. A son is a mirror in which the father sees himself reflected, and the father is also a mirror in which the son sees himself reflected as he will be in the future. But these two rarely contemplated one another thus, for their

---

[1]Dru, *The Journals of Søren Kierkegaard,* 150, §556.

daily intercourse was through a gay and lively conversation. But it sometimes happened that the father stopped and faced his son with saddened visage, let his eye dwell upon him, and said to him, "Poor boy, you are the victim of a silent despair!" Nothing more was ever said, either of what this meant, or of how true it might be. The father thought that he was the cause of his son's melancholy, and the son thought it was he who had caused his father so much grief—but never a word was exchanged between them on the subject.[2]

The father sought refuge in a severe and pietistic religious discipline, which stamped itself upon the family life, and made its deepest impression upon the lively imagination of the boy Søren. "As a child," says Kierkegaard, "I was strictly and most severely trained in the Christian religion. Humanly speaking, this bringing up was a species of madness, for my earliest childhood was made to groan under impressions too heavy even for the melancholy old man who laid them upon me."[3] And again, "I have never enjoyed the happiness of being a child."[4] And still again, "To force the life of a child into conformity with decisive Christian categories, is to offer it violence, be the attempt ever so well meant."

Nevertheless, the mad and well-meant attempt served only to bind the son still closer to the father in the ties of a passionate filial piety. It is moving to note the stereotyped regularity with which each succeeding volume of Kierkegaard's religious addresses was inscribed "To my deceased Father, Michael Pederson Kierkegaard, formerly a woolen merchant here in town."

But it was not only an undertone of religious melancholy which Søren inherited from his hypochondriac father. Successful in his business, the father had retired from its active management at the age of forty, and devoted himself assiduously to reading and study; it was with especial zeal that he applied himself to the works of Christian Wolff, a German philosopher, well known as Kant's prototype for the dogmatist. He was endowed with an unusual talent for disputation, and a strong and vivid imagination. In his family he was something of a martinet, and Søren learned from him the virtues of punctuality, order, and absolute obedience. The following quotation, from the second part of *Either-Or*, is undoubtedly based upon Kierkegaard's personal memories:

> I joined the other boys at school, and heard with astonishment that they complained of their teachers; I saw with the utmost surprise that a pupil was taken out of school because he could not hit it off with his teacher. Had I not already been so thoroughly disciplined, such an experience might have had a demoralizing influence upon me. But as it was, I was protected. I knew that it was my business to attend school, and to attend the school to which I had once been sent. Though all things changed, this could not change. It was not only fear of my father's severity that gave me this impression, but a high and lofty conception of my duty. If my father had died, and I had been placed under the guardianship of some one whom I could have influenced to take me out of school, I should never have dared or even desired to do so; for I had received so strong an impression of the infinitude of man's duty, that no lapse of time could have erased the memory of the fact that I had disobeyed his will.[5]

On account of his physical frailty, and consequent lack of ability to participate in the more violent sports of the playground, and also because of a certain old-fashioned peculiarity in the clothing which his father provided for him, Søren was frequently the butt of the practical jokes

---

[5]*Either-Or*, II, 224

of his companions. When brought to bay, he would attack his tormentors with a stinging tongue-lashing, armed as he was, even in boyhood, with the powers of satire and wit. This revenge he frequently purchased at the cost of a severe physical beating. Though a studious boy, he did not impress his companions with the remarkable gifts he was later to show the world; his chief forte was in Latin composition. In Danish, on the contrary, he showed no unusual proficiency, and Professor Holst, the poet, relates that he used to write Kierkegaard's Danish themes for him in return for Kierkegaard's services in writing the Latin compositions for him; he further states that he really translated into Danish, Kierkegaard's first book, a criticism of Hans Christian Andersen as a novelist, which Kierkegaard had written in a curious Latin-Danish language, full of participles and involved constructions. It therefore aroused general surprise among his schoolmates, when almost at the very inception of Kierkegaard's literary career, the superior excellence of his Danish style received such prompt and general recognition.

Kierkegaard's preparatory school course was completed at the age of seventeen. In the letter of dismissal written by the principal of the Latin school, he was described as late in coming to maturity, possessed of an almost inordinate desire for freedom and independence, having excellent natural gifts, but lacking in seriousness of purpose; his nature is characterized as "very gay and frank." This rather remarkable view should be compared with an entry in Kierkegaard's journal, for the year 1837: "I am a *Janus bifrons*, with one face I laugh, and with the other

I weep.''[6] Certain it is that he possessed a very strong impulse to exercise his powers in the play of wit and intellectual gymnastics, and that he frequently conveyed the impression of unbounded gayety and irresponsibility. This was a reaction from his melancholy and served in some degree to conceal it. At the University of Copenhagen he studied philosophy and theology, indulging his intense craving for reflection in many different directions, but it was many years before he found himself.

Kierkegaard's father wished him to follow in the footsteps of his elder brother and enter the church, but he made no very definite progress in this direction as long as his father lived. He entered into the social life of Copenhagen, playing the role of a rich man's richly gifted son. This period of his life he later came to look back upon with penitence, as a period of demoralization, but there is no evidence to show that he ever gave himself up to the coarser forms of dissipation. From the year 1833 on, the entries in his diary indicate that he was much interested in the great mythical personifications of medieval times—Faust the doubter, Don Juan, the incarnation of sensuality, and The Wandering Jew.[7] Mozart's opera, *Don Juan,* was at that time frequently to be heard in Copenhagen, and Kierkegaard was intensely stirred by it. "In a certain sense," he writes, "I can repeat as my own what Elvira says about Don Juan, and call him the 'murderer of my happiness'; for in truth, this opera has laid hold of me with such diabolical power that I can never forget it; it has driven me, like Elvira, out of the deep shades of the cloister."[8] After having worked on the idea of Faust several years, he makes the following entry

[6]Dru: *Journals,* 47, §140.
[7]*Ibid.,* 26, §49.
[8]*Ibid.,* 76, §296.

in his diary: "How unhappy I am! Martensen has just
written an essay on Lenau's *Faust*."[9] In his esthetic writings, however, there are many echoes of these early studies, notably the criticism of Mozart's *Don Juan* in the
first part of *Either-Or*,[10] and the tremendous figure of
The Seducer in the same volume.[11] During this period
he also tried his hand at writing political satire for the
newspapers. In 1836, a series of three articles was published in Heiberg's *Intelligencer* over the signature of
Kierkegaard, in which he attacked the anonymous re-
formers who wrote in the liberal papers to demand freedom of the press. But he could find no abiding interest
in anything in this period, least of all in politics. He suffered much physical and mental anguish, of which his
journals give us vivid glimpses. He asks himself:

What shall I do? Shall I publish my suffering to the world,
and still further augment the evidence for the wretchedness and
sadness of the times, perhaps discover a new dark spot in human
life, not hitherto brought to the attention of men? I might even
earn renown thereby, like the man who discovered the spots on
the sun. If my whole treasure be but a Pandora's box, would
it not be better for the world and myself if I never opened it?[12]

From the entries in the year 1835, written at the age
of twenty-two, I select the following analysis of his personal situation in the realms of thought:

I cannot deny that the natural scientists have made a most
beneficent impression upon me. They strive to find the Archi-
medean point not to be found in the world. The peace, harmony
and joy realized by these men is elsewhere rarely to be found. I
have always been enthusiastic about the natural sciences, and am
so still, yet it seems to me that I cannot make them my principal

---

[9]Dru: *Journals*, 41, §106.
[10]*Either-Or* I, 37 ff.
[11]*Ibid.*, I, 251 ff.
[12]*Ibid.*, I, 22.

study. It is the life of the spirit, life as lived in the power of reason and freedom, that engages my deepest interest, and my wish has always been to explain and solve its riddles. . . . Theology seems to be the field that lies nearest to my heart, but here I meet with great difficulties. Within Christendom itself, I am confronted with such great contrasts that a calm and free survey is rendered very difficult. Orthodoxy, I have grown up in, so to speak, but as soon as I began to think for myself, the huge Colossus began to totter. Rationalism, on the whole, seems to cut rather a sorry figure. It receives its essential coloring through Christianity, and yet tries to stand on another footing. It does not constitute a system but rather a Noah's ark into which the clean and the unclean animals are crowded side by side. . . . Its procedure resembles that of Cambyses in his campaign against the Egyptians, when he sent the sacred fowls and cats before him, but, like the Roman consul, it is ready to throw the sacred fowls overboard when they refuse to eat. The trouble is that it bases itself upon the Scriptures when they are in agreement with it, but otherwise not, and thus we get two heterogenous standpoints. . . .

What I really want is clearness with respect to *what I ought to do,* not what I ought to know, except in so far as knowledge must precede every action. I need to understand my place in life, what God really wants me to do; I must find the truth which is a truth for me (for then first does a man receive inner experience) ; I want to find *the Idea for which I can live and die.* And what would it profit me if I found the so-called objective truth if it had *no* deeper significance *for myself and for my life?*[13]

After reviewing in turn the prospects of jurisprudence and the stage, he returns to his main theme:

In order to live a complete human life, and not merely a life of knowledge, I need something which I still lack, something that shall be intimately connected with the deepest roots of my existence, something that shall unite me with the divine, something to which I could cling if the whole world collapsed. This is what I want, and this is what I strive to attain.[14]

---

[13]Dru: *Journals,* 6-8, §16; 15, §22.
[14]*Ibid.,* 16, §22.

The inclusion of this long selection may be pardoned in view of the light it throws upon the universality of our philosopher's orientation. We see here, also, the energy with which even thus early, he grasps what was to be the fundamental idea of his message to the world, viz., that the truth is—not the truth, but the individual's relation to the truth—not objective, but subjective.

While Kierkegaard was a student at Copenhagen, philosophy was represented at the University by F. C. Sibbern and P. M. Møller, men of personal weight and force of character, with whom Kierkegaard became very friendly and intimate. The Hegelian philosophy was represented in Denmark by J. L. Heiberg, a critic and dramatic poet, the unquestioned literary leader of the day. Converted to the Hegelian system of philosophy during a short sojourn in Germany, Heiberg had become an enthusiastic exponent of the philosophy that, for the rising generation of students at least, was to be the ruling fashion. Kierkegaard read Hegel, of course, and with great avidity. He translated the hardest passages into Danish, in order to make them clearer to himself, and he read and re-read the *Logic* over and over again. Both his philosophical style and his terminology show the influence of Hegel, but he was never able to acknowledge the validity of Hegel's central idea. He freed himself gradually from the dominating influence that the great name of the German master had exerted upon his youthful and enthusiastic mind, and was destined to give to the world the most thoroughgoing and absolutely destructive criticism that the Hegelian philosophy has, to my knowledge, ever received.[15]

---

[15]*Unscientific Postscript*, 99-108, *et passim*.

In 1838 Kierkegaard's father died. The event made a deep impression upon him, roused the religious life within him, and became, among other things, the signal for a concentration upon his theological studies. As long as his father lived, he had shown little inclination to enter the service of the church; now that his father was dead, it became a pious duty for him at least to take his theological degree, for as he said, "You cannot dispute with a dead man." In 1840 he became a candidate in theology.

In the meantime he had published a little book in criticism of Hans Christian Andersen. Andersen had written a novel, *Kun en Spillemand,* the theme of which was that unfortunate and untoward circumstances frequently combine to crush out the genius of youth. This was more than Kierkegaard could stand, and he replied by presenting a thoroughgoing criticism of Andersen's literary personality, hurling at him the passionate assertion that "What goes to wrack and ruin in Andersen's novel is not a genius, but a sorry wretch who Andersen assures us is a genius." Some time later Andersen answered by writing a farce in which he makes a comic Hegelian figure recite a few passages out of Kierkegaard's little book. The following from the diary may serve as an example of Kierkegaard's polemic style:

One moment, Mr. Andersen! They tell the story of Till Eulenspiegel, that he was once sent to town by his mistress to buy ten pennyworth of vinegar. He was three years on the way. Toward the end of the third year, he stumbled in at the door, broke the flask, and spilled the vinegar, crying, "Well, well. This haste is surely of the devil!" In somewhat the same way, to my no little fright, Mr. Andersen now comes rushing into the literary world with about ten pennyworth of polemics, which he has, I suppose, been carefully gathering during the two years since I wrote my little piece, and acted upon the unlucky idea that is now so ruthlessly punished.

A year after having passed his theological examination, he presented his doctor's dissertation: *"On the Concept Irony, with Especial Reference to Socrates."* This essay is an important contribution to our understanding of the Athenian Sage, and reveals Kierkegaard as an independent and original thinker. He had chosen this subject because of a certain kinship with Socrates which the progress of his thinking had begun to make him feel, and which he continued with increasing intensity to feel as long as he lived. The concentration of Socrates' philosophical interests upon the field of the moral life, and his consequent desertion of the natural sciences; the adoption and artistic development of an indirect maieutic method, the Socratic questioning, the keen desire to maintain some sort of relation with every man, no matter how plain and simple, which drove Socrates to philosophize in the streets and in the market place, with shoemakers and tanners as well as with Alcibiades; the ironical attitude of Socrates toward the arrogant pride of knowledge displayed by the Sophists, and the still deeper irony of his know-nothingness; analogies to all these motives were powerfully operative in Kierkegaard's mind and life. "There was once a young man," says an entry in the *Journal,* "endowed with the rich gifts of an Alcibiades; he sought among his contemporaries for a Socrates to give him instruction and training, but all in vain. Nevertheless, the gods heard his prayer, and he was himself transformed into a Socrates."[16]

But he had not yet fully come to his own. He was first

---

[16]Dru: *Journals,* 111, §414.

to live through a bitter personal experience which served to give his life definite momentum and direction. On the tenth of September, 1840, he became engaged to Regina Olson, the eighteen-year-old daughter of a good family, her father a government official. She was pretty, happy, and bubbling over with life; and she worshipped Kierkegaard. But Kierkegaard himself soon began to notice that there was something amiss. Not that he did not love her —entries in his *Journals* for the last year of his life, show what depths of tender feeling surged up within his soul at the memory of her. But he was scarcely fitted for wedded life, least of all to be the husband of a child of sunshine and fortune. As Brandes says: "The mere mention of the engagement sounds strangely in our ears. It is as if some one said: 'On such and such a day, in such and such a year, Saint Simeon Stylites stepped down from his column, offered his arm to a young lady, and invited her to step up with him on the top of the column in order to share with him his narrow standing-room.' "

Kierkegaard was terrified to find that he had made a mistake. He was astonished to find that he was happier in thinking about her while absent, or in writing to her, than in her physical presence. She had awakened and given form to poetic faculties within him, but he had long lived too spiritually not to find her physical presence an embarrassing surplus. The whole relation between them was transubstantiated, and surcharged with an atmosphere of reminiscence in the spirit of Paul Møller's beautiful lines:

> There comes a dream from the springtime of youth
> To me in my easy chair,
> And a tender longing steals over me,
> O rarest of women, rare!

But the worst obstacle was his melancholy, and the constant physical and mental suffering to which he was subjected. We know very little of the nature of the disease which held him in its grip, but it was undoubtedly of nervous origin. He found it impossible to share this trouble with his fiancée, and without sharing it he found it impossible to live with her. And when his physician told him that an eventual cure was highly improbable, he decided to break the engagement, an event which took place on the eleventh of November, 1841. The young girl protested that a separation would kill her, and her father, though a very proud man, visited Kierkegaard to beg him to reconsider, but Kierkegaard was immovable, and purposely somewhat brusque, in order, if possible, to make it easier for her. There is scarcely one of Kierkegaard's literary productions in which we do not find echoes of his experience, and the *Journals* bear constant testimony to the intensity with which his mind seized upon all sides of this abortive and painful experience. Eight years later, after the young lady had been happily married six years, he makes the following entry in his diary: "My will is unchanged. After my death the writings are to be dedicated to her, and to my deceased father. She shall have a share in their history." As for her marriage, he never ceased being grateful to her for what he called her high-mindedness.

Of course the engagement and its sorry ending became an inexhaustible topic for conversation in polite circles in Copenhagen. Kierkegaard enjoyed the honor of being regarded as a rascal, intent upon experimenting with the emotional life of a young girl, and was considered all the more interesting because he was so clever and so bad.

He faced the music for two or three weeks, and then fled to Berlin. Here he listened to Schelling's lectures, and worked with feverish intensity upon his great book, *Either-Or*. He returned to Copenhagen in the spring, and with the exception of another brief visit to Berlin, did not again leave Denmark. From this time he belonged to his life's Idea, the Idea he had sought six years before, and which now in its outlines at last stood clearly before him. He was free! No wife called him from his work, no friends had claims upon his attention, no social purpose diverted him, no economic necessities hindered him, no finite ambitions blinded him. He was a free man, bound only to the Idea.[17] To this Idea he was to render a service of such loyalty and disinterestedness, such industry and self-sacrifice, such enduring faith and single-minded devotion, that the story of his life, if told as a poet might tell it, should make the blush of enthusiasm mantle the cheek of every youth that heard it.

There now came a period of literary activity that for the brilliance and variety of its productions, finds few counterparts in the history of literature. In February, 1843, were published the two large volumes of *Either-Or*, and in February, 1846, the tremendous attack upon speculative philosophy, entitled, *Concluding Unscientific Postscript to the Philosophical Fragments*. In the brief interval of less than three years that intervened between these two publications, there had appeared in addition, *Fear and Trembling, Repetition, The Concept of Dread, Philosophical Fragments*, and *Stages on the Way of Life*, making, as Brandes says, an epoch in Danish literature. Although it soon became noised about that

---

[17] *Repetition,* 145

Kierkegaard was the author of all these works, no official acknowledgment of the fact was given to the public until 1846, in a "First and Last Explanation" added to the *Postscript*. They were all published under various pseudonyms: Victor Eremita, Johannes *de silentio*, Constantin Constantius, Frater Taciturnus, Hilarius Bookbinder, and Johannes Climacus. Kierkegaard is careful to explain that he is not to be held personally responsible for the views expressed by this array of authors. He is not the author of their opinions, but only the responsible individual who has given poetic life to the authors, each one of whom speaks for himself.

One guiding idea runs through the maze. His purpose is to explain and solve the riddles of the life of reason and freedom. Not, however, in such a way as merely to increase the store of human knowledge. He had diagnosed the evil of his day as a confusion of knowledge with life, and he did not intend to contribute to this confusion by adding a few more paragraphs to help make a systematic result. It was necessary to teach men what it means to live, and to this end he wished to place before them living personalities who think and speak for themselves. Thus would be clarified for the reader the various stages or moments or representative attitudes toward life, which in actual life are rarely so distinctive as to be separately and clearly seen. In *Either-Or*, for example, we have two authors. One represents an esthetic view, or rather an esthetic attitude toward life, an attitude governed by the categories of the pleasant and the unpleasant, the interesting and the dull. The other author represents the life of morality, life as governed by the categories of duty and self-realization. The first is endowed with all the seductive gifts of intellectuality and culture, and expresses himself in a series of brilliant esthetic essays upon a great variety of topics—"Mozart's *Don Juan*," "Ancient and Modern Tragedy," "Psychological Sketches of Literary Heroines" like Elvira, Antigone, Margaret in Goethe's *Faust*, and finally "The Diary of a Seducer," this wonderfully beautiful but terrible picture of a diabolically clever but thoroughly unmoral personality, an analogy to Don Juan, clothed in the garb of a high intellectuality. The second author is a man of dignity and poise, who writes letters of warning and ethical admonition to the author of the first part, discussing marriage and selfhood with a firm, if not a brilliant, touch. No finite choice between the two standpoints is indicated; the reader cannot tell whether A convinced B, or B convinced A. They stand before him—he is free to make his own choice.

The subsequent volumes employ essentially the same method, but make an advance toward throwing light upon the religious life. *Fear and Trembling* and *Repetition* deal with certain psychological situations that predispose toward religion; *Stages on the Way of Life* recapitulates *Either-Or*, with great literary daring, and then goes on to attack again the problem of delineating psychological situations that are pre-disposing and transitional toward the religious life. *The Concept of Dread* discusses the consciousness of sin, and is the only one of these works which is direct and dogmatic in its method of communication. The *Philosophical Fragments* gives in an abbreviated form the logic of Christianity, but without naming Christianity itself, ironically assuming the whole to be a genial invention of the author's, a hypothesis of his own creation. The giant volume of *The*

Postscript reviews objectively the ground already traversed, and defends it against the confusions of speculative philosophy, and especially against the Hegelian logic and philosophy of religion. All this literary output Kierkegaard refers to as esthetic, viewing it as a necessary preliminary outpouring of his nature, paving the way for a distinctively religious productivity in his next period.

To this latter productivity, Kierkegaard affixes his own name, and for its views he assumes personal responsibility. There had indeed appeared from the very beginning a series of religious addresses by Kierkegaard, published simultaneously with the appearance of his esthetic works, in order to signalize that the whole authorship was from the start a religious phenomenon, and had a religious ground.

In 1845, while Kierkegaard was reading the proof-sheets of the *Postscript,* an event took place which became a determining factor in the transition to the period of religious authorship. There was published at that time in Copenhagen, a politico-satirical journal after the style of journalism that had received considerable development in Paris. This journal was *The Corsair,* and its publisher was a somewhat talented young Jew by the name of Goldschmidt. It dealt in attacks on public men, in caricatures and satires, and even exploited the secrets of private life. Evidence is not wanting that it frequently descended to the level of blackmail. No one respected it, but everyone feared it; it was read everywhere, by high and low alike. Writers in this sheet had immortalized Kierkegaard, or rather his pseudonyms, and had praised *Either-Or* and Frater Taciturnus to the skies. One of the

contributing editors was P. L. Møller. This man introduced into a bit of literary correspondence in another
publication a review of *Stages On the Way of Life*. "It
was a frivolous and dishonorable article," says Brandes,
"frivolous, because the writer had made no attempt to
understand the subject he was writing about; dishonorable, because under the sham pretense of criticism it re-
tailed the current town gossip about Kierkegaard's private life, and accused the hero of the third part of the
Stages of placing his fiancée on the dissecting table, and
torturing the soul out of her, drop by drop—accusations
written as if aimed at Kierkegaard himself."

Kierkegaard wrote a scornful and biting reply, mixing
with his esthetic criticism, as he says, a good dose of ethical indignation. His answer concludes by characterizing
certain parts of the Møller article as "one of those
wretched *Corsair* attacks upon peaceable, respectable
men"; and he goes on to express the hope that he might
be attacked in the *Corsair,* which had just before said that
Victor Eremita would never die. Kierkegaard calls this a
shame and an insult, and declares that it is very hard for
a poor author to be marked out as the only apparently
respectable man in Denmark not vilified in the pages of
the *Corsair.* Goldschmidt took up the challenge. For several months thereafter, there appeared little articles in
the *Corsair* satirizing one or another feature of the pseudonymous writings. The articles were illustrated with
pictures of Kierkegaard walking through the streets, his
umbrella under his arm, and one trouser leg depicted
as considerably longer than the other. The result of this
campaign was that Kierkegaard could not show himself
on the streets without being followed by a gaping and

howling mob of boys and young men. So deeply did the attack sink into the popular consciousness of Copenhagen that we have from Brandes a narrative of how his nurse used to bring him back from the error of his ways, whenever his clothes were not properly put on, by pointing at him a warning forefinger and saying reprovingly, "Søren, Søren!"

The judgment of respectable society was that Kierkegaard had only himself to blame for his unpleasant predicament. Yet respectable society had just a little while before kept repeating that something must be done about the *Corsair*. Kierkegaard had taken the step, and had publicly condemned it, with the result that Goldschmidt subsequently found the task of editing it somewhat difficult, and finally abandoned the project, preparatory to attempting to enter the ranks of the respectable.

Upon Kierkegaard's work the situation produced an indelible impression. It served to awaken and direct a new literary productivity in Kierkegaard's soul, a productivity having a distinctively religious stamp. The experience became fruitful to him of a more profound understanding of the Christian categories of innocent suffering, and heterogeneity with the world. He stayed in Copenhagen, and became a religious author. During the next five years there were published works whose scope may be indicated by the citation of the following titles: *The Works of Love, Edifying Addresses, Christian Addresses, The Lilies of the Field and the Birds of the Air, The Sickness Unto Death, Introduction to Christianity, The Gospel of Suffering, For Self-Examination.* Of the intellectual dignity, the sympathetic human fellowship, the lofty inspiration, and the passionate religious warmth

of this comprehensive literature, it is utterly impossible
for me to give any real impression. I shall, however, cite
a passage from the *Works of Love*, not because it fairly
samples the literary level of these works, but because it
reveals one of the points of view that we may with assur-
ance ascribe to the aftermath of his collision with the
Corsair.

> A merely human self-denial thinks as follows: give up your
> selfish wishes, desires and plans, . . . and then you will be hon-
> ored and respected and loved as just and wise. It is easy to see
> that this sort of self-denial does not lay hold of God, but remains
> on the worldly plane of a relationship between men. A Christian
> self-denial thinks as follows: give up your selfish wishes and
> desires, give up your selfish plans and purposes, in order to work
> for the good in true disinterestedness . . . and then prepare to
> find yourself, just on that account, hated, scorned and mocked,
> precisely like a criminal; or rather, do not prepare to find your-
> self in this situation, for that may become a necessity, but choose
> it of your own free will. For Christian self-denial knows before-
> hand that these things will happen, and chooses them freely.
> Human self-denial rushes into danger without fear of the conse-
> quences for itself, . . . a danger where honor awaits the victor,
> and the admiration of his fellow-men lures him on to dare. It
> is easy to see that this self-denial does not lay hold of God, but
> is delayed on the way, in the relativities of human life. Christian
> self-denial rushes into danger without fear of the consequences
> for itself, into a danger that the environment cannot understand
> will yield any honor to the victor, because this environment
> is itself blinded, entangled, and guilty. Thus there is here a
> double danger, for the contempt of the spectator awaits the hero,
> whether he wins or fails.[18]

Once more, and for the last time, an external event
was to be the occasion for a change in Kierkegaard's life,
and to betoken the adoption of a new role, the role of an
agitator. Bishop Mynster, who had ruled the Church of

---

[18]*Works of Love*, 1, Chapter 5

Denmark for many years with a strong hand, died in
1853. A few weeks after his death, Professor Martensen
preached a memorial sermon in which the late Bishop
was eulogized as forming "yet one more link in the holy
chain of witnesses for the Truth, stretching from the days
of the apostles unto our own times," with more of the
same tenor. This idealization of Bishop Mynster seemed
to Kierkegaard to be a demoralizing falsification of the
Christian categories, and he set down at once a passionate
protest, under the caption: "Was Bishop Mynster a Witness for the Truth . . . Is this the truth?" The protest was
written in February, 1854; in December of the same year,
after Martensen had received the appointment to the
vacant bishopric, the article was published in *Fædrelandet,* a political daily newspaper in Copenhagen. Needless
to say, coming from such a source it created a sensation,
and awoke a storm of protest. Kierkegaard was accused
of attacking the memory of the dead, and of violating the
sanctity of the grave. He brushed the objectors and the
objections aside as if they had been a cloud of mosqui-
toes, and continued to hammer away in the newspapers
at his main theme: the comparison of what passed for
Christianity in the Established Church, with the ideals
of New Testament Christianity as exemplified in Christ
and the apostles. The agitation thus begun was continued
in *Fædrelandet* until the end of May, 1855, in upwards
of a score of articles appearing at irregular intervals. The
case was stated with an increasing intensity, rapidly approaching a terrific climax. The agitation finally over-
flowed the columns of *Fædrelandet,* and Kierkegaard
started an organ of his own entitled *The Moment,* of
which ten numbers were published, the last of which

appeared in September, 1855, nine months after war had first been declared.

"He was a great agitator," says Brandes. "His soul was full to the brim with a living indignation; he had the language completely in his power; he had by his religious writing trained himself to speak the plain man's tongue, and his quiver was full of the sharpest arrows of wit. He was just the man to carry on an agitation, such as the nineteenth century will hardly see paralleled, for he united the personal weight of a La Salle to the eloquence of an O'Connell and the biting scorn of a Dean Swift. It is impossible to describe his procedure. One must see him chisel his scorn into linguistic form, hammer the word until it shapes itself into the greatest possible, the bloodiest possible, injury—without for one moment ceasing to be the vehicle of an idea."

What was the burden of his agitation? It was, that so far from the church's being prolific and virile enough to produce one witness for the truth in the person of its Bishop, or a thousand witnesses for truth with titles equally as good, in the persons of its clergymen, Christianity did not really exist in Denmark.

Kierkegaard says:

There is nothing here to reform. What must be done is to throw light upon a state of affairs that from the Christian stand-point is a revolting crime continued through the centuries . . . .

Whoever you are, whatever your life may be, my friend, by refusing hereafter (if you have participated hitherto) , to take part in the public worship as it now is (with the claim of repre-senting New Testament Christianity) , thereby you assume the burden of one less guilty crime upon your conscience, for you take no part in making a mockery of God.[19]

---

[19] *Samlede Værker,* XIV, 83.

To those who asked him what he was driving at, he answered:

What do I want? I want honesty! I do not represent Christian severity over against a given form of Christian mildness. By no means, far from it: I am neither severity nor mildness, I am human honesty. And if the human race or my contemporaries desire to do this: honestly, sincerely, frankly, openly, directly, to rebel against Christianity, and to say to God, "We cannot and will not yield ourselves subject to this power," well and good, provided, mind you, that the thing is done openly, frankly, and sincerely; however strange it may seem for me to say this, I am with them, for I want honesty.[20]

In October, 1855, he fell in a faint upon the street, and was carried to Frederik's Hospital. The young interne who wrote the record of the case, has incorporated into it certain expressions of the sick man. The following from the very first day: "He considers his disease mortal; his death is necessary to the cause he has used all the powers of his spirit to further, for which alone he has lived, and which he considers himself especially called and fitted to serve; whence the great intellectual powers in connection with so frail a body. If he lives he must continue his religious struggle, but people will then tire of it; if he dies, on the contrary, the cause will maintain its strength and, as he thinks, its victory." And a few days later: "He continues to assert his approaching death."

On the eleventh day of November, 1855, he died, forty-two years and six months old.

The ultimate significance of Kierkegaard's thought and life, the place which a final accounting, if any such ever takes place, will give him in the world's history, depends absolutely upon the fate of Christianity—ulti-

---

[20] *Samlede Værker*, XIV, 55, 57. *Fædrelandet*.

mately he stands or falls with this great world force. Its cause was the cause for which he unremittingly gave all the powers of his life, and he himself believed that he had succeeded in the task he had set for himself: to clothe the Christian religion in the garb of philosophical reflection, complete and entire, without modification or distortion. He gives us a final summary of himself in a posthumously published work:

> Here is a literary productivity, whose total idea is—the problem of becoming a Christian. . . . But the author has thoroughly understood from the beginning, and consistently developed the consequences of the fact that the situation is in Christendom. . . . To become a Christian in Christendom is tantamount either to becoming what one already is, and this requires reflection in the direction of inwardness and subjectivity, or else it means to be freed first from the grip of illusion, and this cannot be done without reflection. The problem is: being in a certain sense a Christian, to become a Christian.[21]

To present an estimate of this, his absolute significance, is not possible here, but I desire to call attention to some less decisive, though not unimportant, features of his thought, wherein he is characterized relatively.

His claim to originality as a thinker is bound up with his choice of subject-matter. He set himself the problem of mapping out the life of the spirit, the subjective life of the emotions and the will. It is fair to say that among the great thinkers of the world, the philosophers of the first rank, he had in this task no predecessor except Socrates. When we pass in review the great names in the history of philosophy, we find that they have, almost without exception, devoted their great powers to the objective domains of metaphysics, epistemology, and the system of nature. The inner life has been neglected. So true

---

[21]*The Point of View*, 42-43.

is this, and so accustomed have we become to this neglect, that in the popular consciousness the life of the emotions has become identified with a necessary and unavoidable vagueness, dimness, and lack of clearness. It was an uncharted sea that Kierkegaard set out to map, a task for which, as he says himself, he could find no guidance in books. To have shown us by a thoroughness of execution, and a conscientiousness of workmanship having few parallels in philosophy, that the life of the spirit has a structure as definite as the law-governed, inorganic universe, and an organization as specialized as that of the highest living thing; if there be any philosophic merit in having rendered this service, then that merit belongs unqualifiedly to Kierkegaard as a pathfinder and pioneer. I cannot here detail the closely reasoned and vigorously outlined presentation he gives us of the various typical attitudes toward life: the esthetic, the ethical, and the religious, including both the immanent and the transcendental phase of the latter; together with the transitional or boundary attitude of irony and humor, the former standing between the esthetic and the ethical, and the latter between the ethical and the religious. Suffice it to say that he gives us not only the objective recipe for each, and this is the place where an ordinary thinker would have stopped; but he gives us also a poetic visualization of each attitude in character and situation, creating figures who think and feel and speak themselves out with a consistency that shies at no consequence however drastic. It is in this point that we face one of the peculiarities of Kierkegaard's genius. His thinking is not only sharply defined as that of few philosophers in the history of thought, but it is at the same time present in the situation, concrete, and poetically imaginative. He possesses as much imagination as he possesses dialectic, and as much dialectic as imagination. In this respect we have to go back to Plato to find a genius which parallels his.

In closing, I wish to call attention to one only of the fundamental categories of Kierkegaard's thought, the category of the individual. "My ethical significance as a thinker," says he, "is unconditionally bound up with this category of the individual." In his metaphysics this individualism reflects itself in the proposition that the only reality is the individual's own ethical reality; and that this reality is grasped, not by thinking it, but by living it. Reality is concrete and individual, and thought cannot assimilate the concrete in its concreteness, nor the individual in its individuality. To conceive a reality is to lift it out of the realm of the actual into the realm of the potential, out of the realm of the individual into the realm of the universal. Hence there can be no such thing as a philosophical system embracing potentialities or meanings; partly for the reason just mentioned, and partly because a system presupposes a closed finality, while real life is something we are always in the midst of. We think backwards, but we live forwards; hence our thought is necessarily intermittent and fragmentary. The fact then that thought always operates with generalities can have no influence upon the nature of reality, which remains individual and concrete. Thought and being are not, as the Hegelian philosophy assumes, identical, but thought bears the same relation to reality that a plan not yet realized bears to its actual realization. This does not mean that reality is to be identified with the bare external fact; for the motive, the inner interpretation, the idea, the subjective attitude, is the life of every decision, and he who clings to the external fact alone is content with an empty shell. But this motive, this inner interpretation, is in the last analysis accessible only to the individual himself; hence the individual's own ethical reality is the only reality of which he is in possession; all else is only possibility.

Ethically, the individual is his own highest end and aim. If this were not so, we should be in the throes of an unavoidable ethical scepticism. The good is freedom. The problem is to potentialize one's own subjectivity to the highest maximum. Existence is a struggle of contradictions, and when these are accentuated to their utmost, there appears the paradox of the eternal as a *telos* for realization within the temporal order. But wherever there is contradiction there is passion, and wherever there is a paradoxical contradiction there is the maximum of passion. The ethical task is therefore to keep the subjective pathos of one's life alive at the level of maximum intensity and highest possible quality. Such a subjectivity is at the same time the truth, the only truth possible for an existing individual. The Truth is, not to know the Truth, but to be the Truth; to know the Truth only, is to be enmeshed in error.

The various religious attitudes are to be ranked in accordance with the degree of subjectivity which they stimulate and presuppose. Christianity ranks as highest, for it accentuates life paradoxically, and lends it the maximum possible earnestness. It conceives life in such a way as to make the issues at stake in life the greatest possible; for it presupposes that the moment in time becomes decisive with respect to the winning or losing of an eternal happiness; which is a paradoxical view of life, since no moment can be commensurate with an eternity. The peculiar type of subjectivity which Christianity presupposes is called faith. It is possible to define this faith subjectively, without reference to any object, but in so definite a way that there can be only one object that corresponds to it—namely, the God-man, in whose historical existence, with all that this implies, the Christian believer is infinitely, subjectively, and passionately interested.[22]

This thoroughgoing individualism carries with it as its obverse side a rejection of all political and social aims except in so far as we assign to them a merely relative importance. In reply to a friendly mention by Dr. Rudelbach, which Kierkegaard feared might lead to a misunderstanding, he enters the following passionate protest against politics:

So that is now to be my significance, that I attack the State Church or fight for the emancipation of the church. In Ursin's Arithmetic, which was used in the schools when I was a boy, there is a reward offered to everyone who finds an error in any of the examples of the book. I too offer a reward to any person who can find in the whole array of my books, one single proposal looking toward any outward change, or even the slightest hint of such a proposal, or anything that for the most shortsighted individual at the greatest possible distance, might seem to resemble the faintest hint of such a proposal, or something that might in the most distant manner suggest that I believed that the trouble lies in something external, that an outward change is indispensable, that an outward change would help us.

Christianity is inwardness, subjectification. If at any time the forms under which we have to live are not the most perfect, well, if it is possible to obtain better forms, well and good. But, essentially, Christianity is inwardness. Just as man is distinguished from the lower animals by the fact that he can live in

---

[22]*Unscientific Postscript*, 169-220.

any climate, so the degrees of perfection in Christianity range according to the fulness of life that can be developed under the most imperfect forms. This worldly spirit, this Tantalus-like striving for outward change, is Politics.

Dr. Rudelbach believes that the salvation of the church and of Christianity depends upon the establishment of free institutions. If this faith in the saving power of free institutions, obtained by political means, is a part of true Christianity, then I am no Christian, nay, worse, I am a real child of the devil; for I have, frankly speaking, even a suspicion of these free institutions, to be obtained by political means, especially of their saving and regenerating power. . . . I have never concerned myself with Church and State, these things are too high for me, . . . I have never fought for the emancipation of the Church, nor for the emancipation of women, or the Jews, or the trade with Greenland. As an individual, I have, keeping the individual in mind, and aiming at a subjectification of Christianity in the individual, fought my fight against the illusions with the weapons of the spirit, and with these weapons alone. And just as in my opinion it is an illusion for one to imagine that the outward form hinders him in becoming a Christian, just so it is also an illusion for one to think that the outward forms will hold him as a Christian.[23]

Each one of Kierkegaard's religious works contained a stereotyped reference to the "individual, whom with joy and gratitude I call my reader," and the posthumously published explanation of his authorship contains a note on the Individual, from which I quote the following:

There is a view of life which holds that where a multitude is, there is also the Truth, and that there is need on the part of the Truth itself to have the multitude with it. There is another view of life; it holds that wherever there is a multitude, there is Error, so that, to put the idea for a moment to an extreme test, if each individual, every one for himself, in stillness had the Truth, if they came together as a multitude (so that this fact

[23]*Samlede Værker*, XIII, 474-477.

received any decisive, balloting, noisy significance whatever),
then Error would be present at once. The multitude is a lie—
not this or that multitude, of rich or poor, of living or dead,
or high or low. . . . But the multitude itself: viewed as a category;
for it always gives unaccountability and irresponsibility. A multitude is an abstraction without any hands; every individual
ordinarily has two hands, and when he lays these two hands on
Caius Marius, then it is this individual's own two hands, not
his neighbor's, and much less the multitude's, which has no
hands. . . . To win a multitude does not require very great skill;
there is needed only a little talent, a certain quantity of dis-
honesty, and a little knowledge of human passions. But no witness for the truth—and this is what every human being ought to
be, you and I included—dares to have anything to do with the
multitude. . . . Those who speak to the multitude as authority, he
considers to be in error. . . . For the mode of procedure, which in
politics and in similar spheres, sometimes has entire validity,
sometimes partial validity, becomes a lie when it is transferred
to the sphere of the intellectual, the spiritual, the religious. . . .
By truth, I understand eternal truth, but politics has nothing to
do with "eternal truth." A political system which in the sense of
the eternal truth attempted earnestly to bring the eternal truth
to bear upon actuality, would that same moment prove itself to
be in the most eminent degree the most impolitic thing that can
be imagined.[24]

Such was Kierkegaard's individualism. In the posthumous publication referred to above, he has given us
an estimate of himself:

When my poet comes, he will assign me a place among those
who have suffered for an idea; he will say about me, "The martyrdom which this author suffered was due to the fact that he
was a genius living in a trading town. . . . In Eternity it will
be his comfort that he has suffered voluntarily, and not supported
his cause by the help of any illusion or concealed himself behind
any illusion. His sufferings have been a prudently pious gathering together of savings for eternity: there he has the memory

---

[24] *The Point of View*, 112ff.

that he was faithful to himself and to his first love, with which he has loved all those who have suffered in the world. . . . The dialectical structure that he completed, he could not dedicate to any human being, much less to himself. If he should dedicate it to anyone, it would have to be to Providence, to whom, indeed, it was consecrated, day after day, year after year, by the author, who, to speak historically, died of a mortal disease, but, to speak poetically, died of a longing for Eternity, where he desires nothing better than that he might there without ceasing give thanks unto God."[25]

---

[25]*The Point of View,* 100-103.

II. SØREN KIERKEGAARD—A DANISH SOCRATES

THE English-speaking world has of late years mani-
fested a considerable interest in the literature of
the Scandinavian countries, the more prominent
figures in that literature are well-known, and many of
their works have found eager readers in English translations. Such contemporary figures as Ibsen, Strindberg,
and Høffding, and one or two names from an older generation, like Oehlenschlager and Tegnér, to say nothing
of Ludwig Holberg, have begun to exercise a measure of
influence upon our reading public, though in widely
different degrees. Under these circumstances it is a
strange freak of fate that the man who stands high above
all others in the literature of the Scandinavian north, the
only original philosophical genius of which it can boast,
a man who must be placed in the very front rank as a
master of style, as an interpreter of the emotions, and as
a keen dialectician, Denmark's greatest prose writer, and
her greatest spiritual force—it is a curious freak of fate
that this man should as yet scarcely be known even by
name to the English-speaking world.[1] But though the
course of fame for true genius, like the course of true
love, may not run smooth, it is bound sooner or later to
overflow the narrow boundaries of language and country.

The productions of talent usually yield themselves to

---

[1]The above was written prior to 1930. Since 1935 English translations of
practically all of Kierkegaard's more important works have appeared, or are
about to appear, and he is being recognized by philosophical and religious
thinkers in England and America as well as in Germany where he has long
been known.

interpretation in terms of current and accepted classifications; genius breaks through all categories. "Talent
infuses warmth and life into the old, and therefore fills
a place in the world at once," says Kierkegaard, "but
genius brings that which is new, and is therefore a paradox to contemporaries."[2] The current classifications and
viewpoints afford a very inadequate means of laying hold
of the significance of Kierkegaard's thought. The time-
honored antitheses between Realism and Idealism, between Empiricism and Rationalism, and the current conceptions of Absolutism, Pragmatism, and Voluntarism,
all seem somewhat lame and in need of revision when
they are confronted with Kierkegaard's vital thought, this
luminous reflective energy that is embodied in the vast
Kierkegaardian literature. The fact that he is his own
best interpreter, nay, perhaps his only interpreter; the
fact that no thinker has yet succeeded in embalming him
in a category which he has not himself suggested and discussed, or salted him down satisfactorily in a neat array
of paragraphs—this is a tribute to his greatness, an indirect expression of the fact that he is fitted to play the part
of a teacher on the stage of the world's thought.

When, therefore, I propose to draw a parallel between
Kierkegaard and the Sage of Athens, I have not invented
this interpretation, but merely accepted a point of view
which derives from Kierkegaard himself. If it is not
wholly a misunderstanding to speak of a disciple in connection with such a figure as Socrates, then it must be
acknowledged that Kierkegaard stands a great deal nearer
to such discipleship than does Plato, who was Socrates'
poet, indeed, but not his follower. It is clear that no one
could become a disciple of Socrates merely by the accep-

---

[2]Dru: *Journals,* 500, §1313.

tance of one or more Socratic propositions, or by entering upon some external imitation of his career; it is because Kierkegaard reveals an inner sympathy with him, an understanding of the Greek thinker which is unexampled for its intimacy, and because he seems to have fulfilled, in relation to his own time and age, an ethical task analogous to that which Socrates fulfilled in Greece, that we are justified in calling him a modern Socrates. It is this conception which I hope to be able, in the course of this paper, to invest with some degree of clarity and concreteness.

For the degree of *Magister artium* at the University of Copenhagen, Kierkegaard presented a dissertation entitled: *On the Concept Irony, with constant reference to Socrates*. It was a comparative study of the so-called Romantic irony, as expressed in the life and writings of Tieck, Schlegel, and others of the German romanticists on the one hand, with that Socratic irony which was for Socrates no mere mode of speech or passing mood, but the essential form of his personal life. Written in 1841, when Kierkegaard was twenty-eight, it was a mature work, suggesting, if not entirely disclosing, Kierkegaard's powers and standpoint. Kierkegaard himself frankly confesses that this, his early conception of Socrates, was at some important points vitiated by the too great influence of Hegel, and by the spirit that was in those days the modern spirit; as the years passed, and as he grew into a more profound understanding of himself, his early enthusiasm for Socrates was deepened and intensified, he drew closer and closer to him, and the thought of the Socratic irony, the Socratic ignorance, the Socratic zeal, the Socratic maieutic, became an ever more intimate companion of his mind and heart. I shall cite two passages expressive of this relation; the first of these is from an entry in the diary, written immediately after the publication of *Either-Or*, his first great work:

There was once a young man, happily gifted as an Alcibiades. He went astray in the world. In his distress he looked about him for a Socrates, but among his contemporaries he found none. Then he prayed that the gods might transform him into a Socrates. And behold, the young man who had been so proud of being an Alcibiades, was so shamed and humbled by the grace the gods bestowed upon him, that just when he had received that of which he might well have been proud, he felt himself the least important of men.[3]

Twelve years later, in the last months of his life, when he was in the thick of a powerful agitation, one which, though concerned purely with ideal values, yet stirred Denmark to its depths, so that Kierkegaard even apprehended the possibility of arrest and imprisonment, he wrote as follows:

The point of view which I have to represent and expound is so absolutely unique, that in the eighteen hundred years of the history of Christendom there is, quite literally, nothing analogous or corresponding to which I might link myself. In this sense also—over against the eighteen hundred years—I stand alone.

My only analogy is Socrates. My task is a Socratic task—to revise the conception of what it means to be a Christian. I do not call myself a Christian (keeping the ideal free) but I can reveal the fact that others are still less entitled to the name than I am.

O noble, simple sage of antiquity, the only human being that I acknowledge with admiration as a thinker: there is but little that has been handed down concerning you, true and only martyr of the intellect, equally great as character and thinker; but that little, how infinitely much! How I have longed amidst all these battalions of so-called Christian thinkers . . . for one short hour of conversation with you! . . .

---

[3] Dru: *Journals*, 111, §414.

Our so-called Christian civilization is sunk to a depth of sophistry far, far worse than that which flourished in Greece in the time of the sophists. These legions of preachers and Christian docents are all sophists, earning their livelihood—here we have according to the ancients, the characteristic mark of the sophist—by deluding those who understand nothing, into thinking that they know something, and then making this mass, this numerical power, this human majority, the test and standard of the Truth.

But I do not call myself a Christian. That this is very embarrassing to the sophists, I understand very well; and I understand, too, that they would much prefer that I should loudly proclaim myself the only true Christian, and I know very well that the attempt has been made, untruthfully, to represent my agitation in this light. But I will not allow myself to be made a fool of . . . I do not call myself a Christian.

O Socrates! If you had only loudly proclaimed yourself the wisest man in Greece, the sophists would soon have been able to finish you off! No, no, you made yourself ignorant; but at the same time you had the malicious characteristic that you could expose the fact (precisely as being ignorant) that the others had still less knowledge than you, they who did not even know that they were ignorant.[4]

It is quite obvious that this self-interpretation in terms of Socrates was no merely genial idea, struck off in the heat of a passing mood, but a firm and settled understanding, tested and tried in the fire of an intensive life of reflection. Passing over, with a bare mention, such personal though not insignificant parallelisms as the capacity for conversation with the most widely different kinds of people, the inclination toward ironical self-isolation, the ability to apprehend objectively one's own personality, and the impulse to bring himself and his thought into touch with the man on the street,—there are five Socratic features of Kierkegaard's thought, to which I propose to call attention within the limits of this paper.

---

[4]*Samlede Værker*, XIV, 366-368, *The Moment*, No. 10, *Tillæg*.

First, a concentration of interest on ethical problems; *Second*, an intimate contact with the concrete; *Third*, an instrumentalism with reference to the intellectual; *Fourth*, the maieutic method combined with the distinctive use of dialectic for the purpose of clearing the ground; *Fifth*, the generally polemic and aggressive attitude toward contemporary life and currents of thought

Let us then consider these features which link the two thinkers together in this kinship which Kierkegaard feels so vividly. The first and most obvious point of comparison is their decisive concentration of interest on the problems of the ethical and religious life. We all remember how in the dialogue of the *Phaedrus*, Plato makes Socrates say, that as a lover of knowledge he is almost a complete stranger to the surroundings of the country, since he cannot learn from the trees or from the country, but only from men, dwellers in the city; and you may recall the report of Diogenes Laertius, who tells us that Socrates came to the conclusion that the study of physics was not man's proper business, and that therefore he began to moralize in the workshops and in the market-place. In short, though attracted to the study of natural science in his youth, and not unacquainted with cosmological speculations, tradition makes Socrates abandon such studies as irrelevant to a fundamentally human and ethical interest. This general attitude is reproduced in Kierkegaard with decisiveness and energy. Let me cite an entry in his diary, written at the age of twenty-two, where he pauses to take stock, as it were, of himself:

> My misfortune is that I am interested in too many things, and not decisively committed to any one thing, to which I might subordinate everything else.[5]

---

[5]Dru: *Journals*, 6, §16.

In the sphere of the natural sciences, he distinguishes between the industrious collector of facts and the organizing talent that succeeds in gaining a view of the whole. The former seems to him like the rich man in the gospel, gathering into his storehouse a great heap of facts, but to whom science says: "This night thy soul shall be required of thee," in so far, namely, as it is science which determines what significance each particular fact is to have in the whole. The great organizing talents on the other hand, fill him with enthusiasm; but here, too, they fall short:

> It seems to me that I cannot make the natural sciences my chief study. For it has always been the life of reason and freedom that has interested me most, and I have always wished to clear up the riddle of life.[6]

In a similar vein, he discusses jurisprudence and the stage, in both of which directions he had made some preliminary studies, and then he passes on to theology. But he is not satisfied either with Orthodoxy in which he has been brought up, or with Rationalism, which seems to him to cut but a sorry figure. The former he calls a huge Colossus, but one which began to tumble as soon as he learned to think for himself; the latter, a half-hearted compromise.

> What I really need is clearness as to what I ought to do; not so much as to what I ought to know, except in so far as some form of knowledge precedes all doing. I need to understand my place in life, and to see what the Divinity means that I should do; I need a truth which is a truth for me, an idea for which I can live and die. . . . What I need is the power to live a complete human life, and not merely a life of knowledge, in order that my thought may not be based merely upon something objective, something not my own, but rather upon something con-

nected with the deepest root of my existence, something through
which I am linked with the divine, and to which I could cling
if the whole world were to fall in ruins about me.[7]

This extract strikes the fundamental note of his life
and thought; it poses precisely a question clearly Socratic
in its spirit and character, to which his maturity furnishes
the precisely corresponding answer. The idea of a truth
that is essentially a truth for the individual, his own personal truth, expressing his own primitive individuality,
and yet having the universality which links him with the
divine, that was to be the idea for which Kierkegaard did
indeed live and die. It would be a trivial misunderstanding to interpret the predisposition, thus common to Kierkegaard and Socrates, as merely a preference for the study
of ethics and psychology as over against other objective
disciplines. The distinction here is between the subjective and concretely individual on the one hand, and the
objective and abstractly universal on the other hand. It
is a choice between, as distinct from a mediation of, the
antitheses of Spirit and Nature, Self and Cosmos, the con-
centric and the eccentric, the centripetal and the centrif-
ugal, the inner totality and the endless external approximation. "The universe really centers in the individual
man," says Kierkegaard, "because his self-knowledge is a
knowledge of God; and as a subjective thinker the individual makes his own personality an instrument where-
with he may clearly express whatever is universally human."

Taking modern philosophy as a whole, it can scarcely
be denied that the best energies and the keenest dialectical powers have been spent upon the impersonal problems. Now, from a Socratic point of view, the whole of

[7]Dru: *Journals*, 16, §22.

logic and metaphysics constitutes but an introduction to the beginning of real philosophizing. At any rate it is true that the inner life of the personality has been left a comparatively uncharted realm; in the geography of philosophic thought it has been nothing more than the great beyond, the *Outre-Mer*. But it is just here, in this hitherto unoccupied field, that the distinctive significance of Kierkegaard's work is to be found. We are just entering upon a period of systematic discussion of values in philosophy. I here call your attention to the fact that a thoroughgoing and profound philosophy of values has been in existence almost entirely neglected, for more than fifty years; that its distinctions are as clear-cut and precise as mathematical definitions; that it has been elaborated with an extraordinary wealth of poetic intuition, and pulsates throughout with the most exalted ethical passion.

Now for the fundamental purpose of such a philosophy, it may be urged that the concepts and methods of the natural sciences are quite irrelevant, that scientific research is a mere distraction, and that the attempt to apply its results to the interpretation of the life of freedom is a prolific breeder of confusion of thought. So, we may be sure, did Socrates conceive of the matter in his day, and such was also Kierkegaard's interpretation. In his own generation it was the exaggerated emphasis upon a philosophical contemplation of history, a speculative determination of its course in neatly arranged epochs and eras, which was the specifically demoralizing phenomenon; in the next following generation, he prophesied that it would be the study of the natural sciences which would bring the corresponding demoralization in its train. He notes the Mormon theory that God is not precisely omnipresent, but moves with extraordinary velocity from star to star, and he hails it as a symptom of the improvement which theology may look forward to attain, when at last the new discoveries of the nineteenth century, the mechanical inventions, and all the curiosities of the natural order, are made fully available for the purpose of spiritualizing our conceptions of God. On this point his sarcasm is biting, and now that we are in the midst of a reaction from a naturalistic period, the genuineness of his insight may perhaps be acknowledged.

The scientific temper of our own age reveals itself among other ways also in this, that a predilection for the ideas and methods of natural science in philosophy is held to argue the possession of a sense for the concrete and the real, while conversely, a lack of sympathy for this kind of philosophizing is believed to convict one of remoteness from the actual. Now, if there were only these two alternatives in philosophy, an idealism of the post-Kantian type, namely, and a scientific philosophy of the Spencerian type, a student really in search of a philosophic thought genuinely imbued with a sense for the concrete and the real, might well throw up his hands in despair. When the Hegelian philosophy was enjoying its highest fame, Kierkegaard chose to attack it from the rear, by the application of just this category of reality, existence, but, please note, reality and existence in the thinker himself, not outside the thinker.

We smile at the life of the cloister, and yet no hermit ever lived so unreal a life as is common today, for the hermit did indeed abstract from the whole world, but he did not abstract from himself. We know how to describe the fantastic situation of the cloister far from the haunts of men, in the solitude of the forest, in the pale blue of the distant horizon, but the fantastic situation of the so-called pure thought wholly escapes our attention. And yet the pathetic unreality of the solitary monk is far preferable to the comic unreality of the pure thinker; and the passionate forgetfulness of the hermit, which takes the world away from him, is far preferable to the comical distraction of the world-historic thinker, in which he forgets himself.[8]

And when toward the end of his life, he read Schopenhauer, and noted his apt though brutal attacks upon the Hegelians from a somewhat similar point of view, he sets down in his diary that the word which Schopenhauer uses so much in that connection, *Windbeutel,* is a distinctively German word, and corresponds to a distinctively German weakness.

Indeed, how embarrassing it would be for Schopenhauer if he did not have this word, he who has to deal with the Hegelian philosophy, and the whole professorial-philosophy in general. . . . We Danes do not have that word, nor does the fact it signifies seem to be characteristic of the Danish people. . . . But we have on the contrary another, and, alas, a corresponding weakness, for the German makes wind, and we swallow it. . . . If Schopenhauer has had to do with the windbags who produce wind, then I have had to do with a people only too eager to swallow it.[9]

Our time has experienced a reaction from the intellectually aristocratic unreality of the post-Kantian idealists, which has thrown us into the arms of the plebeian unreality of the naturalistic philosophers, whose sense of reality is satisfied by the massive, the extensive, the numerical, the quantitative; and thus we have merely exchanged one abstraction for another. But just as in ancient times the career of Socrates furnished perhaps the best commentary upon what a sense for reality means, so in modern times the life and thought of Kierkegaard offer an illuminating commentary upon the philosophy of the real, or upon realism in philosophy. For the stimulus, the primary stimulus, of all his thinking does not

[8]*Unscientific Postscript,* 283.
[9]Dru: *Journals,* 507, §1324.

come from books or other men's theories, but from his own personal life; and then again, on the other side, he does not seek a refuge in ideas, theories, principles, as places of escape from the crassness of life, but he is, like Socrates, an existential thinker who exists in his thought. This fundamental fact concerning Kierkegaard comes to an expression in his style. The cold, dispassionate brevity of the language of abstraction, the thin knife-edge of the conceptual outline, is usually farther from the warm concreteness of the real than the rich fulness of a poetic intuition; both means of representation may be so employed as to lead to or suggest the real, though in themselves both belong to the realm of imaginative apprehension. But the intuitional and dramatic manner, as I have said, carries us appreciably nearer; and it is a peculiarity of Kierkegaard's genius that he exhibits an equally extraordinary power in both modes of apprehension and expression. It is doubtful whether so eminent a creative and poetic faculty has been joined to so great a dialectical energy since Plato. My purpose in referring to this matter here, however, is merely to point it out as symptomatic of the closeness of the interrelationship between his thought on the one hand, and the realities of life on the other. A brief reference to one or two outstanding circumstances in connection with Kierkegaard's life will perhaps serve further to emphasize and give precision to my meaning.

Born in Copenhagen in the year 1813, the youngest son of a retired merchant, brought up under a severely religious discipline, entering the University of Copenhagen and pursuing there for a number of years esthetic, philosophical, and theological studies, near the age of thirty launching himself upon an extraordinarily brilliant and productive literary career, he died in the year 1855, at the early age of forty-two. Literature was his only pursuit, and since the flow of his productivity was altogether disproportionate to the size of the Danish reading public, his support came mainly from his inheritance, which amounted to a sum of between twenty and twenty-five thousand dollars, and which was found to be completely exhausted at the time of his death.[10] His outward life was in a sense monotonously uneventful, the life of a student and writer. "One being is elevated above another," says Wordsworth, "in proportion as he possesses the capacity to be excited to significant feeling without the application of gross and violent stimulants." This saying might well have been coined as a commentary upon Kierkegaard's life, for events, which in the case of most men would have been allowed to pass off without leaving a ripple on the surface of their lives, produced in him storms that stirred his soul to the depths, and yielded an ethico-philosophical reflection of universal significance.

Two such events marked crises in his inner life. The first was his engagement at the age of twenty-seven, to a pretty young woman, a child of sunshine and fortune, happy and bubbling over with life. The engagement was scarcely a week old before Kierkegaard was terror-stricken to discover that there was something amiss in this relationship. He loved her, he would never love anyone else, but his nature, his individuality, his melancholy, and his health, rose up against him as so many protests against the realization of this love in marriage. For a year he struggled with himself, his mind was torn with anguish, his conscience accusing and then again excusing him, absolutely alone with his doubts and fears. Then

---

[10]Lowrie: *Kierkegaard*, 500-504.

he cut the Gordian knot by breaking the engagement; his sole anxiety being to do it in such a way as to make it easier for her to forget him. She protested that it would kill her; two years later she was happily married. This experience sufficed to launch Kierkegaard on his literary career with a tremendous impetus; it made him a poet in prose. "In one year I have lived more poetry," he said, "than most poets write in a life-time." It was a sympathetic collision that he had lived through, and it gave him an insight into analogous states of mind which he used with telling effect. Not one of his books but re-echoes, now in one way, now in another, this unhappy love affair; yet he never deals with it except with complete objectivity, always preserving an ideal transformation of the facts to serve the purpose of the matter in hand; and the actual facts of the situation remained a personal secret until the posthumous publication of his letters. He did not even entrust these facts to his diary, no, not even the name of his fiancée, his emotion not even allowing his pen to write her name.

The sympathetic and ideal aspects of the love-relationship thus came to serve Kierkegaard as a point of departure for the clarification and exposition of the fundamental religious experiences. It is impossible to convey briefly any adequate impression of the richness, the rarity, and the profundity of the psychological insight thus brought to bear upon the problems of religion, but a passage from the *Introduction to Christianity*, a work from the later period of his authorship, may be cited as giving some intimation of his personal attitude with respect to the use he makes of his experiences.

Now as regards myself, I who strive to describe these things, perhaps I owe to the reader a little explanation. I may sometimes seem to reveal such a knowledge of the secrets of the inner life, such an acquaintance with the sufferings of genuine self-denial, that someone may perhaps conceive the idea that I, though naturally only a man, yet am one of those rare and noble men who serve humanity for an ideal. This is very far from being the case. In a very strange manner, and certainly not for my virtue's sake, but rather as a consequence of my sins, I have acquired a purely formal knowledge of the secrets of existence and mysteries of living, as these exist for the very few indeed. I do not pride myself on the possession of this knowledge, for it did not come to me on account of my virtues. But I strive to use this knowledge honestly in order to throw light upon the genuinely human truth, and the truly human good. And this again I use to call the attention of men so far as is possible, to that which is sacred—concerning which I then invariably add, that this is something which no man can understand, that in relation to this, we must begin and end with worship.—The responsibility which rests upon me, no one understands as well as I do myself; let no one therefore take it upon himself to terrify me, for I stand in fear and trembling before One who is able to terrify me more effectively.[11]

The second critical experience came five years later, in the mid-point of his career as an author. This was his conflict with *The Corsair,* already described in the biographical sketch. The persecution which Kierkegaard suffered as a result of this conflict, his desertion by the respectable classes who should have given him their support, opened his eyes to a new aspect of the religious life, namely the conflict with the environment, as distinct from the inner conflict with oneself. This experience determined Kierkegaard to become a religious author, and gave his thought its distinctively and decisively Christian coloring.

These two critical experiences, then, illustrate from one side my thesis that Kierkegaard's thought stood in the closest possible relation to reality; from the side,

---

[11]*Training in Christianity,* 138f.

namely, that concerns the part played by the real as a stimulus to reflection. A third experience illustrates that thesis from the other side, from the side of bringing this reflection back into closest contact with the actual life, as Socrates philosophized in the shops and market-places, and made himself a gad-fly to the Athenian people. I refer to the grandiose agitation with which Kierkegaard brought his career to a climax during the last year of his life. Mention has already been made of this in the biographical sketch, and it cannot be adequately described without an orientation in the content and movement of the Kierkegaardian literature as a whole; suffice it here to say that it was a passionate protest against the shams, delusions, and hypocrisies of the contemporary religious life of Denmark, of Protestantism, and of our whole Christian civilization, an attempt to bring the ideals to bear through pamphlets and the daily press. I quote a passage from the first number of the *Moment,* the pamphlet periodical which Kierkegaard published as a vehicle for this agitation:

Plato says somewhere in the *Republic* that we can never hope for a good government until we force those to govern who have no desire to govern. This remark also holds true in other relations where there is something to be done in real earnest: provided the person in question is in possession of the necessary abilities, then it is best that he should be unwilling to take the matter in hand; for true earnestness is first introduced in any undertaking when a man who is equipped for the task with the requisite abilities, is constrained against his will by something higher, to take up the work, that is, with the ability, but against the inclination.

Thus interpreted, it is proper for me to say that I am fitted for the task of bringing my work into touch with the present moment; for God knows it is against my inclinations.

To produce literature—well, that is my delight; to be honest

I must even say that I am in love with writing—but, please note, in my own way. And what I have loved, that is precisely the opposite of anything like an agitation; I have loved to stand afar, far from the turmoil of the moment, at this distance from the moment, to trace the thoughts in their interconnection, to entertain myself with the language, as an artist who is in love with his instrument entertains himself, luring from it the expressions which the thought requires.—Oh, happy way of employing myself! I could employ myself thus for an eternity without becoming weary.

But if I am to bring my work to bear upon the present moment, then I must, alas! take my farewell of you, my beloved aloofness, where there was never any hurry, where there was always time, where I could wait hours, days, weeks, to find the suitable expression, while I must now break with all such considerations and all such beloved habits. And if I am to work in the present, then there are people for whose sake I must pay some attention to the trivialities, which mediocrity with a great air of importance puts forth as profound wisdom; to the galimatias which it will read out of my words because it has first read it in; to the lies and vituperation which a man must endure against whom the two great social powers, envy and stupidity, instinctively find themselves arrayed.

Why then, do I propose to exert myself as a force in the moment? Because I should everlastingly rue it if I dared to neglect it.[12]

In this last phase of his life-work, Kierkegaard takes the final step out into the real world, and consolidates himself as an ethical personality. He began as a poetic and philosophical genius; in every such genius the intellectual and the imaginative is disproportionate to the will and the character. Kierkegaard's development was an education of this originally given geniality, tending toward the transformation of it into an ethico-religious character; of this educational progress he was himself conscious, and reflection marked and noted every step

---

[12]*Samlede Værker*, XIV, 103-104.

of the way. It is thus possible to see what Kierkegaard means by reality: it is the ethical synthesis within the individual of the ideal and the actual. Just in so far as a so-called practical man lives his life absorbed in finite ends, insensitive to or forgetful of the ideal which is his own true self, just in so far, he and his life are unreal. And just in so far as a thinker or poet develops or contemplates the ideal in the imagination, without bringing his own actual life into conformity therewith, just in so far he, too, is unreal. Kierkegaard's own life was a process tending toward a greater and greater reality, until finally he entered upon the scene of contemporary life as an individual actor, and, commensurate with the significance of his personality, in bringing the ideal to bear upon himself, he also brought it to bear in the most decisive way upon the whole contemporary age. And thus, like Socrates, he came into Socratic closeness of touch with the real.

A third Socratic aspect of Kierkegaard's thought is found in its instrumentalism, its consistently pragmatic character with reference to theory, expression, and practice. In this connection it is instructive to remember the difference between Socrates and Plato. The dialectic which in Socrates' hands was an instrument to sweep away the cobwebs of illusion to make room for the human ideals, therefore a means of self-discipline and incidentally also of a discipline of others, this dialectic was transformed by Plato, more or less clearly and consciously, into an end in itself, and the abstractions developed by this dialectic therefore naturally became the supreme realities. In short, Socrates was an existential thinker, to use Kierkegaard's terminology, while Plato was a speculative metaphysician. What Kierkegaard es-

pecially admires in Socrates is that he had no objective
result, but only a way, so that it is only by following the
Socratic way that one can reach the Socratic result.

Of a Persian emperor Sardanapalus, it is told, says an entry
in the diary, that he had inscribed upon his tomb, "I took the
pleasures of life with me," to which a pagan had strikingly replied: "How is that possible? You could not even while you lived
hold one single pleasure fast." No, indeed, in that way it cannot
be done. But Socrates, he is the only human being who solved the
problem: he took everything with him into the grave. Wonderful
Socrates! You perfected yourself in an art which will forever be
equally difficult for every successor; you left behind you not one
single loose string of a result that a Professor might be able to
get hold of; no, you took everything with you into the grave.
In the most eminent reflection, you preserved air-tight the greatest enthusiasm, and preserved it for Eternity—you took it all, all
with you. And for this reason it is now being said—O Socrates!—
for this reason it is now being said among the Professors, depreci-
atingly, that you were only a personality, that you did not even
have a system.[13]

In this Socratic sense, Kierkegaard's own thought was
instrumental and pragmatic also. His objective thinking
is everywhere absorbed—absorbed back into the subjective, the personality. His writings are rich in philosophical ideas, but he has no systematic treatise presenting
objectively a logical or metaphysical doctrine. This is
intentional, the expression of a principle. His position
is that the metaphysical and logical categories are not
the categories of Reality; that they do not, strictly speaking, exist as such; for when they exist, they exist as an
abbreviation of, or a priority for, the esthetic, the ethical,
or the religious spheres of life. No human being, therefore, exists in logical or metaphysical categories; but his
existence is always esthetic, or ethical, or religious in its

[13]*Papirer*, XI, 1, 344, §449.

constitutive form. Kierkegaard's writings are throughout permeated with this consciousness, hence this virile humanism. Just as in Reality the logical categories are embedded in life's moral substance, so in these writings, the philosophical and logical structure is concealed and yet revealed by a flesh and blood covering of pathos and imagination, of irony and humor. Instead of a systematic web of paragraphs, he gives us a wealth of mimic and lyric expressions of doubt and despair, of courage and faith, but all interpenetrated with a conceptual and ideal consistency; he gives us not so much thoughts, as a representation of thinking personalities who exist in their thought. He does not content himself with describing abstract logical thought as instrumental, but actually compels it to perform a pragmatic service, holding it every moment in subjection to an aim as realistic as it is idealistic, and as idealistic as it is realistic.

Incidentally, he deals with the logic of what is nowadays called Intellectualism. James, you will remember, characterized Intellectualism as the type of thought which assumes logic to be the final authority in the world of being or fact, and asserts that the logic of identity is the most intimate and exhaustive definer of reality. It is interesting to note that Kierkegaard, half a century before James or Bergson, clearly formulates and consistently develops the counter-proposition that logic does not and cannot define reality, that reality may indeed be pre-disposed by logic for our knowledge, but that it contains elements which no logic can ever assimilate. It is impossible, for example, logically to bridge or construe the transition from one quality to another, as is so clearly shown by Zeno's paradoxes; and it is in my opinion, also, the principal lesson of Plato's dialogue: *Parmenides.* Some modern logicians have indeed imagined it possible to transcend the difficulty by the positive conception of the infinite, but this is, I believe, a confusion and a misunderstanding. The category of transition does not belong in logic; the fundamental principle of logic is the Eleatic doctrine that everything is, and nothing comes into being. But since transitions do take place in Reality, it follows that the historical disciplines, and all the knowledge which rests upon the basis of the historical, and particularly ethics, operate with this concept. But the fact that the concept does not belong in logic makes it impossible to treat transitions as necessary; they obey the principle of cause and effect, but not the principle of ground and consequent. They come to pass by a leap; and wherever the ideal and the actual, the rational and the empirical, the laws or principle on the one hand, and the observed facts on the other, are brought into relation, there we have a transition of thought, identical or analogous with the inductive leap. Every science operates within a certain universe of discourse, a logically immanent system of presuppositions; and it is a temptation, by yielding to which science is not advanced, but only retarded and confused, when the attempt is made to deduce and construe the transcendent principles upon which our own immanence rests; as if physics were to try to demonstrate motion, in the sense of logically construing it; or psychology, consciousness; or ethics, the concept of obligation; or theology, the existence of God; or Christian dogmatics, the consciousness of sin. It is Reality itself which posits such principles as points of departure; and if we do not start with them, presupposing them, and attempting to explain them only in the sense of thinking them through to the end, i. e., clarifying their meaning,—if we do not start with them, we shall never end with them, no matter how ingenious or profound our speculations may be.

Just as actual change, then, is incommensurable with and external to the whole sphere of logic, so the contingent is also unassimilated by the science, although it is an essential ingredient of the actual. We can therefore have a logical system, provided we remember that an absolute beginning is chimerical, and that such a system will thus rest, in the last analysis, upon presuppositions; and provided we are careful not to admit anything which is only because it is actual, or has come into being, i. e., has a historical presupposition and character. But a system embracing reality is for human knowledge impossible. For Reality is for human knowledge something which is always in process of becoming, and hence the necessary systematic finality is an indefinitely postponed *desideratum*. In a logical system all development is immanent, from the same to the same, the whole being implicit in each part. Hence it is dominated by necessity, for the necessary is simply an expression for self-identity and self-relatedness, and for the eternal sameness of the relation which each logical concept or system bears to itself. But change is always contingent, and in the sphere of Reality the fundamental change is that which Aristotle defines as the transition from the possible to the actual; which is a change of being, but not a change of essence; and this is another reason why it cannot be logically construed, since logic deals only with essences, abstracting from factual existence. Hence it is also that factual existence, as distinct from ideal existence, is never capable of demonstration, whether in relation to a stone, a man, or God. For all demonstration or proof operates by means of logical *quales*, essences, ideal entities; in every such proof either the factual existence of these is presupposed or given, or else is abstracted from as irrelevant. I cannot demonstrate the existence of a stone, but only that some existing thing is a stone. The evidence offered in a court of justice does not prove that a criminal exists, but only that the accused, whose existence is naturally granted without proof, is a criminal. And every proof of the existence of God reduces itself in the last analysis to a conceptual development of the consequences which flow from having initially assumed His existence. If God does not exist, we cannot prove that He does exist; and if God does exist, the attempt to prove it is an egregious bit of folly, as if one were to propose, in the presence of another person, to prove that this person exists. This would be an insult, since it amounts to ignoring said person's existence, present existence being higher than all demonstration for it, and requiring a higher form of recognition. The existence of God is a postulate, not in the ordinary meaningless and frivolous sense, but in the sense that the individual's postulation of God is a subjective and personal necessity. "In stories of romantic adventure," says Kierkegaard, "there is frequent reference to a lamp called the wonderful; when this lamp is rubbed, a spirit reveals itself. Jest! But freedom is the true wonderful lamp; when a man rubs this lamp with ethical passion, God comes into being for him. The spirit of Aladdin's lamp is a servant, so wish it then, ye, whose spirit is a wish! But whoever rubs the wonderful lamp of freedom, becomes himself a servant—the Spirit is Lord!"[14] The task I have set myself in the present discussion will not permit further elaboration of this anti-intellectualism. One must read for himself the great super-

---

[14]*Unscientific Postscript*, 124.

dreadnought, as Brandes calls it, which Kierkegaard sent out in combat against post-Kantian Idealism, the book which he calls by the curious title of *The Concluding Unscientic Postscript to the Fragments of Philosophy.* In this the reader will get an impression of the resources of pathos, humor, wit, irony, and dialectic which Kierkegaard employs against an intellectualism which had assumed pretentiously to include and embody all the elements of life in a higher and more rational unity, although it was in reality a brilliantly futile and wretchedly distorted one-sidedness.

But Kierkegaard is Socratic also with respect to the maieutic element in his method. By the logic of the well-known "pugnacious proposition" of the Meno, the principle that Professor Royce called the "religious paradoxes" and which he quite consistently used to destroy the concept of a revelation,—Socrates was forced to assume the doctrine of Reminiscence, that each individual has the essential truth within him, so that it needs only questioning to bring it forth. In analogous fashion, Kierkegaard starts from the principle that the truth is known, that the age does not require a communication of knowledge, but rather a more intimate realization of the significance of that which is already known. And just as the Socratic dialectic was used to eliminate misunderstandings and illusions, to take away the delusion of false knowledge, in order to make way for the underlying truth lying unawares in the potentiality of the soul, so that it might realize itself without hindrance; so Kierkegaard felt it to be his mission to take away knowledge rather than to increase it; to make things more difficult rather than to make things more easy. And while Socrates' contemporaries were living in the secure consciousness that of course they knew what a human being was, and moreover knew it in such a way that they did not feel it worth while to give it a thought, but were busy about other and more important concerns, Socrates made this supposed knowledge a problem, and so seriously, that at the end of many years' reflection over the matter, he could not be quite certain whether he was a more terrible monster than Typhon, or had in his nature a gentler and divine part. Kierkegaard's attitude was precisely parallel. While all knew the Christian truth, as a triviality among a hundred others, having no primitive impression of its significance, the more ambitious therefore being busy with projects to advance beyond it and transcend it, in order to have at least something significant to do—Kierkegaard transformed the being of a Christian into a problem, and so profoundly that at last it became a question whether there existed one true Christian. The Socratic dialogue was a clearing of the ground, a puncturing of the bombastic thoughts and ill-considered opinions of the respondent, to make room for the ideal within; in precisely the same way, the whole Kierkegaardian literature may be viewed as a vast Socratic dialogue with his contemporaries, with Kierkegaard taking it upon himself to interpret the mind of the respondent, spying out everywhere the illusions and exposing the principles of life to view, the entire literature tending toward and making room for the ideal determination of what it means to be a Christian. But this uninteresting and tiresome purpose was by no means confessed in the beginning; Kierkegaard began with the esthetic, where most people have their lives, in order, like a good teacher, to begin with what the pupil understands, and so gradually to lead on to what he does not

understand; though here the task was made more difficult by the presence of a very pertinacious illusion of
knowledge.

Knowledge—a superfluity of knowledge, but possessed
without reality or significance, this was Kierkegaard's
diagnosis of the disease of the age. Christianity had been
transformed into an objective system of doctrine; the age
of the martyrs had long since given way to the age of the
monks; and now finally had come the professorial-scien-
tific age of Christianity, where the ordinary Christian
looked up to the professor as the standard and test of
Christianity, and in which the existential was altogether
forgotten. But if men had forgotten what it means to be
a Christian, they had undoubtedly also forgotten what
it means to live as human beings. Hence it was necessary
to begin far back, in order to leave no loop-hole or difficulties behind. The first task then was to show what it
means to exist as a human being. For this purpose Kierkegaard realized that it would be necessary to avoid communicating what he had to say in the form of knowledge,
which would only be misunderstood, as if to live were
identical with acquiring information on this or some
other point. The method must be "indirect," calculated
to stimulate the reader to self-activity. The first work
having a place in this plan was *Either-Or*. It deals with
the relation between the esthetic and the ethical principles of life. The reader is introduced to two personalities who interpret reflectively their respective standpoints, each being the author of one of the two volumes
of the work. The author of the first volume presents an
esthetic attitude toward life, brilliantly, with a keen and
utterly fearless dialectic, regardless of every consequence,
bound only by ideal considerations of self-consistency.

He expresses himself in a number of essays, critical reviews, lyrical outbursts, and in the famous "Diary of the Seducer." He has no name; his papers are called A's papers. This, then, is one alternative; the attempt is made to let it expose its own inner nature by having it speak and interpret life for itself. The other alternative is an ethical view of life, presented with dignity and enthusiasm by B, a friend of A's, and his two long letters to the latter constitute the second volume. The preface explains that these papers, both A's and B's, had been found by the publisher in an old secretary; thus there is no author, and no decision, even in the preface, between the points of view; the reader is not told whether B converted A from the error of his way, or A converted B; he is confronted with a choice, an either-or.

The keynote of A's papers is romantic, a fiery and passionate romanticism, kindled by an enthusiastic dialectic. The short lyrical outbursts with which the volume opens, called Diapsalmata, express a Byronic despair. The initial paragraph posits a dissonance which is closely in tune with the theme of the entire book: the problem of the book is to solve it. It is often quoted:

What is a poet? A poet is an unhappy being, whose heart is torn by secret sufferings, but whose lips are so strangely formed that when the sighs and the cries escape them, they sound like beautiful music. His fate is like that of the unfortunate creatures whom the tyrant Phalaris imprisoned in a bronze bull, and slowly tortured over a steady fire; their cries could not reach the tyrant's ears so as to strike terror into his heart; when they reached his ears they sounded like sweet music. And men crowd about the poet and say to him "Sing for us soon again"; that is as much as to say: "May new suffering torment your soul, but may your lips be formed as before; for the cries would only cause us anguish, but the music is lively." And the critics come, too, and say: "Quite correct, and so it ought to be according to the rules of Esthetics." To be sure a critic resembles a poet to a hair; he only lacks the suffering in his heart, and the music upon his lips. Behold, therefore, I would rather be a swineherd in the sties, and be understood by the swine, than be a poet and be misunderstood by men.[15]

B, the ethicist of the second part, is not A's equal either in poetic gifts or dialectic power; but he is A's superior in sureness of touch, in dignity, and in ethical pathos. He is a concrete personality, A is only the possibility of a personality. In explaining himself, B also explains A, and corrects his errors. His ethical formula is to choose oneself, through esthetic despair to find oneself by means of a movement of the will, a movement which posits a real alternative between good and evil. It is not a choice between good and evil which he makes primary, but a choice whereby the distinction between good and evil is posited, so that it comes to have significance for the personality. The development is concrete. The first letter deals with marriage, defends its esthetic validity against romantic objections and worldly-wise falsifications; the second half deals with the equilibrium between the esthetic and the ethical in the development of the personality. The primary ethical obligation is to reveal oneself—the esthetic principle is secretiveness,—and hence the central significance of marriage as the most concrete revelation of the personality, whereby time is utilized for the purpose of attaining a new history. The volume ends with a sermon, written by a friend of B's, a clergyman in a country parish—on the theme that over against God we are always in the wrong, and that this is a happy thought, since it makes doubt impossible; the sermon ends by expressing the principle that only the truth

---

[15]*Either-Or*, I, 15.

which edifies is truth *for you; for you* being the characterizing mark of all religious truth.[16]

The limits of space will not permit me to summarize
the contents, or even to name the titles of Kierkegaard's
following publications which formed so many steps forward in what I have called a Socratic dialogue, whose
main theme was: the forms of existence which correspond to Christianity. *Either-Or* had confined itself to
esthetic and ethical categories; even the sermon merely
hinted at the religious, and was fundamentally based on
an ethical conception. The ethicist had saved himself out
of his despair by a choice, without breach of continuity
with himself, and without coming into a personal relationship with the divine. God is thus for him only a
limiting conception, his relation to God is merely a reflex
of his relation to family, state, and so forth. This way of
introducing the ethical was adopted by Kierkegaard because he wanted to take up the various aspects of life
successively, and did not wish to deal with the religious
until he had presented the ethical in its ideality; but he
himself held that a breach of continuity could not be
avoided, that in this breach the individual required
divine assistance, bringing him into a personal relationship with God. In the subsequent publications, therefore,
he turned his attention to faith, taking up one aspect at
a time. The first deals with the particularity, the excep-
tionality, of the personal God-relation, its suspension of
the ordinary form of the ethical obligations, using the
tragic hero as *terminus a quo,* and the hero of faith as
terminus ad quem. In this connection he also uses the
figure of a young man whose love-affair makes him a
poet, so that he cannot marry;—a theme which Ibsen

---

[16]*Either/Or*, II, 294.

considerably vulgarized in the *Comedy of Love*. This takes two volumes; and now he brings up the matter of sin as the decisive and universal point of departure for the religious life, in a psychological essay on the *Concept Anxiety;* simultaneously there appeared the *Fragments of Philosophy,* in which the dialectical structure of Christianity is presented in a form which is an ironical parody of the Hegelian philosophy of religion, the idea being presented as an invention of the author, and no reference being made to Christ or the Christian religion by name until the last page of the book. The next volume, *Stages on the Way of Life,* passes in review the whole previous development of ideas—the esthetic stage by means of a banquet scene *à la* Plato's Symposium, the speeches all being about woman—the ethical stage by an essay on marriage, again emphasizing the ideality of resolution, decision, will—and the religious stage by the unfolding through the pages of a diary of a sympathetic love-collision, closely resembling, but not actually reproducing, his own experience. Finally comes the giant *Unscientific Postscript,* which, in Kierkegaard's phrase, "clothes the problem in historical costume." It dismisses in a brief introductory section Biblical Criticism, the History of Christianity, and the Church, as inadequate objective guarantees for what Christianity is, and then poses the subjective problem: "I, Johannes Climacus, born here in Copenhagen, now 30 years old, have heard that Christianity promises and conditions a highest good, an eternal happiness; I ask now how I may come into relations with Christianity for this purpose."[17] The problem is discussed through five hundred closely printed pages of as

---

[17]*Unscientific Postscript,* 19.

keen dialectic as can be found in any book in the whole history of thought.

All the volumes of which I have spoken were published over the signatures of different pseudonyms: Victor Eremita, Johannes *de silentio*, Constantin Constantius, Vigilius Haufniensis, Frater Taciturnus, Johannes Climacus. The standpoints, from which the books were written were various; Kierkegaard was the author and the creator of the authors, but these were themselves, as ideal personalities, the sole creators of their contents. And secondly, though dealing with religious problems, they all have this characteristic in common, that the problems are presented in an esthetic form, not in the religious form of edification. In order to express his own personal standpoint, and in order to suggest that the whole literature had at bottom a religious motivation, there were published under Kierkegaard's own name, eighteen religious addresses, two or three at a time, the whole series concurrent with the esthetic productivity. These addresses do not, however, attempt to develop or use the distinctively Christian categories; it is their function to try out how far it is possible to go in the realm of the religious without using, in any decisive sense, the idea of sin, salvation, atonement, etc.

The publication of the *Postscript* marked the highpoint of this movement of thought, which I have likened to a Socratic dialogue, where the whole contemporary consciousness, the Spirit of the Age, is made to play the part of the respondent. From now on came the distinctively Christian ideas, developed mainly in the form of sermons—invariably dedicated to "the individual whom I am glad and grateful to call my reader." The development of the Christian ethic is gradual, careful, methodical, step by step advancing to a higher ideality, culminating finally in the decisive enunciation of the position that Kierkegaard does not call himself a Christian, precisely as the Socratic dialectic culminates in the Socratic ignorance and in the doubt as to whether Socrates himself was really a human being. Thus the Absolute Ideal was disentangled from human compromises and relativities; the guiding purpose was to bring into life a greater degree of honesty, humility, and respect for the Ideal and to express the hollowness of the modern pretensions to progress. "I represent neither Christian severity nor Christian mildness," says Kierkegaard; "what I represent is common human honesty. We have abolished place number one, and have advanced to the first rank, place number two or three or four, deceitfully lowering the standards; gentlemen, this process, called progress, must be put a stop to,"—such was the tone of the grandiose agitation in which Kierkegaard's life culminated, and with which his career was brought to a close.

The entire Kierkegaardian literature describes at the same time the author's own personal education and discipline, toward becoming a Christian. It describes the movement in reflection so that the author reflects himself out of everything else, the esthetic, the poetic, the philosophical—in order to become the simple, straightforward, plain, uninteresting, moral personality—a Christian. "If the author had been twice as gifted," says Kierkegaard, "the process would have taken twice as long a time."

Professor Royce in his work, *The Problem of Christianity*, presented a clear and extremely consistent philosophy, which he identified as the Essence of Christianity, as this was developed and perfected in the Pauline

churches. In this view of Christianity, its essence is identified with the speculative idea, the central metaphysical
principle; the central category is the process of interpretation in terms of mediating ideas; its culminating concept is the Community. In these three fundamental
points, Kierkegaard's concept of Christianity constitutes
a precise dialectical opposite. Instead of identifying
Christianity with the speculative idea, he holds that it is,
from the standpoint of all human philosophy, an Absolute Paradox. It is not a temporary anticipation of a
future point in the evolution of the human race, but
permanently transcendent of all human thought and
values, and hence forever incapable of assimilation as the
immanent principle of the human reason, "an eternity
older and an eternity higher than all systems, even that
which ten thousand years from now will be the newest."
Instead of the category of Interpretation, therefore,
Kierkegaard operates with the opposite category of indirect communication, of Faith. With respect to the latter,
he holds that it is essential to distinguish between the
idea of the Greek *pistis,* belief, and the Christian concept
of Faith.

Saint Augustine has done an incalculable harm. The whole
Christian formulation of doctrine through the centuries is
based on him—and he has confused the concept of Faith. He
has simply brought up again the Platonic-Aristotelian definition of this concept, the entire pagan-Greek philosophical idea—
and in so doing has performed a service to Christianity like that
which Holberg's Peter Deacon attributes to Saxo Grammaticus,
who, he says, enriched the Latin language by adding to it many
Danish words, for example—black horse, equus blakkatus. In
Greek philosophy, faith is a concept which belongs within the
sphere of the intellectual (in Plato's *Republic* the idea is clearly
defined, and also in Aristotle's *Rhetoric*). Faith in this sense
corresponds to the probable, and so we get the climax: first, faith,

then knowledge. But in Christianity, Faith does not belong to the intellectual sphere, but to the existential—God did not appear in the role of a docent. Faith is the expression for the relation between personality and personality. Personality is a return upon itself, a *clausum;* a shrine, a retreat; it is a something within, and the highest possible relation between personality and personality is faith. Take, too, the most passionate lovers who have ever loved, even if they were, as we say, one soul in two bodies; it can never come to anything more than that the one believes that the other loves him or her. In the purely personal relation between God as Personality, and the believer as personality, *in existence* there lies the concept: Faith.[18]

In the same way, Kierkegaard's standpoint for Christian ethics is not primarily social, but aggressively and decisively individualistic. The concept of the Community when applied to the present life is an impatient anticipation of the Eternal, an illusion corresponding to the illusion of a triumphant Church, or a Christian civilization. When on the other hand, the Church is recognized as militant, and the warfare it is engaged in, a Christian warfare, a spiritual warfare, then the stress is on the individual, and the individual's personal relationship to God becomes necessarily higher than all human fellowship. The "Community" is in a state of rest what the individual is in a state of unrest and struggle; the community belongs not to Time but to Eternity, where it is the union of all the individuals who as individuals have endured the test and conquered in the fight. God wants primitiveness, individuality;—hence the principle, "first the kingdom of God." No one who makes this his life-principle can possibly become "just like the rest." Each individual is forced to interpret the principle concretely in his own individual fashion—and life has con-

---

[18]*Papirer*, XI, 237.

creteness enough for innumerable millions. It is the
dignity of the human race that each individual has something by which he is essentially different from every other
individual; he has a self. And it is the demoralizing effect
of a misuse of culture and science and the intellectual
in general, to take away the primitiveness, to rob human
beings of their selves.

But if it were not true that one man might under the same
circumstances do just the opposite of that which it is right for
another man to do, and both be equally honest, sincere, just,
God-fearing, then the God-relation would not exist, not essentially, and not in its deepest significance. If one could pass
judgment upon every human being in accordance with a general,
common standard, then God would be abolished, everything
would culminate, as in paganism, in society, or the state; life
would become much easier, but also very empty; neither the
spiritual exertion nor the deepening of self-consciousness which
arises, when in the collision of an infinite misunderstanding, the
God-relationship is developed in the human heart, would be
either necessary or possible. (Abbreviated.)

Lastly, it will perhaps be quite enough merely to call
attention to the fact that Kierkegaard produced no
Apologetic—no defense of Christianity. Christianity was
for him the Absolute—but to defend the Absolute, to
recommend it for three or a thousand reasons, is to betray
it. It is not men who are to judge Christianity, to see if
it fits into their lives; it is Christianity which proposes
to transform the ideas of men and to teach them to live
as spiritual beings. The only defense worth talking about
in this connection, is that men might seek to defend themselves over against Christianity. The tone throughout is
therefore consistently and aggressively polemic. And this,
too, reminds one of Socrates—was there a single trace of
apology in that famous Apology of his before his judges?

If I were to compress into a single word the intellectual significance of the Kierkegaardian literature, I would say that it consisted in mapping out the sphere of the inner life, the subjective life of the emotions, with constant reference to the ideal. And great as has been the energy devoted to reflection in the centuries past, wonderful as the productions of human thought have been, with reference to all the impersonal and objective problems—nature, logic, mathematics, metaphysics, history—it must be confessed that the inner life of the emotions has long been a comparatively uncharted sea. Herein lies Kierkegaard's originality, herein his permanent contribution to thought.

III. THE "LITERATURE"—A RESUME

THE outer aspects of Søren Kierkegaard's career suggest the placid and uneventful life of a student and man of letters. Born in Copenhagen on the 5th day of May, 1813, the youngest son of a merchant of means, he received the humanistic discipline of a classical school, and was enrolled in the University at the age of eighteen. The ten years following were spent in somewhat discursive studies, ranging over the fields of esthetics, philosophy, and theology. At twenty-seven he received the degree of *Magister artium,* and soon thereafter entered into an engagement of marriage, broken after a year upon his own initiative. He remained unmarried and from this time until his death, which took place on the 11th of November, 1855, he devoted himself unremittingly to his literary labors, unfolding an extraordinary productivity.

While the first two chapters in this volume have perhaps familiarized the reader with the main incidents of Kierkegaard's life, there are two phases of his boyhood and of his father's influence upon his mental development that are worthy of special emphasis. In an unfinished metaphysical essay, *De omnibus dubitandum est,* written by Kierkegaard in 1842-1843, his description of the training of Johannes Climacus, the principal character, is undoubtedly autobiographical in nature, and affords to some degree an explanation of the richly imaginative power so characteristic of his work. I quote:

His home life offered but few diversions. He was scarcely ever permitted to go out, and thus he became accustomed, at an early age, to find his diversion in his own thoughts. His father was very strict and dry and prosaic on the surface; but underneath this coarse and unpretentious exterior he preserved a glowing fancy, which not even his extreme old age was able to dull. When Johannes sometimes asked for permission to go out, he was most often refused; but occasionally, as if to make up for this refusal, the father proposed a walk together up and down the room. This seemed at first a poor substitute; and yet, like his father's coarse gray coat, it concealed under its plain exterior something very different from that which appeared on the surface. The proposal accepted, it was for Johannes himself to decide where to go. They passed out the gate and visited a neighboring palace; or went to the seashore, or wandered about the streets, all at the boy's pleasure. For the father's imagination was powerful enough to create a realizing sense of anything and everything the boy desired. While they walked up and down, the father described the sights along the way; they greeted the passers-by; the vehicles rumbled and drowned the father's voice; the dainties displayed by the fruitwoman on the corner seemed more alluring than ever. When they were on ground familiar to Johannes, everything was given a description so vivid and minute that not the smallest detail was overlooked. When the way took them to scenes new and unfamiliar, the father knew how to draw so explicit a picture, and give it so vivid an intuition, that after but half an hour of this promenade Johannes was as tired and overwhelmed by his impressions as if he had been out of doors an entire day. He soon learned how to practice his father's magic art for himself. A dramatic representation supplanted the former epic narrative; for they conversed together on the way. When they walked amidst scenes with which Johannes was familiar, they prompted one another faithfully, lest anything should be overlooked; when the way was strange, Johannes trusted his fancy to combine the elements of his memory into pictures, while his father's all-powerful imagination brought into being every least detail, utilizing every childish wish as an ingredient in the drama. To Johannes it seemed as if he were witnessing, during the course of their conversation, a world coming into being; it was as if his father were the Creator, and he himself a favorite, permitted freely to introduce his own childish fancies into the creative process. For he was never repressed, and his father was never at a loss; every suggestion tendered was made use of, and always to Johannes' complete satisfaction.

With an all-powerful imagination the father combined an invincible dialectic. And hence when at times the father was engaged in argument with a neighbor, Johannes was all ears; and this so much the more, as everything in these discussions was arranged with ceremonious order and precision. His father never interrupted the opponent, but let him speak through to the end; when he appeared to have finished, he always cautiously asked him if there was anything more he wished to say, before he began his answer. Johannes had followed the argument with concentrated attention, and was, in his own way, a truly interested participant. There came a pause, and then the father's reply; all was changed in the twinkling of an eye. How it was changed was a mystery to the boy, but his mind was fascinated by the spectacle. The opponent spoke in rebuttal, and Johannes was still more deeply attentive, if possible, than before; he wanted to bear every point in mind. The opponent approached his peroration, and Johannes could almost hear his own heart beat, so impatient was he to hear the outcome of the argument. Then came the father's reply, and in a moment everything was changed. The things that had seemed clear before, suddenly became inexplicable; the things that had seemed certain became doubtful, and their very opposites were made to appear evident.

What other children possessed in the enchantments of poetry and the surprises of adventure, Johannes had in the calm of a vivid intuition and the swiftly changing perspectives of dialectics. When he became older he had no need to cast his playthings aside, for he had learned to play with that which was to be the serious business of his life; and yet it never lost its allurement. A girl plays with her dolls until at last the doll is transformed into a lover, for a woman's entire life is love. A similar continuity characterized Johannes' life, for his entire life was thought.

In later years Kierkegaard was accustomed to spend days and weeks in practicing on himself different emotional and temperamental states, an exercise which he describes as "a kind of nimble dancing in the service of thought."[1] This making of himself an instrument for the exploration of the passions, by which he attained an extraordinary command of the scale of human feeling, was undoubtedly to a large extent made possible by the strange training of the imagination above described, fantastic as it must seem to all straightforward souls.[2]

The other final and decisive paternal influence was that which had its source in the elder Kierkegaard's sombre religiosity. The sternness of the parental discipline, indeed, gave the boy a lofty impression of duty, for he was trained to a strict obedience. Not that he was enmeshed in the web of a multiplicity of petty obligations, but with respect to the few commands that were laid upon him, it was the parental principle that no evasion was to be tolerated. Kierkegaard's great esthetic sensibility thus received a restraining and balancing counterpoise in the form of a strong sense of the value of obedience, of authority, and even of an uncompromising severity. This left a permanent mark upon his thought. In spite of this severity Kierkegaard was tenderly devoted to his father, and the religious discourses of his authorship were repeatedly dedicated in their successive issues to "my deceased father, Michael Pedersen Kierkegaard, formerly a merchant of this city."

When Kierkegaard was twenty-five, his father died. At this time, so he describes himself, his personality was a strangely developed potentiality. Fortunate in the external circumstances of his life, initiated into all kinds of pleasures, equipped with a superfluity of culture, gifted with imagination and the power of dialectic, he

---

[1] *Philosophical Fragments,* 3.
[2] Perhaps the best examples of Kierkegaard's play of imagination are to be found in the purely esthetic first volume of *Either/Or,* particularly in the "Diary of the Seducer," although it flashes forth in practically all of his writings

was an observer and a student of human nature. His spirit
was high-strung and proud. That he should ever be
defeated in any undertaking seemed to him inconceiv-
able, except that he had no hope of ever overcoming
his melancholy. In his heart he entertained a lively
sympathy for all who suffered oppression and hardship;
and his total attitude toward life was thoroughly polemic.
He had long entertained the ambition to be able to help
others to clearness of thought, especially in connection
with the Christian religion, for which he had never lost
his respect, although troubled indeed by doubts, in many
instances doubts of which he had never even read or
heard. The death of his father, however, had caused a
revival of the religious impressions of childhood, which
he now came to experience in a somewhat idealized and
less harsh form.

A passage from the Journals, written at the age of
twenty-two, reveals the nature of his intellectual orientation. The entire passage is a sort of stock-taking, a review
of his varied interests and ambitions. "My misfortune,"
he says, "is that I am interested in too many things, and
not decisively committed to any one thing, to which I
might subordinate everything else." Along with jurisprudence, the theater, theology, he takes up the claims
of natural science as a possible prospective vocation. Distinguishing between the industrious collector of facts and
the organizing intellectual genius who succeeds in gaining
a view of the whole, he expresses his admiration for the
latter. Nevertheless, he concludes that it does not seem
possible for him to make natural science his chief concern.
The passage continues:

It has always been the life of reason and freedom which has
most interested me, and it has always been my wish that I might
solve the mystery of life. The forty years in the wilderness, before

I could enter into the promised land of science, appear to me too precious; so much the more, since I have an idea that Nature may also be viewed from another side, without requiring an insight into the secrets of science. In a particular flower I may train myself to see the whole world; or I may listen to the many hints and suggestions which Nature offers with respect to human life.

Theology would seem to be the sphere to which my interest most clearly inclines me, but my theological studies have hitherto met with the greatest difficulties. Within Christianity itself such great contrasts present themselves as at least to place obstacles in the way of an impartial survey. Orthodoxy I have, so to speak, been brought up in; but as soon as I began to think for myself, the huge Colossus began to tumble. I call it purposely a Colossus, for it has in the main much inner consistency; and, in the course of centuries, the individual parts of it have been so fused together that it is hard to come to close quarters with them simply as isolated features. There are individual points on which I might be able to reach an agreement with the orthodox doctrine, but these would then have to be regarded as the green sprouts which may sometimes be found growing in the cleft of the barren rock. On the other hand, I might possibly be able to discern the errors and perversities present at other points; but the foundation itself I would have to hold for a time *in dubio*. If the foundation were to be changed, the whole would, of course, have to be viewed in a different light; and so my attention is drawn to *Rationalism*. But Rationalism seems to me to cut a very sorry figure. Insofar, indeed, as Reason consistently follows its own impulses and spirit in the attempt to clear up the relation between God and the world; and insofar as it thus considers man in his deepest and most intimate relationship with God, and hence also comes to take Christianity into account, from its own standpoint, as the religion which for so many centuries has satisfied man's deepest religious need—insofar, indeed, no objection can be urged against it. But this is not what Rationalism proceeds to do. It takes its essential coloring from Christianity, and hence stands on an entirely different footing; it is not a system, but a Noah's ark, wherein the clean and the unclean animals lie down side by side. It makes about the same impression on me as the civilian guard we formerly had here in Denmark beside the Royal Potsdam Guard. It seeks essentially to base itself upon the Scriptures, and sends a legion of scriptural passages before it at every point; but the exposition and development is not itself saturated with this consciousness. The rationalistic theologians behave like Cambyses, who in campaigning against Egypt sent the sacred fowls and cats before him; but, like the Roman consul, they are quite ready to throw the sacred animals overboard when these refuse to eat. . . . . What I really need, however, is a clear mind regarding what I ought to do; not so much as to what I ought to know, except insofar as some sort of knowledge precedes all doing. I need to understand my place in life, and to see what call the divine power has for me; I need to discover a Truth which is a Truth for me; I need to find the Idea for which I can live and die. For what would it profit me if I discovered some so-called objective truth; if I worked my way through all the philosophical systems, and could pass them in review when necessary; or if I were able to point out the inconsistencies within each particular school of thought; what would it profit me if I were able to develop a theory of the State, to combine scattered facts gathered from many sources into a totality, and thus construe a world in which I did not live, but only held up to the gaze of others; what would it profit me if I could expound the significance of Christianity, and explain many of its particular phenomena, if it had no deeper significance for me and for my life? . . . . What I need is the power to live a complete human life, and not merely a life of knowledge; lest I come to base my thought upon something so-called objective, in any case something not my own. I need something that is connected with the deepest root of my existence, something through which I am linked, so to speak, with the divine, and to which I could cling even if the whole world were to fall in ruins about me.[3]

It is in these closing aspirations that the key-note of Kierkegaard's subsequent life and thought is clearly struck.

Since the details of Kierkegaard's engagement to Regina Olsen and its subsequent rupture have already been outlined in Chapter I, it is unnecessary to repeat them here, but the effects of this experience upon Kierke-

---

[3]Dru, Selections from *The Journals*, §§ 16, 22.

gaard's subsequent development were so far-reaching that they cannot be passed over, since it was this experience which placed him almost at a stroke in the full possession of his esthetic and literary powers. The wealth of feeling which derives from it and centers about it constitutes a rich vein in the Kierkegaardian literature, and is one of its prime claims to distinction. The experience had probed deep. That he should have ventured upon an undertaking which he could not fulfill, and that he had been compelled to sacrifice his honor in the breaking of a solemn pact, stirred his sense of pride and self-feeling profoundly. A passage in *Either/Or* reflects one of the moods in which he reacts on the experience.

What I need is a voice as penetrating as the eye of Lynceus, as terrifying as the sigh of giants, as persistent as the sound of nature, as full of derision as a frosty wind-gust, as malicious as Echo's heartless mockeries, of a compass from the deepest bass to the most mellifluous soprano, modulated from the sacred softness of a whisper to the violent fury of rage. This is what I need in order to breathe, to get expression for what is on my mind, to stir the bowels of my compassion and my wrath.[4]

What the estheticist in *Either/Or* thus desires, Kierkegaard came to possess in the fullest measure; for his unhappy love-affair had made him an imaginative writer of the first rank.

But the experience had, according to his own interpretation of it, also a deeper import. It gave his life its definite and final direction. "When I broke with her," he writes, "my impression was: either sensuality in extremest measure, or else absolute religiosity, and that according to a standard quite different from the clergyman's *mélange*."[5] The latter alternative was at bottom

---

[4] *Either/Or*, I, 19.
[5] Kierkegaard's *Papirer*, X:5, A149, 18.

already chosen, prepared for by his father's discipline, and matured by the very motives operating to bring on the crisis above described. He came to make a beginning in two different places at one and the same time, namely, as a poetic and as a religious nature; such is his own epigrammatic description of the situation.

Because of my previous religious training the fact in question [the broken engagement] took hold of me in a far deeper manner than would otherwise have been possible; it annihilated, to a certain degree, in religious impatience, the "poet" that had been born within me. The poetic within me therefore became something essentially foreign, something that had merely happened to me; the religious awakening, on the other hand, though not indeed produced by myself, nevertheless came to possess the most intimate relation to myself. That is, in the "poet" I did not recognize myself in the deepest sense; but rather in the religious awakening.

However, the poetic endowment demanded expression. The religious side of his nature, being the deeper self, took it in charge, and made it serve its own purposes. All the while it stood waiting, as it were, for the esthetic productivity to be got through with as soon as possible. The authorship bears the mark of this situation, since it has from the first a double character—esthetic and religious; and during the production of his esthetic writings, Kierkegaard tells us, "the author himself lived in categories that were decisively religious."

The number of external influences to which Kierkegaard reacted was considerable. An author may gain a certain degree of originality through mere exclusion, but the individual stamp and coloring so highly characteristic of the Kierkegaardian literature is the consequence rather of an intensiveness in the personal reaction, and of an energetic assimilation of the given influences. What an author is able to write the day after his library has been burned has been suggested as a crucial test of his resourcefulness. Almost every line of Kierkegaard's seems to meet such a condition, so little is it the product of a bookish erudition, and so completely is it the expression of a free creative energy. Nevertheless, many general intellectual influences reveal themselves in his work and enter deeply into its form and structure.

As a true son of his native land, his inheritance included the full wealth of Danish culture as expressed in its literature. But of all Danish writers, he appears to owe most to Holberg, the great pioneer of Danish comedy. Holberg's humor is something which Kierkegaard may almost be said to have absorbed *in succum et sanguinem*. The Holberg comedies served him for a veritable language; and the more technical philosophical treatises are replete with references to Holbergian characters and situations, giving substance and mass to the delicate comedy of their fine-spun polemic.

Kierkegaard offers many points of contact with romanticism. The style of the esthetic pseudonyms has an emotional intensity and abandon, a lyrical effervescence, at times an extravagance of feeling and statement, verging close upon the limits of the rational. By way of contrast, the religious discourses are written in a style noticeably sober, even, and restrained. The involved literary structure of the pseudonyms, with one author inside another like the compartments of a Chinese box, has also been cited as a romantic trait. More significant, however, is the strong attraction which Kierkegaard felt, in common with most romanticists, for the primitive in folklore, ballads and sagas. He made systematic studies of the great representative figures that stand out so strongly for the medieval imagination: a Don Juan, a Faust, The Wandering Jew, a Robin Hood. And he shares with the German romanticists an unbounded admiration for Shakespeare. Of the rich Shakespearian insight he makes liberal use for his own delineation of the passions. Though he may be said to have had a sympathetic appreciation of the German romantic movement, his dissertation, *On the Concept Irony*, reveals him as a severe critic of its aberrations. His attitude was on the whole too objective and analytic for him to be classified as a romanticist.

Kierkegaard's relation to Hegel was that of a student sufficiently docile to absorb the master's teaching, but whose matured criticism just on that account became all the more dangerously destructive. To Hegel he owes his mastery of a precise and finished philosophical terminology, and Hegel's influence may perhaps also be traced in the frequent reversion to an algebraically abstract style, clashing somewhat strangely with expressions vividly poetic in their concreteness. But undoubtedly the most important and the most intimate influence leaving its mark upon Kierkegaard's work and thought, was the personality of Socrates. His dissertation was an interpretation of Socrates from the point of view of the Socratic irony. This study reveals a sympathetic appreciation of the Athenian sage and became the point of departure for an increasingly deeper understanding, culminating in the sense of an intimate spiritual kinship. Kierkegaard recognized in his own life-work the fulfilment of an ethical and intellectual task analogous to that which Socrates performed for ancient Greece.[6]

Kierkegaard was unique in the degree to which his enormous energy of reflection was directed back upon

---

[6]See pp. 36-39.

himself. Subsequent criticism has uncovered very few points of view for his interpretation not already suggested either in the literature itself, or in the wealth of comment which the Journals afford. In the *Unscientific Postscript*, his pseudonym, Johannes Climacus, reviews the esthetic literature, and assigns to each work its place in relation to his own central thesis. Some years later, after the bulk of the religious literature had appeared, Kierkegaard wrote a literary autobiography to serve as an interpretation of the whole. The latter work, however, was not published during his lifetime, only a brief abstract of it appearing in pamphlet form.

It was Kierkegaard's purpose, so he tells us in the course of this self-criticism, to formulate a definition of what it means to live, and to make this formulation fruitful and suggestive for life, stirring the reader to a degree of self-activity that might help him to find himself. He believed that the age suffered from an over-abundance of knowledge. Life was being made increasingly unreal, since living was being confused with knowledge about life. In this situation it would be superfluous and even harmful merely to increase the store of knowledge already existing, even if it were possible to attain a considerable improvement upon current conceptions; this would only tend to promote the disease it was intended to cure. Kierkegaard therefore resolved systematically to eschew the abstract, objective, didactic, systematic, scientific form, and to choose instead the subjective and incidental form characteristic of a knowledge completely assimilated to the personality. In other words, he presents knowledge-in-use, as distinct from knowledge in the form of potentiality-for-use.

To delineate different standpoints and ideals of life in this way is to present personalities "existing in their thoughts," and thus revealing through self-expression the personal significance of the standpoints they occupy. As a consequence, the esthetic literature is pseudonymous and polyonymous; the different authors are Kierkegaard's creations, but "their words, their views, and even their prefaces, are their own productions," their standpoints nowhere precisely coinciding with Kierkegaard's own. Being ideal personalities only, they can express themselves "with a disregard for consequences in good and evil limited only by the requirements of an ideal consistency, a freedom that no actual author speaking in his own name could appropriately claim."

The work with which the literature was launched is *Either/Or, a Fragment of Life,* by Victor Eremita (1843). An ethical view of life is here contrasted with a purely esthetic attitude. There are two authors, an estheticist and an ethicist. Victor Eremita is merely the editor and publisher of the material, which has fallen into his hands by accident. The estheticist is the author of the papers that constitute the first volume, and is designated as A; the ethicist B is responsible for the second volume, consisting of letters written to A, couched in terms of friendly admonition. The title of the work suggests that the reader is confronted with a decisive alternative; he is invited to weigh and choose for himself. The style of the first volume is impassioned, and throughout the work, the thoughts presented glow with the warmth of personal appropriation. The alternative presented is thus characterized both in its emotional and in its intellectual significance, and the service rendered to the reader is the Socratic one of formulating the question proposed with the greatest possible clarity and precision.

The estheticist is purposely made the more brilliant of the two authors. His glowing fancy, his hectic eloquence, and his dialectic power, are all devoted to the exploitation of a quasi-byronic despair. A group of lyrical aphorisms introduces the work. The first of these gives expression to the inner discord of a poet's life,[7] while the last has a certain symbolic character, a hint of Kierkegaard's determination to utilize the comical as a factor in his literary program. I quote the latter here. They are typical of the tense eloquence characteristic of the entire volume.

Something wonderful has happened to me. I was carried up into the seventh heaven. There all the gods were assembled together. As a mark of their especial favor I was granted a wish. Said Mercury: "Will you have youth, or beauty, or power, or a long life, or the most beautiful of maidens, or some other of the many grand things we have here in the chest? You may choose what you will, but only one thing." For a moment I was at a loss, but quickly recovered myself and addressed the gods as follows: "Honorable contemporaries, I choose always to have the laugh on my side." None of the gods answered me by a single word; on the contrary, they all began to laugh. This I interpreted as a sign that my wish was to be fulfilled, and I perceived that the gods knew how to express themselves with taste; for it would hardly have been suitable to the occasion for them to have answered me solemnly: "Your prayer is granted."[8]

The essays which make up the bulk of the volume deal with a variety of topics. There is a criticism of Mozart's *Don Juan,* which seeks to exhibit this opera as a classical expression for sensuous geniality; an essay on the topic of "Ancient and Modern Tragedy," including a sketch of a modified Antigone; psychological stud-

[7]See quotation, pp. 60-61.
[8]*Either/Or,* I, 34.

ies of Marie Beaumarchais, Donna Elvira, and Margaret in Goethe's *Faust;* an oration on "The Unhappiest Man"; a criticism of Scribe's comedy, *The First Love;* an essay entitled "The Rotation Method," describing how one may best escape being bored; and finally the "Diary of the Seducer," in all respects a most amazing and brilliant production, a study of a reflective Don Juan, a highly complicated esthete who has concentrated himself upon the enjoyment of the feminine in all of its various nuances.

B is a gentleman into whose house the young man who is the author of the preceding papers frequently comes as a welcome visitor. This gives occasion for the two long letters that make up the second volume; the subjects discussed are those which have been touched upon in conversation between them. Himself married, the ethicist writes in defense of marriage, presenting it as the deepest and most concrete manifestation of life, and hence as essentially fitted to bring out the ethical in its true significance. A second letter discusses "the equilibrium between the esthetic and the ethical in the development of the personality." His ethical formula is: the choice of one's self, a choice by which the absolute distinction between good and evil receives validity for the will. In choosing himself the ethicist also becomes manifest to the world, and enters into the life of the community so as to realize its social tasks. Time is interpreted as an ethical category, since it is the condition which makes a history and a development possible for the personality; the individual thus achieves an ethical continuity. The specifically ethical enthusiasm constitutes the individual's victory over esthetic secrecy, selfish melancholy, illusory passion, and despair. Such a view of life, he asserts, does not destroy the esthetic, but preserves it and ennobles it.

When I view life from the ethical point of view, I see it in its beauty. Life becomes rich in beauty, and not poor, as it really is for you. I do not have to travel round the globe to find traces of beauty here and there, or to rove about the streets. I do not have to choose and select, to criticize and reject. To be sure, I am not blessed with as much leisure as you are possessed of; for since I am in the habit of regarding my own life from the standpoint of its beauty. I always have enough to do. But sometimes, when I have an hour free, I take my stand at the window and observe the passers-by; and every human being that I see, I see as having beauty. Let him be ever so insignificant and humble, I can nevertheless see his beauty; for I see him as this particular individual who is at the same time the universal man. He has his concrete task in life; he does not exist for the sake of anyone else, even though he be the humblest of wage-servants; his teleology is self-contained. He realizes his task, he conquers, and I can see his victory. For a brave man does not see spooks, a brave man sees everywhere victorious heroes. It is only the coward who can see no heroes, but only spooks.[9]

At the close of the work is a sermon, the fruit of the meditation of a country parson, a friend of B's. It gives expression to that religious enthusiasm which overcomes the incommensurability existing between the infinite and the finite, removing the obstacles caused by the misunderstanding between God and man by resolutely braving this misunderstanding out. Its theme is "the happiness to be derived from the thought that as over against God we are always in the wrong." The final word of this sermon has a peculiar significance. The sermon ends, namely, with the epigrammatic proposition that "only the truth which edifies is truth for you."[10] This is a pragmatic principle on a higher level, and serves as a concrete

[9] *Either/Or*, II, 230.
[10] *Either/Or*, II, 294.

expression for Kierkegaard's ethical individualism. The appeal to edification is not, as might perhaps be imagined, a refuge for vagueness of thought, since Kierkegaard gives the concept of edification itself an elaboration precise and definite.

The ethic presented in the second part of *Either/Or* is an ideal ethic. It ignores the possibility of a radical evil. It assumes that the individual may find himself, even in his despair, without breach of continuity with his former self, and without the necessity of a new point of departure. Now this is a view of the matter that Kierkegaard did not at the time hold; but he tells us that he wished to develop the implications of an ideal ethic before taking up the problem of evil. When a man has reached a point in his experience where the ethical ideal exists for him in all its infinitude, then and not before will he be prepared to have his attention called to the fact of the evil will. Here the strictly religious crises begin, for here the individual needs divine assistance.

An immanent ethical doctrine of life necessarily assumes that man finds his individual duty and destiny commensurate with the life of the community. The ethical and the universal are for such a view coincident. In the realization of his ethical task the individual is consequently manifest to all and intelligible to his social environment. The individual neither needs nor experiences any private relationship with the divine, a relation distinguishable, that is to say, from the relationship which he sustains to the community; the community is for him essentially identical with the divine. God is like the horizon of the landscape, or like the point outside the picture which determines its perspective; but God does not enter immediately into life as an individual factor. When the fact of sin is acknowledged, however, the whole situation is changed. An individual relationship to God becomes a life-necessity, and it is only by a transcendence of the old immediacy, and of the social relationships grounded therein, that the ideal self can be found in its reality. Such a personal relationship between God and the individual is by Kierkegaard identified with the Christian concept of Faith.

The clarification of this concept thus becomes the next problem in his literary program. By means of three successive volumes he advances, step by step, to a psychological motivation of faith: *Fear and Trembling, a dialectical lyric* by Johannes *de silentio* (1843); *Repetition, a psychological experiment,* by Constantine Constantius (1843); and *The Concept of Dread, a simple descriptive psychological inquiry, with a view to the elucidation of the dogmatic problem of Original Sin,* by Vigilius Haufniensis (1844). The last named was published on the same day as the *Philosophical Fragments,* and constitutes, from the point of view of content, a companion volume.

Fear and Trembling uses the story of Abraham's sacrifice of his son. Abraham is not a tragic hero, for he cannot claim, like Jephthah or the Roman consul, a higher ethical justification for his deed. His intention to sacrifice his son has a purely personal motivation, and one which no social ethic can acknowledge; for the highest ethical obligation that his life or the situation reveals is the father's duty of loving his son. Abraham is therefore either a murderer, or a hero of faith. The detailed exposition elucidates Abraham's situation dialectically and lyrically, bringing out as *problemata* the teleological suspension of the ethical, the assumption of an absolute duty toward God, and the purely private character of Abraham's procedure; thus showing the paradoxical and transcendent character of a relation in which the individual, contrary to all rule, is, precisely as an individual, higher than the community. A number of examples of the tragic hero are delineated to form a background for the exposition.

Repetition attacks essentially the same problem, but modernizes the situation. A young man falls in love; he discovers to his surprise and chagrin that he has become a poet, and cannot fulfill his engagement to marry the young woman who was so unfortunate as to have awakened the poetic productivity within him. He struggles with himself for a while, and finally flees the field without leaving any word of explanation behind. His honor has received a blow and his pride is wounded to the quick, but he is not conscious that he could have acted otherwise. In eloquent monologues he voices his despair and his sense of the bitter injustice that life has visited upon him. In his agony he discovers Job, whose plight seems to fit his case precisely—"if Job is a fictitious character, I hereby assume full responsibility for his words." The story of Job helps him first to give vent to his emotions; later it suggests the possibility of a solution. Without having any clear idea as to ways and means, and with the probabilities of the case completely against him, he begins to expect a thunderstorm that will clear the air, give him back his honor, and show him that the whole experience is merely a trial. This expectation constitutes his analogy with Abraham, and gives him a resemblance to a believer. The actual resolution of his difficulty comes in a somewhat different form, with the news, namely, that his former fiancée has married another. This liberates him for a poet's career. The experience was transitory. Its result is a religious awakening which does not quite break through but registers itself in a profound but unutterable religious undertone.

The author of the book, Constantin Constantius, follows the development of the young man's love-affair in
the role of a consulting psychologist. He is himself occupied with the problem of a "repetition," which he interprets esthetically as the problem of whether an experience gains or loses in esthetic value by being repeated.
He comes to the conclusion, based upon experience, that
a satisfactory repetition is altogether impossible, and seeks
comfort in a cynical self-limitation. The young man of
the love-affair illustrates the same problem, but in the
form of a religious experience. He wins a "repetition"
as a redintegration of his personality, and as the restoration of his consciousness to its integrity in a higher form.
It is in this latter sense that the concept of Repetition
becomes the chief subject-matter of the book. The essential purport of this concept is the same as the Christian
idea of a "new creature," but viewed as if from afar and
with a certain ambiguity, in hints and suggestions, in distant gleams. The alternation between the esthetic and the
religious points of view gives occasion for dealing with the
category in a variety of moods, mingling jest with earnest;
in order, says the author, "that the heretics may not be
able to understand me." Repetition is described as "the
interest of metaphysics, and at the same time the interest
upon which metaphysics makes shipwreck; the solution
of every ethical view of life; the *conditio sine qua non* for
every dogmatic problem." A psychological characterization of the concept is given in a beautiful passage which
I shall here quote *in extenso.*

Hope is a new garment, starched and stiff and glistening; but
it has not yet been worn, and hence one does not know whether
it will fit, or how it may become one. Memory is an old garment,
and useless, however beautiful; for it has been outgrown. But
repetition is an imperishable garment, fitting closely and tender-

ly; it neither flutters too loosely about the person nor presses the body too close. Hope is a beautiful girl who slips away through your fingers; memory is a handsome old lady, never quite serving the purpose of the moment; but repetition is a beloved wife of whom you never tire, for it is only the new that tires. The old never tires, and when the mind is engrossed with the old it is happy. Only he finds a true happiness who refuses to yield to the delusion that repetition ought to give him something new; for then he will be bored. Hope is a prerogative of youth, and so is memory; but it requires courage to will the repetition. Whoever is content to hope is a coward, and whoever is content to remember is a pleasure-seeker; but whoever has the courage to will the repetition is a man, and the more profoundly he has known how to interpret the repetition to himself, the deeper is his manhood. But whoever fails to comprehend that life is a repetition, and that this constitutes its beauty, condemns himself, and deserves no better fate than that which will eventually befall him, which is: to be lost. For hope is an alluring fruit that fails to satisfy; and memory is a miserable pittance that fails to satisfy; but repetition is the daily bread that not only satisfies but blesses. When a man has circumnavigated the globe, it will appear whether he has the courage to understand that life is a repetition, and the enthusiasm to find his happiness therein. Whoever does not circumnavigate the globe before he begins to live, does not begin to live. Whoever makes the journey, but is overtaken by weariness shows that he had a poor constitution. But whoever chooses the repetition, lives. He does not run here and there to catch butterflies, like a child; nor does he stand on tiptoe to behold the glories of the world, for he knows them. He does not sit like an old woman at memory's spinning-wheel, but he wends his way through life calmly and quietly, happy in the repetition. And what indeed would life be, if there were no repetition? Who could wish to be a tablet on which every moment Time writes a new inscription, or a mere memorial of the past? Who could wish to be subject to everything that is new and flighty, and to permit his soul ever and again to be engrossed with an ephemeral pleasure? If God had not willed the repetition, the world would never have come into being; for He would either have permitted His fancy to pursue the easy plans of hope, or recalled it all, and kept it only in the memory. But this He did not do, and therefore the world stands, and stands because it is a repetition. In repetition lies the reality and the earnestness of life. Whoever wills to repeat, proves that his earnestness is full-grown and mature.[11]

In the two volumes above described, Faith is delineated in some of its more abstract and formal characteristics. It is described as it appears in exceptional situations, and with a psychological motivation that falls short of the concrete and decisive background which, according to the Christian teaching, it has for every man in the experience of sin. The advance to a more concrete treatment is made in the last of the above-mentioned volumes, *The Concept of Dread;* and the *Philosophical Fragments* occupies itself with the logic of the same situation that *The Concept of Dread* psychologically describes.

In the interval between the *Philosophical Fragments* and its continuation, the *Unscientic Postscript,* Kierkegaard produced a new poetico-psychological treatment of the problems already dealt with. This résumé, which seems to have all the lyrical vitality and freshness of his first handling of the subject, is called *Stages on the Way of Life, studies by various authors, collected and published by Hilarius Bookbinder* (1845). The volume is divided into three parts, corresponding to the three spheres of life which Kierkegaard regarded as fundamental—the esthetic, the ethical, and the religious. The first part is a reminiscent reproduction of a banquet-scene, "In vino veritas." Five estheticists discourse on the subject of woman. Their speeches invite comparison with the similar discourses of Plato's Symposium, and neither in beauty of form nor in pregnancy of thought do they suffer by the comparison. The second part of the book deals with marriage and its problems from the standpoint of B, the ethicist of *Either/Or.* To the esthetic proposition

_____
[11]*Repetition,* 4, 5.

put forward in the first part, that the significance of woman culminates in the moment, the ethicist opposes the view that her beauty grows with the years. The ideal resolution with which marriage begins, and by which it is sustained, is eulogized as constituting the true ideality of human life; and the validity of marriage is defended against attacks from both the esthetic and the religious side. The third part, comprising the bulk of the book, is a "psychological experiment" by Frater Taciturnus, "Guilty or not Guilty?" This is again the story of an un-happy love-affair and a broken engagement, presented in the form of a diary. The subject of the experiment is equipped at the outset with a high-minded ethico-esthetic view of life, which his experience shatters. In his despair he is made to approach as near as possible to the prob-lem of the forgiveness of sin; but without finding rest in a Christian interpretation of himself and his situation. Frater Taciturnus dissects him psychologically and indi-cates his idiosyncrasies, expounds the tragedy and the comedy of his situation, and points to a view of life, re-ligious in character, and in advance of his own stand-point as a humorist, as being deducible from it all. The sympathetic collision described is brought home to the reader with tremendous force in a beautiful lyrical prose. In Kierkegaard's own view, this book is emotionally the richest of all his writings, but too ideal to become widely popular.

Then came the continuation of the *Philosophical Frag-ments* with its strange title: *Concluding Unscientific Postscript to the Philosophical Fragments, a mimic-pathetic-dialectic composition, an existential present-ment,* by Johannes Climacus (1846). It discusses briefly the objective approaches to Christianity through Biblical criticism, the authority of the church, philosophical spec-

ulation, the evidences of Christianity's historical achieve-
ments. It dismisses all these modes of approach as incommensurable with the problem of Christianity, and as
tending to subvert its significance. The rest of the book,
through five hundred pages of dialectic, humor, pathos,
and irony, is devoted to the elucidation of the following
subjective problem: "I, Johannes Climacus, born and
brought up here in Copenhagen, now thirty years old,
assume that there exists for me as well as for a servant-girl
or a professor of philosophy, a highest good; I have heard
that Christianity conditions its attainment. I ask the question: How do I enter into relations with Christianity?"[12]
The exposition of this personal question develops a philosophy of religion and, incidentally, an analysis of the
concepts of Reality and Truth. It is here that Kierkegaard makes up his final accounting with the Hegelian
philosophy, and with the interpretations of Christianity
which rest on a Hegelian basis. The work is sustained
polemic not only against Hegelianism, but against all
system-making in philosophy, taking its stand upon an
ethico-dynamic conception of reality, and emphasizing
the categories of existence, actuality, life. Over against
the subjective thinker, "the Greek philosopher, whose
life is an artistic embodiment of his thought," it sets by
way of contrast the objective thinker, "the German professor of philosophy, who feels bound to explain everything à tout prix," and delivers him over to a comic interpretation.[13]

The *Unscientific Postscript* is an extraordinary book.
Its polemic coloring and the tremendous power of its
dialectic naturally suggest the simile of the huge battle-
ship, with which it has been compared by Brandes. Its

---

[12]*Postscript*, 19
[13]See quotation on the world-historic thinker, pp. 43-44.

easy conversational tone, its aptness in anecdote and
humorous characterization, the playful facility with
which it handles the most difficult of abstractions, and its
ironical self-depreciation, mark it as embodying a quite
novel species of philosophical writing. It is a philosophical introduction to Christianity of a most original kind.
It describes "the way from philosophical speculation back
to Christianity, from the profundity of philosophical
thought to the simplicity of Christian faith, just as the
previous esthetic pseudonyms had described the way
from the poetic to the religious, from the interesting to
the simple." In a personal note affixed to the *Unscientific
Postscript,* in which note he acknowledges the authorship
of the pseudonyms, Kierkegaard says of these works:

> Whatever actual significance the pseudonyms may come to
> have in the world is absolutely not to be found in the making of
> any new proposal, or in exploiting any unheard-of discovery, or
> in beginning any new movement, or in taking up any advanced
> position. Their significance lies in the precise opposite, in the
> renunciation of all claim to significance, and in the mere attempt
> to read through again, *solo,* at a distance of double reflection, the
> scriptures of our human, individual, existential relations, the old
> and well-known scriptures handed down to us from the fathers;
> if possible, reading them through again with increased inward-
> ness.[14]

Of the twenty-one religious discourses issued from time
to time under his own name, while the above esthetic
pseudonyms were being published, all but the last three
strike the universal religious note, i.e., they attempt to
exhaust the possibilities of edification in the religious
sphere without drawing upon any of the conceptions
peculiar to Christianity. The last three, however, run
parallel to the exposition of the *Fragments* and the *Post-*

---

[14]*Postscript,* "A First and Last Explanation."

script, and deal in edifying form with the considerations which these works introduce problematically and esthetically. The Kierkegaardian literature has thus far brought its reader merely to the threshold of the Christian view of life, marking the end of the first phase of a most unique literary undertaking.

Despite the isolation which the unremitting labor of his authorship naturally imposed, Kierkegaard managed to keep in closest touch with his contemporaries. Although he received no visitors at home (except such as came to him for assistance, to whom his door was always open) he spent much time on the streets, talking with the acquaintances he chanced to meet, professors at the University, editors of Copenhagen newspapers, politicians and officials, writers and students and men about town, or striking up a conversation with some casual passer-by. In this way he took his recreation of an afternoon, when he did not vary the program by one of his frequent carriage-rides into the country. He took pains to make himself generally accessible, and the promiscuity of his intercourse was noticeable. This contact with men on the street had a considerable personal significance for him; among other things, it helped to enrich his literary vocabulary. "What you have vainly sought for in books," says Frater Taciturnus, "is suddenly illuminated for you while listening to a servant-girl as she talks with another servant-girl. An expression that you have vainly attempted to torture out of your own head, you hear in passing; a soldier-boy says it, and he does not dream how rich he is." He felt that this mode of life tended to undermine the ideal conception of an aloof greatness which the public might otherwise have formed of him. He notes Shakespeare's testimony, in *King Henry IV,* to the method by which "a great host of kings and emperors and spiritual dignitaries, Jesuits and diplomats and clever people of all kinds" have known how to profit by the illusion of distance, so as to enhance their personal reputation. But he would not adopt this method, preferring to give the situation the stamp of truth. "All the unselfish witnesses for the truth have always been accustomed to mingle much with men; they have never played hide-and-seek with the multitude."

Simultaneously with the completion of the *Postscript,* Kierkegaard ventured upon a step that resulted in placing him in a still more conspicuous position before the Copenhagen public. He became a standing comic figure in the most widely circulated journal of the town, *The Corsair.* This sheet had obtained a considerable ascendency as a vehicle for ironical, levelling attacks upon well-known men, and was much feared. Kierkegaard thus describes its influence:

> The whole population of Copenhagen had become ironical and witty, especially in proportion as it was ignorant and crude; there was nothing but irony first and irony last. If the matter had not been so serious, if I could bring myself to regard it from a purely esthetic standpoint, I should not wish to deny that it was the most ridiculous phenomenon I had ever witnessed. I believe that it would be necessary to travel far and wide, and even so be favored of fortune, before one could find anything so fundamentally comical. The whole population of a town, all these many thousands, became "ironical." They became ironical by the aid of a journal which, again, ironically enough, by the aid of straw men as editors succeeded in striking the dominant note and the tone struck was—the ironical. I believe it impossible to imagine anything more ridiculous. Irony presupposes a specific intellectual culture which in every generation is very rare—and this chaos of people was ironical! . . . .
>
> But the matter was only too serious. This irony was of course nothing but, in essence, vulgarity; and in spite of a not inconsiderable degree of talent in the man who was its originating

force, by passing over into these thousands of people it became, essentially, a mob trait, a trait which is always only too popular. In view of the proportions of the little country, it threatened a complete morál dissolution. One must envisage at close range how no attack is so much feared as that which singles one out as an object of laughter; how even one who would bravely risk death for a stranger, is not far from betraying his own father or mother when the danger is that of being laughed at; for such an attack isolates the victim more than any other, and at no point does it offer him the support of pathos. Frivolity and curiosity and vulgarity grin; the nervous cowardice which itself trembles for fear of such an attack cries that it is nothing; the wretched cowardice which by the use of bribery or good works protects itself cries that it is nothing; and even sympathy says that it is nothing. It is a terrible thing when in a little land idle prattle and vulgar grimaces threaten to constitute public opinion. (Abbreviated.)

The publisher of the sheet in question was a talented young man who was himself an admirer of Kierkegaard, and *The Corsair* had more than once praised the pseudonyms to the skies. Victor Eremita had been pronounced immortal; from a sketch in the Journals at the time, it appears that Kierkegaard had projected a reply to this pronouncement, asking to be spared the distinction. A little later an opportunity offered itself, apropos of an article published in P. L. Møller's literary year-book, *Gaea,* in which Møller had made some irresponsible animadversions upon the third part of *Stages on the Way of Life,* bringing it into connection with the gossip current in Copenhagen about Kierkegaard's engagement. This gentleman had described himself in the Dictionary of Authors as a regular contributor to *The Corsair,* author of pieces "both lyrical and satirical." Frater Taciturnus replied to the criticism, taking a very superior tone, and took advantage of the fact just mentioned to add the following remark at the end:

Now may I soon be put into *The Corsair*. It is pretty hard for an author to be so singled out in Danish literature, that he (assuming that we pseudonyms are one) is the only one who is not vilified in its pages. My own principal, Hilarius Bookbinder, has been flattered in *The Corsair*, if my memory serves me right; and Victor Eremita has even had to endure the disgrace of being immortalized—in *The Corsair!* And yet, have I not already been there? For *ubi spiritus ibi ecclesia, ubi* P. L. Møller *ibi The Corsair.* Our literary tramp therefore characteristically winds up his "Visit to Sorø" with one of these wretched *Corsair*-attacks upon peaceable and respectable men, who in honorable seclusion follow their vocations in the service of the state; excellent men, in many ways deserving well, and in none having made themselves worthy of ridicule.[15]

Nothing daunted by the delicacy of its own situation, *The Corsair* took up the gauntlet flung at it, with an attack on Frater Taciturnus, the silent brother, who could not restrain himself, but had to reveal the secrets of *The Corsair*, entrusted to him in confidence. Frater Taciturnus countered with a summary article: *"The dialectical result of a piece of police work."*

With respect to a sheet like *The Corsair*, which, though read generally and by all sorts of people, has hitherto enjoyed the distinction of being ignored and despised, never answered, absolutely the only thing that could be done in a literary way was for one who had been praised and immortalized in its pages to ask to be vilified, thus expressing the moral literary order of things as reflected in the contrary order which this sheet has done its best to establish. I assume that the procedure adopted has met with success. One can therefore engage vilification at the hands of *The Corsair*, just as one can hire a hurdy-gurdy to make music. . . . .

I can do no more for others than this—to ask to be attacked myself. The fallen cleverness of *The Corsair*, and of its collective secret helpers, the professional tradesmen of wit and vulgarity,

---

[15]*The Fatherland*, December, 1845.

ought to be and shall be ignored in our literature, just as in civic life one ignores the public prostitute. . . . .

The way is now open, and, as the pseudonyms say, the method is changed. Everyone who is insulted by receiving the praise of this sheet, can, if he happens to learn of the fact, reply, and thus testify to the judgment that decent literature has passed on *The Corsair*. It is to be permitted to pursue its livelihood by way of vilification and attack as much as it likes; but if it dares to praise, it shall meet with this brief reply: "May I ask to be attacked; it is an unendurable disgrace to be immortalized in *The Corsair*."

Kierkegaard did not pursue the polemic further, but *The Corsair* kept up a steady fire of satire and caricature for many months. Kierkegaard was not insensible to the attacks, and the Journals show how profoundly the experience affected him. As usual, his reflections explored all its various phases in an objectifying and idealizing manner. We have, as a by-product, profound estimates of the press and its influence on public opinion, probing its anonymity and its irresponsibility in relation to characteristic features of modern life. On the other side, the aloofness and indifference which he met in relation to the matter from the side of the higher circles in which it had previously been urged, privately, that something ought to be done about *The Corsair*, but where there was now maintained the most complete silence, leaving Kierkegaard to bear the brunt of the attack alone—this prudent aloofness confirmed Kierkegaard in his view of the mediocrity of the world, and gave a characteristic coloring to the religious literature that followed. In his subsequent description of the religious life, the inner collision, by which a man comes into conflict with himself, a collision which had been the chief burden of his early delineation, began to yield precedence to the external collision, in which a man in the pursuit of his duty comes into conflict

with his environment, a conflict whereby the perform-
ance of this duty becomes an act of true self-denial.[16]

A volume of literary criticism, devoted to the interpretation of a Danish novel, and notable for its characterization of the contemporary age as against the background
of the revolutionary period, followed close upon the publication of the *Unscientific Postscript*. From the beginning, Kierkegaard's plan had not included a distinctively
religious authorship, but rather an introduction to such
an authorship. The underlying religious motivation was
something he had intended to express by taking a charge
as a clergyman in some country parish. But now, influenced partly by the trouble with *The Corsair*, partly by
a sense of his own unfitness for an official position, and
partly by the acquired momentum of his productive impulse, he determined to devote himself to religious writing, and thus his authorship entered upon its second
phase. To the first half of this period belong *Edifying
Discourses* (1847), the *Works of Love* (1848), and *Christian Discourses* (1848). Though each religious discourse
is complete in itself, the individual themes are logically
connected, and the methodical and systematic advance,
so noticeably characteristic of the esthetic productions,
finds its counterpart here in a gradual approach to more
and more concrete conceptions, and to an increasingly
severe judgment of the actual contemporary life in the
light of the ideals delineated.

Edifying Discourses deals, in a first section, with the
unity of the ethical ideal—"that the heart can be clean
only when it has a single aim," and that this singleness
of aim is possible only for one who chooses the good, and
actual only when he chooses the good in truth; in a second
section, with the lessons to be learned from the lilies of

---

[16]See quotation, page 22, from the *Works of Love*.

the field and the birds of the air—contentment with our common humanity, an appreciation of its glory, and an understanding of its blessedness, which consists in first seeking the kingdom of God; and thirdly, with the gospel of suffering, the happiness to be derived from the thought of following Christ, how the burden can be light though the sorrow is heavy, that the school of suffering prepares for eternity, that it is not the way which is narrow but the narrowness which is the way, that in relation to God we always suffer as those who are guilty, that eternity outweighs in its blessedness even the heaviest temporal suffering, and that the spirit of courage in suffering takes power away from the world, and transforms derision into honor, defeat into victory.

The *Works of Love* presents the elaboration of a social ethic on the basis of Christianity. It makes no attempt to formulate an ideal organization of society, nor does it so much as even give a suggestion of a hint of any external polity; but it deals profoundly with the attitude of the individual toward his fellowmen:

> These are Christian reflections and therefore not about love, but about the works of love. They concern the works of love, not as if all its works were herein enumerated and described, far from it; not as if the particular works herein described were now described once for all—praise God that this is impossible! For that which in its whole wealth is *essentially* inexhaustible, is also in its least expression *essentially* indescribable, because it is essentially present everywhere in its wholeness, and essentially incapable of being described.[17]

The beauty and simplicity of the language, the tender persuasiveness of the idealism, and the universality of its appeal, make this perhaps the most popular of all Kierke-

---

[17]Preface to the *Works of Love.*

gaard's religious writings; it forms a striking contribution to the world's sermonic literature.

Christian Discourses contains in the first part a treatment of the anxieties of the pagan mind, "the anxieties of poverty, of wealth, of lowliness, of high position, of presumption, of self-torture, of doubt, inconstancy and despair," devoting a discourse to each; second, a series of discourses on the Christian gospel of suffering; third, a number of discourses critical of the prevailing religious situation under the caption: "Thoughts which wound from behind—in order to edify"; and fourth, a treatment in sermonic form of the Christian doctrine of the Atonement, seven discourses on the Lord's Supper. The following significant motto is attached to the third section:

Christianity needs no defense, and cannot be served by means of any defense—Christianity is always on the offensive. To defend Christianity is the most indefensible of all distortions of it, the most confusing and the most dangerous—it is unconsciously and cunningly to betray it. Christianity is always on the offensive; in Christendom, consequently, it attacks from behind.

Here we meet with the first definite anticipation of the attack which Kierkegaard was soon to make upon the open or tacit assumption, current in Christendom, of an established Christian order.

A little esthetic article from Kierkegaard's pen, "The Crisis in the Life of an Actress," saw the light in a Copenhagen journal during the summer of 1848, to serve notice upon the public that his exclusive devotion to religious themes for the past two or three years did not have its ground in an obtuseness to esthetic values. In the spring of the following year there were published anonymously two remarkable theological essays: "Has a man the right to allow himself to be put to death for the truth?" and

"The difference between a genius and an apostle"; the former with an indirect bearing upon the Atonement, and the latter attempting to clear up the Christian concept of Authority.

To the second half of Kierkegaard's religious authorship may be assigned the following volumes: *The Sickness Unto Death* (1849;) *Training in Christianity* (1850); and *For Self- Examination* (1851). In these writings Kierkegaard presents the Christian teaching in its highest ideality, and with a reference to the prevailing state of religion in the Christian world. The ideal is presented sharply and clearly, without compromise. But the consequent judgment on Christendom is formulated as gently as possible, urging nothing but admissions in the interests of sincerity, "in order that we may learn to take refuge in grace, even with respect to the manner in which we use grace." *The Sickness Unto Death* marks the appearance of a new pseudonym, Anti-Climacus. The standard for human life here delineated is so ideal that Kierkegaard did not wish to present it in his own name and character, as if his personal existence embodied it; it was therefore presented in the light of a poetic and imaginative rendering—for the ideal ought at least to be heard—under which Kierkegaard wished to humiliate himself *qua* reader. Too much the poet to be a reformer, he preferred to represent himself as a spy in the service of the ideal, his mission being the Socratic one of detecting and exposing illusions. The Journals from these years show the intensity of his feeling about what passes for Christianity in Christendom, his unmeasured contempt for its paltriness and its mediocrity; they disclose also the long-continued self-examination which preceded all these publications, and his anxious fear lest he should assume too high and authoritative a role, and say more than he had a right to utter.

Training in Christianity was written in 1848, but held back from publication for two years, while Kierkegaard was debating in what form it ought to appear, or if it ought to appear at all. It was finally published as by the pseudonym, Anti-Climacus, and the preface virtually appeals to the authorities of the Danish church to make the admission that the religion preached and practiced in the church was really a modification, several degrees lower than the Christianity of the New Testament. With such a concession publicly made by the highest authority, Kierkegaard felt that the established order could be made to embody a sufficient measure of sincerity and truth, so that it would be unnecessary for him, at least, to make any open attack upon it. No such admission was forthcoming, and Bishop Mynster found means to let Kierkegaard know, indirectly, that he regarded *Training in Christianity* as a vicious and dangerous exaggeration, not to say distortion, of Christian teaching; but he refused to discuss the matter with Kierkegaard personally, and publicly maintained silence. *Training in Christianity* is perhaps the clearest and most precise exposition of the Christian dogma in its pragmatic significance and meaning for life to be found in any literature. It was published in a form carefully calculated in its bearing upon the concrete contemporary situation in Denmark.

The Sickness Unto Death is a psychological study of despair in its various forms, conscious and unconscious. Its point of view is that despair is a universal disease of the spirit, so that every man who has not been cured of it, suffers from it whether he knows it or not. And despair is an imperfect expression for sin; on a higher level of consciousness despair reveals itself as the consciousness of sin.

For Self-Examination, two series of discourses, of which the second was not published until after Kierkegaard's death, presents a critical estimate of Lutheran Protestantism, acknowledging the significance of Luther's mission as a corrective, but condemning modern Protestantism for taking advantage of Luther's one-sidedness to leave out the deeper ethical implications of Christianity, ignoring the requirement of following Christ, and "taking the grace of God in vain."

The ideas which were to play a part in the grandiose agitation that followed some years later, as the climax of Kierkegaard's career, were now laid down in the religious literature as a whole. But as yet they were brought to bear at a distance from the actual situation, in the form of imaginative delineations, suggesting no other requirement to the reader than concession, admission and personal humiliation under the ideal.

From September, 1851, to December, 1854, there was a pause in the steady stream of publications flowing from Kierkegaard's pen ever since the year 1843. His reflection had not become sterile, but its energy was consumed in self-preparation for a new role, one more decisive than any he had yet played, as the Journals of the period bear witness. He was engaged in probing the distance between modern life and the ideals which it professes; and, particularly, his reflection seized upon the difference between the life of Christendom and the Christianity of the New Testament. As always, his thought was impassioned, pregnant with indignation and scorn. Financial worries, which had assailed him for some time, helped to mature his personality, and there are indications that Kierkegaard began, during this period, a course of self-discipline by means of ascetic exercises, to replace the somewhat luxurious life he had permitted himself earlier to lead.

Then, in the year 1854, came an opportunity which, in view of his previous publications, appealed to him as a challenge that must be squarely met. In the fall of 1853, Bishop Mynster died. He had been a pulpiteer of great ability, and as bishop he had ruled the church with a strong and conservative hand. Kierkegaard had maintained close personal relations with him, Mynster having been his father's pastor. He admired his ability, and had frequently defended him against attacks which he deemed unjustified. But he had not hesitated to let him know where and how far he differed from him. A few weeks after Mynster's death, Professor Martensen (whose *Christian Dogmatics* had at one time so wide a vogue in theological circles) preached a memorial sermon in which the late bishop was eulogized as "one more link in the holy chain of witnesses for the Truth, stretching all the way from the days of the apostles to our own times." This idealization of Bishop Mynster seemed to Kierkegaard an impudent falsification of the Christian ideal, symptomatic of that demoralization to which Christendom as a whole was subject. He wrote at once a brief but emphatic protest. Professor Martensen was a candidate for the vacant bishopric, and hence Kierkegaard postponed publication until the appointment was announced, so as to avoid entanglement with political cross-currents and other irrelevant considerations. Martensen received the appointment, and in December, 1854, the article was published, in the columns of a daily newspaper in Copenhagen. It places in question the truth of the assertion that Bishop Mynster was a witness for the Truth, maintaining that both as regards the content of his preaching and the form of his personal life Bishop Mynster fell far short of the Christian ideal of a witness. It accuses Professor Martensen of *playing* at Christianity, just as children play at being soldiers. This decisive attack upon the ideal legitimation of the established order created a sensation, and naturally awakened a storm of protest. Kierkegaard was accused of attacking the memory of the dead, and of violating the sanctity of the grave; of a lack of earnestness of purpose; of an overweening personal pride; of being insane; and of whatever else the wounded feelings of his antagonists could invent. But Kierkegaard brushed objections and objectors aside, keeping straight to his main theme, and maintaining it with increasing intensity. For four months, publishing altogether a score of articles at irregular intervals, Kierkegaard kept up the agitation in the columns of *Fædrelandet*. It quickly became clear that here was no attack upon the reputation of Bishop Mynster, as that phrase would be ordinarily understood, but that Denmark was confronted with a most searching critique of the whole established order which Bishop Mynster represented.

If Bishop Mynster is a witness for the Truth, then every clergyman in the country, as even the blindest can see, is also a witness for the Truth. . . . What we call being a clergyman, priest, or bishop, is a means of livelihood, just like every other in the community; and a means of livelihood carried on, if you please, within a community where all call themselves Christians, where there is therefore not the slightest danger connected with the preaching of the Christian doctrine, but where on the contrary this situation in life must be regarded as one of the most respected and attractive. Now I ask: Is there the slightest resemblance between these clergymen, priests, bishops, and what Christ calls His witnesses? Or is it not ridiculous to call such clergymen, priests, bishops, "witnesses" in the sense of the New Testament— as ridiculous as to call field maneuvers in time of peace, war?

But Bishop Martensen persists in calling them witnesses, witnesses for the Truth. If the clergy understood their own interests in the matter, they would without delay petition the Bishop to give up this terminology, which puts the whole profession, to say the least, in a ridiculous light. For I know several most respectable and able, very able, clergymen; but I venture to say that in the whole kingdom there is not one, who when viewed in the light of a witness for the Truth does not present a comic figure.

With rapid strides and bold strokes Kierkegaard advanced to the position that the notion of a Christian people or nation is an illusion, that a Christianity with official sanction and authority is directly contrary to the teaching of Christ, that Protestantism in general is a slily dishonest perversion of Christianity, and that New Testament Christianity is so completely non-existent in modern states that it is nonsense even to talk of a reformation, there being nothing to reform. In two separately published leaflets the situation was intensified almost to the breaking point.

Whoever you are, my friend, and whatever your life may be, by refusing any longer to take part (if you have hitherto done so) in the public worship as it is now conducted, with the pretense of being New Testament Christianity, you will have one less crime, and a heavy one, upon your conscience; for you will no longer take part in making a mockery of God.

Shortly after this pronouncement, he sharply called the attention of the public to the fact that the clergy were bound by oath to the New Testament; and then went on to apply the words of Christ in Matthew 23:29-33 and Luke 11:47-48, without reservation, to an official Christianity of every description, and particularly to that of the Danish church.

The last week in May, Kierkegaard began the publication of a pamphlet called *The Moment,* of which altogether nine numbers appeared up to the end of September. A tenth number was made ready for publication, but its appearance was delayed by Kierkegaard's last illness, so that it came to be published posthumously. In these stirring pamphlets the agitation is carried on to its ultimate consequences, and the measure of the distance between the Christian ideal and the actual life of the Christian world, is taken with a certainty and an accuracy that leaves no illusion unexposed. His purpose was ideal. He had no finite end in view, no proposal of a changed organization, no displacement of authorities, no derogation of persons, nothing but a clarification of consciousness in the direction of greater honesty and sincerity. For those who wondered what his motive might be, he replied:

I want honesty. I do not represent Christian severity as over against Christian mildness; by no means. I represent neither severity nor mildness, I stand for human honesty. . . . . And if the human race or my contemporaries wish honestly, sincerely, frankly, openly, to rebel against Christianity, and to say to God, "We cannot and will not subject ourselves to this power"—well and good; provided this be done openly, frankly and sincerely, then, however strange it may seem for me to say this, I am with them; for I want honesty.

It would be interesting to speculate upon the reputation that Kierkegaard might have attained, and the extent of the influence he might have exerted, if he had written in one of the major European languages, instead of in the tongue of one of the smallest countries in the world. An idealism more powerful and more consistent than that of either Emerson or Carlyle, a democratic individualism as thoroughgoing as the aristocratic individualism of Nietszche, and presented with an equally passionate intensity, an ethical voluntarism clothed in a literary form as persuasive as that of Schopenhauer's philosophy, and a species of pragmatism more carefully and thor-

oughly worked out than that of either James or Bergson
—these qualities must have attracted world-wide attention. And yet he himself believed that the limitations
under which he was compelled to labor, and the consequent lack of any effective opposition from the outside,
were a necessary factor in the peculiar development of
his personality, and one demanded by his peculiar task.
Had he written in English or in German there would
naturally have been enough significant opposition to
have consumed a great part of his energy in external
polemic. As it was, the outward opposition was negli-
gible; he was compelled to set his own standard and to
be his own critic. His reflection was thus turned inward
in a greater measure than would otherwise have been
possible; this he regarded as essential for the kind of
literature it was his mission to produce. This literature
will always remain in one sense a luxury; it does not have
the kind of one-sidedness which would adapt it for the
foundation of a school or the promotion of a movement.
Nevertheless it is bound to have an enduring significance, for it "delineates the essential thought-determina-
tions of life, and of individual existence, in a manner
more dialectically precise and more emotionally primitive
than anything comparable to be found in any modern
literature."

IV. THE EXISTENTIAL DIALECTIC OF SØREN KIERKEGAARD

A SENSE of intellectual bankruptcy impelled the reputed father of modern philosophy to seek a radical reconstruction of the basic concepts of science. With respect to the problems of life and conduct, however, Descartes tells us with simple frankness that he was content to follow a less radical procedure. He will observe the laws of his country; he will accept the tenets of the religion in which he was nurtured; he will model his conduct upon that of the most respected and moderate of his contemporaries. As for theology, since the way to heaven is open equally to the wise and to the ignorant, he will not presume to bring its problems to the test of a personal reflection.

In Kierkegaard we have a thinker who completely reverses the Cartesian distribution of emphasis: he reflects where Descartes accepts, and accepts where Descartes reflects. He took his point of departure in something deeper than an abstract intellectual doubt, namely, in a concrete personal despair. In this despair, which was ironically witty and articulate, he questioned the meaning and truth of human life in its whole range of substantial values. The struggle to find solid ground under his feet was undertaken with a concentration of all his faculties, intellectual and passional; and, in gradually achieving this task for himself, he brought into being a revision of the basic categories of human existence. The revision is such as to have significance also for others, and it has been given expression in a literature of surpassing artistry and rare moral power.

The contrast between these two modes of emphasis in choosing problems for reflection was in ancient times brought to the fore by Socrates, who came to the conclusion that "physics was not man's proper business," and became a moralist haunting the gymnasia, the workshops and the market-place. Kierkegaard poses the problem of the highest use of the energies of reflection in the following manner: The wise man ought surely to understand what the plain man understands and needs to know, before allowing himself to become absorbed in the distant, the abstract, and the highfalutin. In seeking such an understanding he will make a significant discovery, namely, that what is relatively simple for the plain man becomes for the reflection of the wise man extremely difficult and complicated, capable indeed of fully engaging all his faculties. So occupied, he finally comes to glimpse a beautiful and humane principle that grips him with profound emotion and reconciles him with life in its entirety. For he begins to perceive that between the wisest man and the simplest human being there exists but the vanishing little difference that the plain man knows what is essential, while the wise man gradually comes to know that he knows it or comes to know that he does not know it. But what they both know is the same.

The existential dialectic is the instrument of such a wise man in thinking about his own existence. The problem of the existential thinker is namely to understand himself as an existing human being, essentially like all other human beings in status and task. His thought is thus a concrete thought, in that it has an essential reference to the thinker and deals with a particular something which the thinker seeks to apprehend. Abstract thought, on the other hand, proceeds by way of abstracting from the thinker and from all concrete particularity; it contents itself with seeking to explain reality in general. The concrete thinker sets himself a much more difficult task. He must seek to understand what it means for him that this particular something is a reality, by interpenetrating it with thought. This thought is necessarily dialectic in character, since the existence in which he moves is not a closed system, but is one which confronts him with open possibilities.

The brief abstract which this paper proposes to present will be expository of certain outstanding traits of the existential dialectic, as Kierkegaard has determined them in scattered portions of his writings—chiefly in the *Unscientific Postscript,* where the matter is dealt with at some length. But I cannot here or elsewhere reproduce the varied and artistic form in which Kierkegaard has clothed his thought. This mingling of jest and earnest; this alternation between humor and irony and pathos; this illustration of abstract categories by the use of stories and anecdotes taken directly from the streets of Copenhagen; this constant shifting back and forth between logical abstractions and poetic imagery; this incorporation of a category in an imagined personality, who is permitted to speak for himself so that we may see him as he is; this succession of different pseudonymous authors, each representing a distinct nuance of position; this teasing personal relationship which the style seeks to establish between the author and the reader, after the manner of a Socratic gadfly—all this is not mere idiosyncrasy of a versatile and capricious writer. It is rather a reflective maieutic, the sign of an author who has something more profound in mind than a mere appeal to the abstract understanding of the reader. For Kierkegaard writes as one aware of the dialectic of the process of communication, understanding this as a reflection of the dialectic that is grounded in the very existence of the individual.

In connection with all knowledge that is merely objective and that claims no other significance (logic, mathematics, metaphysics, history) the task of communication has been fulfilled when the thought has received a suitable expression in the word, mediating a meeting of minds in something objective. But in relation to the ethical and to the ethico-religious this principle does not hold. Such truth is essentially something to be done, to be realized in the subject, to be assimilated in inwardness. For a real understanding, as distinct from an illusory appearance of knowledge, there is here required a "double reflection." In the first stage of reflection, the thinker finds a universal principle; in the second stage, he discovers a particular application of this principle to his own individual person and situation. The first stage of ethical reflection, for example, is a search for the universal man as norm and ideal; the second stage is directed to the incorporation of this abstraction in this concrete particular individual. This last reflection, which clears the road for action, is not and cannot be a co-operative enterprise but is rather something which each individual has for himself—an essential secret. By this reflection the individual isolates himself, since it makes the truth into something that belongs to him and to him alone. The ethical teacher will thus seek to hold the individuals discretely apart, lest they fuse into a mere mass in their concentration upon something objective to the forget-fulness of themselves.

A consciousness of this double reflection and its essential character will transform all ethical and ethico-religious communication into a maieutic art. Objective thought in this field fails to apprehend this necessity and hence takes the process of assimilation frivolously for granted. Objective thought presumes the readiness and adequacy of the individual to accept the truth as soon as it has been objectively determined, a presumption which but proves its naiveté. In the maximum of objectivity it dismisses the individual as a vanishing and accidental appendage; the objective result is everything, the individual is nothing. But the spirit of the ethical is precisely the contrary: the individual is everything, and what is outside him is accidental and vanishing.

The principle that there is an essential relationship in this field between form and content is given expression in a passage from the *Postscript:*

> Now if anyone wishes to object that this is mere declamation [the preceding paragraph is an expression for ethical enthusiasm], that all I have is a little irony, a little pathos, and a little dialectic, my reply would be: What else should anyone have who proposes to set forth the ethical? Should he perhaps seek to frame it objectively in a formal paragraph structure, fit to be learned and recited by rote, so as to contradict himself by his form? In my opinion, pathos and irony and dialectic are *quod desideratur,* when the ethical is *quod erat demonstrandum.*[1]

Kierkegaard is quite inexhaustible in tracing the comic collisions which ensue when this matter of the dialectics of communication is neglected, and a naive faith in the value of publicity for reforming the world—a faith not

---

[1]*Unscientific Postscript,* 137.

wholly unknown to our own age—gives itself free rein in action. Thus, if a man came to entertain the conviction that no human being ought to have any disciples, it would not be long before, as a result of saying this in season and out of season, he would have on his hands a dozen applications from would-be disciples, all offering for the smallest of stipends to go out in the world to win disciples for this doctrine, the doctrine that no man ought to have any disciples. And such a campaign would have success, no one noticing the contradiction; while the artistic and consistent and indirect method would achieve results very slowly and precariously, thus requiring self-restraint and true self-sacrifice in the teacher.

The existential dialectic operates primarily with value-judgments. It could not be otherwise, since human existence is essentially a search for satisfactions, and every satisfaction embraces for a thinking being a real or imaginary value. Value-judgments are for Kierkegaard subject to a true-false dialectic, as are the corresponding conceptions of satisfaction and happiness. It is assumed that such judgments are matters of insight, and that precisely as value-judgments. To say that they are matters of insight *qua* value-judgments is a precautionary qualification, since Kierkegaard is wholly unaware of those current theories of meaning which in this sphere, and in the sphere of perceptual judgment as well, seek a radical and emasculating correction under the guise of furnishing an explication. It is fortunate, perhaps, that this correction remains a paper speculation which cannot be carried through in daily life where it scarcely occurs to the theorist that the attempt should be made. Were he to make trial of his theory here, he would soon have experiences which would give him pause.

The existential dialectic moves within three chief spheres of value, or types of value categories: esthetic, ethical, and religious. All human existence is in terms of one of these categories or in some combination of them. No one can possibly live, for example, in logical or scientific categories, though these may be utilized as instrumentalities of life. Nor does anyone live in metaphysical categories. These latter are of course present everywhere; but when they exist, they exist as constituting a formal structure for the esthetic, the ethical, or the religious.

The normal life-movement for an existing individual is *from* the esthetic, *through* the ethical, *to* the religious. But this movement is not completed once for all, since existence poses the task of its incessant renewal. The existing thinker has esthetic passion enough to give his life content, ethical enthusiasm enough to regulate it, dialectics enough to interpenetrate it with thought. The esthetic is the raw material; the ethical posits the requirement and constitutes the principle of regulation; the religious is the fulfilment, but again not once for all, but as renewal, reinstatement, and impulsive energy for the forward movement of existence.

The existential dialectic bears *qua* dialectic the stamp of its origin as a philosophical term in the dramatic dialogue. It is, namely, a mutual confrontation of opposites in their logically developed consequences. As existential it seeks to mediate a clarification of the issues of life, paving the way for a decisive personal commitment, a fundamental and therefore passionate choice. In this it presents a close analogy with that Socratic dialectic which issues in a confession of ignorance, to the accompaniment of the insistent Socratic refrain: One thing at least is certain, that we cannot afford to remain as we are. The dialectic is the unrest in the forward movement of learning, the existing individual being always a learner in the sense. that his life is a constant striving.

For Plato dialectics was a process of exploring the logical relations subsisting among the forms, tending toward an intellectual-esthetic intuition of the Form of the Good as crown and summit of the whole. This purpose makes of the Platonic dialectic a speculative and not an existential instrument, in so far as it envisages an ultimate taking of the individual out of existence to live a life of contemplation. For Aristotle the dialectic is essentially an inductive process of learning, sharply contrasted with that demonstrative science for which it constitutes a psychological propaedeutic. Its purpose is to stimulate an activation of the speculative reason, which then realizes a final scientific insight. The Aristotelian stress upon dialectics as a process of learning yields an intellectualistic analogy to the existential dialectic with its predominantly ethical emphasis. But it is only an analogy, since the existential dialectic is not a movement in the direction of science, but a movement in the direction of decisive choice and fulness of life.

The Hegelian dialectic is no mere subjective process, but the form taken by the self-evolution of the Idea as a logical system, and is *ipso facto* embodied as the work of the objective reason in the historical process. But for Kierkegaard the realm of the logical is not subject to any form of evolution, transition, or movement; its eternal expression is the principle which the Eleatics by a misunderstanding transferred to the realm of existence: Everything *is*, and nothing comes into being. Negation has no creative force and is not to be confused with a contraposition; mediation can have no place in logic, since it presupposes transition, which is a transcendence that logic excludes. The transition-category is historical, not logical. The incompatibility of logical necessity, on the one hand, and all forms of becoming, on the other, is argued at length in the *Philosophical Fragments*. The qualitative transitions brought about in the individual by dialectical deliberation and consequent choice come under the head of what Kierkegaard has called "pathetic" transitions, whereby the individual through strain and suffering becomes what he becomes, such becoming being the form of all ethical and ethico-religious existence.

The Hegelian dialectic is relevant to an observer contemplating the world-process; the existential dialectic is relevant to an individual who confronts the future as an active participant in life. The two points of view yield a contrasting consciousness. A merely contemplative consciousness sees nowhere, for example, any absolute oppositions; and this is the reason why the Hegelian dialectic registers a compromise or synthesis of opposites which is supposed to preserve the essence of both while annihilating them in their separateness; its watchword is: "both-and." The existential dialectic operates with qualitative distinctions and discovers absolute disjunctions which cannot be mediated; its watchword is therefore: "either-or."

When the "both-and" point of view comes to dominate existence as well as contemplation, it is the death of spirit; *"either-or* is the key to heaven," says Kierkegaard with epigrammatic incisiveness, *"both-and* is the road to hell." When the individual takes himself out of existence and contemplates himself as he is, statically, he perceives that he *is* both good and bad. But when he again plunges into existence and confronts the future ethically, he cannot *become* both good and bad at the same time, but he must move either in the one direction or in the other. The ethical relativist either occupies the irrelevant standpoint of a disinterested observer, in which case he cannot see the issue, or he is bankrupt of ethical enthusiasm. Without the passion of subjectivity there are nowhere any decisive distinctions in life. But when the individual has once chosen to exist in ethical categories, the distinction between good and evil comes into being for him in all its absoluteness, being essentially the distinction between realizing and failing to realize his own deeper self.

Again, from the standpoint of an immanent abstract contemplation there are no alternatives at all, relative or absolute. For such contemplation abstracts from the process of becoming as it is in real time, merely viewing the event as given in the abstract form of time. It therefore neglects, as immanent contemplation, the unrealized possibilities which were present in the real process of coming-to-be, and which constituted alternatives for the wills of the participants.

When contemplation finds a dialectical or causal structure in the given, and then puts together again the factors into which the event has been analyzed, this synthesis necessarily reproduces the event precisely as it was before it was analyzed. This self-relationship is the source of the necessity which contemplation finds; as Aristotle says: "That a thing is what it is, and will be what it will be, is necessary." But on this account to impute necessity to the process of becoming itself, the transition from possibility to actuality, is a paralogism. The expressions of freedom wear an aspect of necessity, when we reflect only upon their structure in the *sub specie aeternitatis* of contemplation, which they do not in the least have when we reflect upon their coming to be.

For the existing subjective thinker who confronts the future in passionate decision, there exists inevitably an absolute disjunction. Kierkegaard therefore says that in arguing with one who denies the existence of real alternatives one must be careful in choosing one's ground. One must not seek to import an "either-or" into the sphere of an immanent contemplation of what is taken as given; for there no alternatives can exist, and Hegel is absolutely right in rejecting them. But in so far as Hegel seeks to take alternatives away from existence, he fails utterly; since the effect of taking them away is to annul existence, and hence they are not taken away from existence. A philosopher who denies alternatives in existence must be asked if he is a human being, or if it is possible for a human being to become speculative philosophy in the abstract; let him be asked if he was perhaps born *sub specie aeternitatis* and has lived in that condition ever since, even when blowing his nose or drawing his monthly salary; let him be asked if he ever confronts the future so as to act with passion and decisiveness. If he answers this last question in the negative, he must forgive an ethical individual for asserting with indignation and dramatic truth that such a philosopher is a nincompoop. But if he answers in the affirmative, he will be compelled to admit that there is then for him an "either-or."

Kierkegaard thus treats the problem of freedom without resort to a *liberum arbitrium,* without rejecting a universal causal structure or a principle of continuity in events. He seeks to trace the locus of the necessity which contemplation discovers, and he appeals positively to an experience which cannot be repudiated without self-stultification.

Let us now consider the existential dialectic in its most crucial application, when it faces the problem of truth. Logicians tend to regard truth as exclusively a quality of propositions. The logical content of a judgment constitutes an ideality which is true or false according to the nature of its relationship to a relevant reality. But the speech of daily life enshrines another, and no less important, usage, whereby truth or falsehood comes to be attached to realities: a true man, a true statesman, a false friend, a false diamond. Here, too, a relationship is present as between an ideality and a reality, namely, between an ideality of worth and a relevant reality which either realizes this ideality or fails to realize it. When Kierkegaard asks: In what direction is the truth to be sought by an individual who is conscious of being in existence and subject to the claims of existence? he has this entirely natural and deeply ingrained duplicity in mind. And the bearing of this duplicity upon the paradoxical principle that subjectivity is truth is sufficiently evident.

A speculative idealism might seek to answer the question about truth by proclaiming the identity of thought and being. But this answer cannot be pertinent to existing individuals, the very terms of whose empirical existence in time and space separate thought from being, just as they separate striving from fulfilment. The idealistic answer that this is true for the finite understanding and for things in a lower realm of being, but not true for pure thought—and pure being—is merely a sign that philosophy has forsaken the realm of existence altogether and has emigrated to a sixth continent, where thought is sufficient to itself, where truth is not a quest but a finality; a realm where every problem has its solution and every doubt its cure and whatever else one pleases to say; that is, philosophy has become fantastic.

If the inquirer resists this temptation, his reflection will reveal to him two alternative possibilities. The search for truth may be pursued either in an objective or in a subjective manner. In the objective reflection the first step consists in an abstraction from the subject and his subjective interest. At the maximum of objectivity the truth becomes subjectively indifferent, as in the case of mathematical truth, for example. As the quest proceeds farther and farther in this direction the inquirer loses his real subjectivity more and more, until he finally becomes nothing but an abstract form for the objectivity that has come into being. The need for a decision has vanished, as well as every decisive result. And besides, the objectivity that has come into being for him is never anything more than an approximation, a stage in a never ending process; from the subjective standpoint his result is a hypothesis. Thus the inquirer has been brought into contradiction with himself, in so far as the search was prompted by a passionate interest in the truth, with a view to existing in it when found.

For the alternative subjective reflection the task is so to interpenetrate the subjectivity of the inquirer with thought that the inwardness thus developed may be the truth, a truth especially relevant to existing human beings. Here the individual sloughs off his objectivity more and more, until only subjectivity remains. The mode of procedure accentuates existence and tends to make it increasingly significant; the other is a flight from existence, and in so far as the inquirer still cannot help existing against his will, his situation is comical—as is that of everyone who tries to be what he is not. And the subjectivity that remains to him tends to become trivialized, exhibiting that "sometimes pitiful professorial figure" which Kierkegaard satirizes. A talented thinker sometimes builds a magnificent palace of thought, but it is one in which he does not live, apparently preferring for his personal domicile a dog kennel at the side of the palace. What marks the mature and significant thinker is the precision and stringency of the categories in which he has his daily life; but such a thinker will also be a subjective thinker.

A passage in the *Postscript* defines the two modes of reflection as follows:

When we inquire about the truth objectively, our reflection is objectively directed to the truth as an object to which the knower stands related. Reflection is not focussed upon the relationship, but upon the question whether it is the truth to which he stands related. When this something has been made out to be the truth, then the inquirer is supposed to be in the truth. But when we inquire subjectively into the truth, reflection is focussed subjectively upon the subject's relationship. If the mode of this relationship is a valid one, then the individual is in the truth, even if that to which he so stands related be untruth.[2]

Thus, for example, in connection with the knowledge of God: If a man enters the temple of the true God, with an intellectually correct conception of God in his understanding, but prays to Him in a spirit of falsity; and another bows down before an idol, but pours out his whole soul in the passion of the infinite; and we now ask where most truth is to be found, there can be only one answer for everyone who has not been altogether demoralized by science and scientific objectivity.

---

[2]*Unscientific Postscript,* 178.

An objective reflection inquires into the truth of the God-idea and raises the question of God's existence; a subjective reflection inquires into the subjectivity, the mode of existence, of the individual, asking whether he is related to something in such a manner that his relationship is a true God-relationship. The objective inquirer contemplates nature and human history; he sees much that suggests wisdom and omnipotence but also much that disturbs him and makes him doubtful. He can never overcome all these doubts and, even if he could, must fear that something might happen tomorrow which would shatter his little bit of proof to pieces. The inquiry is thus a never ending approximation, whose sum total is indecisiveness. Nor could he ever bring God objectively before him for still another reason. God is namely spirit, and spirit is subjectivity, and subjectivity is an inwardness which is revealed only to a corresponding inwardness in the seeker after God, an inwardness which the objective temper makes to vanish.

The thinker who chooses the subjective way appreciates to the full and in all its pain the dialectical difficulty that he must use some time, perhaps a long time, to find God objectively. He is aware that he may die tomorrow or before the search is ended, and that every moment is lost in which he does not have God—needing God even in order to be able to search for Him. In the moment of realizing this passionately, he has God, not by virtue of any objective deliberation, but by virtue of the infinite passion of his inwardness. For God is that of which each individual has an infinite need, and the passionate understanding of this is the very form of the true knowledge of God, the true God-relationship in inwardness.

Here then is the parting of the ways, where the road

traveled by the subjective thinker swings away from the road taken by the speculative philosopher. It is not the intellectual content of the latter's philosophy that makes the essential difference, but the fact that his mind comes to rest and his life culminates in an objectivity. A mediocre thinker and a mediocre personality will, of course, seek to compromise this dialectical issue, halting on both sides or walking alternately both ways. The greatness of Kierkegaard as a religious thinker lies among other things in his decisive and unwavering choice, his intensive concentration upon subjective reflection as the road to the highest truth. He has thus effected for theological thinking a veritable Copernican revolution, one in my opinion infinitely more significant than the much heralded astronomical one, the same Copernican revolution which is effected in the soul of every man when he becomes mature in the consciousness that it is not so much he that cross-examines existence, as existence that cross-examines him.

The rationale of the subjective procedure is not that there is no object or any objective reference; this is' a misunderstanding. Kierkegaard means by the objectivity that he rejects, an impersonal and disinterested temper of mind on the part of the subject; he does not mean that reference to an object which is the universal character and distinguishing mark of every intellectual function, one which professional empiricists and logical positivists tend altogether to neglect, to the confusion of their epistemology. But Kierkegaard assumes that there exists in the world of the spirit a situation which does not obtain in the world of finite ends and values, namely, a one-one correspondence between object and subjective attitude.

The concept of immortality, for example, has as its

only subjective correlate an infinite, passionate, personal, ethical interest—the fully developed potentiality of the individual's latent subjectivity. The possibility of this interest is the possibility of his immortality. And the interest verifies itself when it becomes the ruling passion of the individual's life in time, absolutely transforming it, and reducing every finite value to a relativity subject to resignation. Money can be attained in a thousand ways, the money remaining the same value; but there is only one way to obtain the highest good, and that is to risk every lower good for its possession. In the absence of such an interest, inquiry into immortality is an affectation of curiosity.

The existence of God becomes real only for the individual who is fully persuaded that he can of himself do nothing, neither rightly rejoice in his day of gladness nor rightly sorrow in his hour of grief. As long as he lives in the illusion that he can of himself do everything or something, God does not really exist for him, no matter how orthodox his theistic credo. This self-annihilation of the individual before God is man's truth and his highest perfection as human being, a perfection, moreover, open to all men.

The revolution of which we have spoken consists in the shift of attitude from the common presupposition that we must begin by obtaining true opinions, when the subjective assimilation will come of itself (which, however, it never does), to the making the question of man's true subjectivity primary, the truth of the objective correlate then following of itself. For a view of life it is pathos and ethos which constitute the decisive factors: pathos first, and then the ethos that springs from this pathos. The "how" of the subjective mode of existence indirectly determines the "what" of the truth and is the point of application for fruitful inquiry.

In the issue of this dialectical situation God becomes a postulate for the subjective thinker. But not in the usual empty and otiose sense, that God is objectively needed to explain and justify human ideals. This would make of God something like an imaginary point outside the picture of life, having the function of giving a theoretical unity to its perspective. But for the religious man God is not outside life, but within it, as its all in all. When the passionate concern of the individual is maximally developed, faith breaks forth in his consciousness as a postulation of God necessary to the individual, a life-necessity, since God is the resolution of his despair.

The above considerations apply only to ethical and ethico-religious truth, whose essence it is to have an essential and inseparable relationship to human existence. Other truth, whose relationship to human existence is external and accidental, requires as a matter of course objectivity in the inquirer; and Kierkegaard insists merely on the primacy of the ethical. That an individual thinker here and there should devote his life to objective research, as a relativity among other relativities, meets with no criticism from Kierkegaard; he rather goes out of his way again and again to express his profound respect for science and scholarship. But each individual, whether philosopher or scientist or butcher or baker or candle-stick-maker, needs first and foremost to understand himself and the disposition of his powers in the ethical; for the ethical is the universal foothold for each individual existence, the one indispensable bond of human fellow-ship, in which and before which we are all equal. The ethical is jealous for the purity of its own quality, not being in the slightest degree impressed by the utmost quantity of talent and power and fortune; it requires itself of the humblest man and the greatest genius on the same terms. It is not science, but the sophistical use of science to emasculate the ethical and confound existence, against which Kierkegaard directs the arrows of his wit and satire.

We have called this dialectic an existential dialectic partly because it everywhere accentuates existence and partly because it reflects the fundamental traits of existence. What then is existence, in Kierkegaard's use of this term as a category? It is first of all a synthesis of status and task. The task may be evaded or shabbily executed; but the existence of the individual as a matter of status remains to plague him with its unfulfilled requirement and to render his situation comical. There are many who exist after a fashion, succeeding bestially enough in becoming objective, though they still remain subjects, also after a fashion; just as a drunken driver who lets the horses take him home is also a driver.

Existence is a synthesis of the temporal and the eternal which posits a process of becoming and hence involves an incessant striving. When Plato says in the *Symposium* that love is the child of poverty and plenty, and hence is always in want, a seeker after satisfaction, he evidently means by love human life taken in its entirety; and the synthesis of poverty and plenty is an analogy to the synthesis of the temporal and the eternal. It is the eternal that gives continuity to the striving; the eternal becomes concrete in the individual in the culminating moment of his idealizing passion. To exist without passion is impossible, if one is to become conscious of the terms of one's existence; the passion of the infinite within a man yields in its culmination the highest realization that can be had in time. But the next moment the temporal conditions of existence are again enforced upon the individual, and his life again becomes a striving in which thought and being, striving and fulfilment, are separated from one another. An existing individual cannot remain in the eternal, but can at the most repeatedly arrive; renewal and reinstatement thus become the goal of life as long as life lasts.

The existential dialectic, being grounded in this situation, will therefore be utilized to dissolve away every form of illusory finality, which would in one way or another put an end to the striving which is life's content in its truth. It will discover and explore and accentuate the elusiveness, the insecurity, the uncertainty, the risk, inseparable from existence; for existence and objective security do not jibe. The subjective thinker will thus be active in discovering the negativities of existence and will be as negative as he is positive, holding both in an equal balance.

Intellectually, the subjective thinker will not permit his mind to rest in that supposed certainty of sense knowledge, for example, that deceives the sensuous man in his stupor. Nor will he come to rest, as if he had reached finality, in any form of approximation-knowledge, historical or natural-scientific. He will have no system as his final result, since system and finality are one and the same thing, and since life, for the living individual, comes under the head of unfinished business. He will avoid the sense of security which comes from credulous trust in the permanence of the customary and will actively bring home to himself, as a daily discipline, the precariousness of every established order. He will not so trust in his own cleverness, his power to calculate the probabilities, as to imagine that he has tamed and confined the incalculable energies of the possible. He will permit the consciousness of the possibility of death at any moment so to pervade his thought as always to be present in the background, transforming every ever-so-solid security into an uncertainty in relation to himself.

Morally, he will not permit his life to become petrified in a respectable routine, turning the rest of his moral existence into the slightest of marginal notes appended to a text long since finished. (If a friend who has had time to investigate this matter is right in reporting that cases of conscience are extremely rare in academic circles, then it would seem that this is a form of finality especially tempting to college professors.) He will not so cling to an institution, or to an established order of any kind, as to find in such an objectivity a guaranty that his striving has reached its end. Newman spent a good part of his life in seeking an answer to the question of which is the right church. Had he posed the question subjectively, he would have asked instead how his subjectivity should be constituted, in order that the fellowship of those like-minded with him might constitute the true church. And, in view of the circumstance that no individual is finished, he would have been compelled to postulate the true and ideal church as an invisible and spiritual order. The fixation of the religious life about a formula or an institution as a final resting-place that decides once and for all the issues of life is an illegitimate objectivity which the subjective thinker uses his dialectic to avoid. To keep the ardor of the spirit alive, the dialectic must actively discover the precarious and the uncertain. For the uncertain is the perpetual unrest in the dynamic of subjectivity, the guaranty that faith is a real victory of the spirit and not a delusive dream.

I quote as summary a footnote from the *Postscript:*

> In general, it is the distinctive mark of the infinite reflection in which alone the subjectivity of the individual can have the appropriate concern for an eternal happiness, that it is everywhere accompanied by the dialectical. Let it be a word, a proposition, a man, or whatever else you please—as soon as this is made to constitute a limit such that the limit itself is undialectical, we have narrowness of mind and superstition. There exists in every man an indolent as well as anxious desire to have something so entirely fixed and certain that it can exclude the dialectical; but this desire is really cowardice, and treason toward the divine. Even the most certain of all things, a divine revelation, becomes dialectical the moment I set myself to appropriate it; even the most fixed of all commitments, the infinite negative resolve, the infinite form for the existence of God within the individual, becomes at once dialectical. The moment I take the dialectical away I become superstitious, and cheat God of what He requires of me, namely the constant, repeated and strenuous reacquirement of that which has once been acquired. But it is of course much easier and more comfortable to be objective and superstitious, proclaiming this thoughtlessness as the highest wisdom.[3]

The general purport and spirit of this passage is reflected in the remarkable Socratic saying that even if a man knew how to make himself immortal, it would do him no good as a means to happiness, unless he also had the wit to use his immortality rightly after achieving it.

The great abundance of thought in the Kierkegaardian writings is only misunderstood if it is regarded as a contribution to the world's objective scholarship, an addition to learning, a *gefundenes Fressen* for budding Ph.D.'s and scholarly professors. It is directed to the human

---

[3]*Unscientific Postscript,* 35 n.

being who is so often submerged in the scholar and who seeks to make his life more significant. In the figure of the "professor" Kierkegaard personifies the tendency to translate everything into terms of objective knowledge and thus to rest in the illusion that one really possesses everything for which one has a classification; as if one were to seek satisfaction for hunger by contemplating a meal ticket, or rather, as if one's hunger had become so attenuated as really to be satisfied by such contemplation. Kierkegaard prophesied that the professor of the future would inherit him also, just as he has in a sense inherited all the best wisdom that has been wrought out in the world, in strenuous application, in agony of spirit, in fear and trembling and suffering, in tears and in blood. In another sense the "professor" cannot inherit, since he excludes himself from the realm of spirit by evading the claims of inwardness, passion, and decisive action.

With biting irony Kierkegaard has traced three stages in the evolution of Christendom. In the first stage the martyr was the representative Christian; in the second stage it was the monk; and then came the modern age, the flowering of science and culture, when the representative Christian has become the learned professor. There is in the professor an obstinate and almost inextinguishable persistence in apprehending everything as knowledge, just as a certain type of Englishman in his spleen looks at everything as subject for a wager. This professor in us, says Kierkegaard, is longer than the longest tapeworm; only God can extirpate him, so as to make a man.

Let me close with a typical Kierkegaardian anecdote, used by him in the *Journals*[4] to illustrate this point: A raw recruit is being instructed by a corporal in the bear-

---

[4]Dru: *Journals,* 471, §1269.

ing and behavior of a soldier. "You must hold yourself erect in the ranks," says the corporal. "Aye, aye, I understand that," says the recruit. The corporal continues: "And then you must not talk while under arms." The recruit: "Oh, is that so; very well, I am glad you have told me, so that now I know about it." "What the devil," says the corporal, "did I not tell you to keep your mouth shut!" "Aye, but do not be angry with me; now that I understand it I shall be sure to remember it."

V. THE ANTI-INTELLECTUALISM OF KIERKEGAARD[1]

THE aim of the present paper[1] is two-fold: to give an introductory characterization of Kierkegaard's individuality as a thinker, and to elucidate in some detail the epistemological position from which the paper takes its title. This position I have characterized as anti-intellectualism, in order to establish a point of contact with present-day currents of thought; but I warn the reader that Kierkegaard resists a facile classification, and that one cannot, without danger of misunderstanding, transfer impressions derived from a study of James or Bergson, unmodified, to the interpretation of this most profound and original thinker. The introductory section of the paper deals briefly with Kierkegaard's style and method of writing, in its relation to his philosophical ideas; with his doctrine of "indirect communication," as the consistent form of a reflectively conscious protest against intellectualism; and with the method and program of his constructive philosophy of values.

I

Although the author of a literature rich in philosophical content, Kierkegaard wrote no systematic treatise on pure logic or metaphysics. It most often happens that philosophical writers who thus wear the less professional

---

[1]A paper presented before the American Philosophical Association at Philadelphia, December, 1915.

air, have their treasures of truth so submerged in feeling, or so suffused with imagination, that their position is not abstractly clear, and consequently not readily susceptible of a sharp definition. But in Kierkegaard we have a rare combination of dialectical power with an imaginative and dramatic intuition, so that picturesque characterization in the concrete is to be found in his writing, side by side with exact and algebraic definition. His native dialectical powers were disciplined by a serious study of Hegel; and though emancipating himself from the tyranny of Hegel's dominant influence, he acquired through his aid the mastery of a precise and finished terminology. The absence, therefore, of any systematic treatise covering the logical and metaphysical disciplines, is due not so much to a limitation or a peculiarity in his genius, as to the nature of his philosophical position; indeed, it is the deliberate expression of a well-considered choice, the carefully planned application of a corrective against a one-sided and abstract intellectualism.[2] This feature of his thought makes his ideas extremely difficult to convey at second hand, since the task resembles the translation of poetry, where the form is inseparable from the content. One is constantly exposed to the danger of utterly failing to interpret the spirit of his philosophy, in spite of having correctly transcribed its chief salient propositions—a danger which the reader will note is somewhat ironical in its nature.

Kierkegaard calls himself a subjective thinker. His meaning may perhaps be conveyed, in one of its aspects, by calling him also an artist-thinker. For he strove constantly to reduplicate his reflection in an artistic form, attempting to assimilate and transmute its objective con-

---

[2]*Unscientific Postscript*, 223-224, 312.

tent so as to make it serve the purposes of a communication in which due regard should be had both to the giver and to the receiver. This care for the subjective elements in communication demands that thought should be doubly reflective; by the first reflection it then attains to its ordinary and direct expression in the word or phrase, and by the second reflection it receives an indirect expression in style and form, as the concrete medium of human intercourse.[3] Such an indirect expression, inasmuch as it is the result of reflection, is artistic; and such a thinker is therefore an artist in another and higher sense than that which is implied by the possession of mere literary skill. Kierkegaard maintains the validity and necessity of this two-fold reflection, whenever the subject matter to be communicated concerns Reality in its most concrete aspect, as rooted in the very nature of Reality itself, and as grounded in the fundamental relation between objective thought and real existence. Reality is such that a form of communication may be chosen which contradicts the very thought that it assumes to convey, thus "transforming the supposed communication into a non-communication."

I cannot undertake to convey, within the limits of this paper, an idea of the literary resourcefulness, the reflective ingenuity, the keenness of irony and profundity of humor, the variety and multiplicity of forms and devices, that give to Kierkegaard's writings their peculiar individuality of stamp and coloring, as a consequence of the method described as "double reflection." One expression of the method is the absence of a volume of pure logic or metaphysics from the list of his published works; the

---

[3] *Unscientific Postscript,* 68-74.

principle by which this choice was guided I wish briefly to explain.

The problem of Reality is of course, in one sense or another, the problem of all philosophy, and it was also Kierkegaard's central problem. As a student of the philosophy of his day, he soon began to feel, like many other students in his day and our own, the inadequacy of what philosophers are accustomed to say on this all-absorbing topic. "What philosophers say under the head of Reality," he complains in one of his aphorisms, "is sometimes as illusory as a sign displayed in a window, 'Clothes pressed here.' If you enter the shop to have your clothes pressed, you are disappointed to learn that the sign is held for sale, and that clothes are not pressed on the premises."[4] Philosophers tend to forget that the categories which are usually the first to attract their attention, and to which objective thinking is apt exclusively to devote itself, namely the logical and the metaphysical, are not as such the categories of Reality. The entities of metaphysics and the forms of logic do not exist *as such;* when they exist, they exist as imbedded in the flesh and blood of the esthetic, the ethical, and the religious. Their reality or being is not identical with the reality of factual existence, but they constitute an abbreviation of, or a *prius* for, the above three fundamental spheres of existence. Hence it is that no man lives in categories that are purely logical or metaphysical, but exists on the contrary in categories that are esthetic, ethical or religious in their nature.[5] A philosopher thoroughly conscious of this fact should be impelled to give his intercourse and his writings the stamp of a broad and sympathetic humanism;

[4] *Either/Or* I, 25.
[5] *Stages on Life's Way,* 430.

he will certainly wish to bear in mind that a philosopher is not only *sometimes* a man, as a Greek sceptic once frankly confessed, but always and essentially a man. In the attempt to express this consciousness, Kierkegaard made his work approximate, as nearly as possible, the essential features of the living reality. Now, in the concrete, the logical both is and is not, being imbedded in life's moral substance; hence the skeleton of Kierkegaard's own logical position was likewise imbedded and hidden in a certain "thickness," to use a significant expression of James. It was wrapped up in a covering of humor, wit, pathos, and imagination, and interwoven with mimic and lyric expressions of doubt, despair, and faith; so that we have presented before us, instead of a mere logical web of paragraphs, a thinking personality who exists in his thought. The subjective is shown appropriating and using the objective; on this account the style has a certain breadth, an unsystematic lingering ease of conversational tone; and there is displayed a pregnant and decisive energy of acceptance or repudiation which is unusual in philosophical composition, but which brings us incomparably nearer to the breath of life.

Pascal has noted that there are few who show themselves able to speak of doubt doubtingly, or faith believingly, or modesty modestly. It is no slight tribute to the noble simplicity of William James as a thinker, that he put in practice so large a measure of what he had learned to understand, and actually taught pragmatism in a pragmatic spirit. A student of Kierkegaard is in like manner impressed by the fact that his doctrine and method and spirit are consonant, and may be called genuinely pragmatic in a high and noble sense. In Kierkegaard, abstract logical thought is not merely dogmatically described as

having an instrumental function, but it is actually made
to perform its duty as instrumental; it is every moment
held in subjection to a realistic aim. Moreover, so concrete is the conception of this realistic aim, so reflectively
apprehended are the difficulties in the way of its actualization, that the problem which it sets gives rise to a
philosophic theory of the art of communication respect-
ing it. This theory seeks to define the nature and limits
of the mutual dependence of individuals upon one another, in such a way as to exhibit and respect their real
and ultimate independence. The theory is expressed
and summarized in the category of "indirect communication," which is the logical outcome of the method of
double reflection, and the consistent consequence of the
thoroughgoing anti-intellectualism which Kierkegaard
represents.[6]

That communication on the subject of the highest and
most concrete phase of Reality must necessarily be indirect, has its ground, according to Kierkegaard, in the fact
that the actualization of the real is always in process, and

---

[6] A study of Professor Royce's *Problem of Christianity* reveals an interesting parallel between the category of "interpretation" as developed by him,
and Kierkegaard's doctrine of "indirect communication." These two categories
play analogous and central roles in two antithetical views of life and reality.
Kierkegaard's conception of Christianity is therefore the precise opposite, at
every essential point, of that offered by Professor Royce. Interpretation is
direct and positive, is an expression for objective certainty, and is related,
despite strenuous efforts to avoid the implication, to an essentially static view
of life. Indirect communication is a negative expression for an underlying
positive principle, involves the denial of objective certainty, and is related
to an essentially dynamic view of life. To take one illustration of many:
Royce has a doctrine of the Spirit in the Community, but does not make
paramount the question of how the Community *comes to be,* since for him
it simply *is;* he does not ask how the Spirit comes to constitute the Community, or to dwell in it. When this question is raised and answered, as
Kierkegaard would answer it, by an insistence upon the primacy of the
individual, and a recognition of the fact that the Spirit must first come to
dwell in the individual in order to dwell in and constitute the Community,
instead of *vice versa:* then the life of the individual is turned inward rather
than outward, and is made inwardly, and therefore radically, dynamic; the

also in that independence of the individuals which makes any essential discipleship a false relation; it is an expression for the ethical isolation which makes it impossible to judge of an individual justly, or with unconditional certainty, by means of any code of general rules or laws; finally, it is a consequence of the metaphysical incommensurability between the particular and the universal, language being the vehicle of the abstract and the universal, Reality being essentially concrete and particular. When communication deals with the abstract, or with such aspects of the concrete as can be apprehended through essentially valid analogies, *i.e.,* the whole realm of purely objective thinking, there is no good reason why it should not be direct and positive; but when it attempts to deal with the absolutely individual and concrete, *i.e.,* the realm of the ethico-religious inwardness, its apparent positive and direct character is illusory; such communication becomes real only on condition that its negative aspect is brought to consciousness, and embodied in the form. A lover, for example, may feel the need of telling others of his love, though he also feels that he neither desires to convey, nor is able to express, its deepest and most intimate secret. And that which is only relatively true in the case of the lover, since the lover's experience has analogies, is absolutely true for the ethico-religious individual. A concrete subjective thinker, like Socrates, has no positive result that can be truly or adequately conveyed by a formula or a sum of propositions; he has only a way, he is never finished, and he cannot therefore positively communicate himself.

A protest against intellectualism needs a category of

relation to God becomes prior to, and fundamental to, the relation to humanity, instead of an ambiguous variant expression for the latter, or a powerless shadow of it; and the distinction between pantheism and theism receives its true significance.

this kind in order to free itself from the last vestige of subservience to the dominance of the principle of identity. In my opinion, Kierkegaard was the first critic of intellectualism who burned his philosophical bridges behind him, and thereby liberated himself from the trammels of the intellectualist application or misuse of logic in the world of life and reality. Certainly not the first to discover the category in question, or the first to use it, he was nevertheless the first, as far as I am aware, to give it a clear and dialectical formulation. What I have said about it here is simply for the purpose of calling attention to the concept, and does not pretend to play the part of an exposition.[7]

James characterizes intellectualism as the claim that conceptual logic is the final authority in the world of being or fact, and as the assertion that the logic of identity is the most intimate and exhaustive definer of the nature of reality.[8] Kierkegaard meets this claim and assertion by the proposition that logic does not and cannot define reality; that it merely predisposes reality for our knowledge without itself coming into contact with its actuality.[9] With this proposition his anti-intellectualism begins, but it by no means ends there; and although this attitude toward logic is the primary concern of the present paper, I wish also to indicate, very summarily and only by way of introduction, the philosophical advance which he has made in the application of this initial proposition to more concrete problems.

The chief forms of positive objective knowledge—mathematics, the historical disciplines, sense perception and the natural sciences which rest upon perception, and

---

[7]*Training in Christianity,* 155-179.
[8]James: *A Pluralistic Universe,* 213-220.
[9]*The Concept of Dread,* 9.

metaphysics—are subjected to a critical estimate, in the endeavor to establish the fundamental fact that these disciplines, despite their real and obvious value (Kierkegaard is no obscurantist), when viewed as revelations of Reality, suffer from two fundamental defects of abstraction. First, they are either entirely hypothetical in their application to reality, as in the case of logic and mathematics, or they are endless approximations to the truth, as in the case of history and the natural sciences. Secondly, they are, and indeed wish to be, purely objective disciplines; as such they realize a knowledge which from the standpoint of the real knower is non-essential, since it does not express his actual and concrete position in existence. Hence they do not essentially concern him, but concern merely a fictitious objective subject-in-general, not identical with any concrete human being; in the last analysis, the degree and scope of such knowledge are a matter of indifference, and only knowledge whose relation to existence is essential, is essential knowledge. No form of positive objective knowledge, no logical system, no metaphysical result (a metaphysical system embracing reality is an illusion), can attain to a Truth in which Reality is adequately and definitively revealed.[10]

If the problem of Truth and Reality is not to be given up in despair, one must seek for a solution elsewhere, and seek for it in another spirit. There is but one other sphere in which such a solution can be sought, and this is the sphere of the subjective attitude of the knower, the realm of the subjective "how" as distinct from the objective "what." Such is the fruitful turn which Kierkegaard gives to an analysis of the adequacy of knowledge that is nearly as old as thought, and which, according to

---

[10]Cf. *Unscientific Postscript*, passim.

the temperament of the philosopher, has served variously as a starting point for scepticism, for positivism, for relativism, for mysticism, or for an abstract idealism. Kierkegaard makes it the point of departure for an elaborate and profound critique of the personality in its chief subjective modes, in order to discover a "how" which shall adequately express and grasp the real in its human accessibility and concreteness. He offers us a delineation of the whole range of typical subjective life-attitudes, describing them in their ideal self-consistency and sharpness of distinction.[11] In this way he presents a variety of esthetic points of view, from hardened understanding to sympathetic-egoistic melancholy; esthetic and ethical despair in many forms; prudent eudemonism and worldly wisdom; executive irony, or irony as a fundmental attitude toward life; ethical self-assertion in terms of moral courage and pathos; marriage as the most concrete ethical realization of life; the struggles of conscience and remorse under exceptional and irregular conditions, for the purpose of throwing light upon the normal; humor and resignation; religion. The forms of the religious attitude are reduced ultimately to two, which Kierkegaard regards as fundamental: immanent religion and transcendent religion, the latter being distinguished from the former by the decisiveness with which it grasps, and the passionate concreteness with which it expresses, the deepest paradox of life.[12] This critique of the personality is evidently equivalent to a philosophy of values. But the uniqueness of Kierkegaard's contribution to such a philosophy lies in the fact that the evaluations of life which form its subject matter are by his method made to reveal

---

[11]*Unscientific Postscript*, 225-267, and the entire literature.
[12]*Ibid.*, 493-498.

themselves, and therefore in a sense to criticize themselves, through representative personalities; they are embodied in the self-expression of a variety of authors or pseudonyms, whose ideas constitute typical and rival views of life.

The results of this dramatic and imaginative exploration of the personality are abstractly summarized, and culminate in a definition of Truth, as *Subjectivity raised to the highest intensity of which it is capable;* or, in order to make explicit its negative relation to the objective, as *the objectively uncertain, held fast in subjective inwardness with the highest possible degree of passionate appropriation.*[13] This formula also defines Faith, which is the subject's mode of apprehending the Truth, *sensu eminenti.* A more concrete and epigrammatic characterization of the Truth is embodied in the maxim: "Only the Truth which edifies, is Truth for you."[14] This is evidently a concrete way of acknowledging the individual himself as the test and standard of Truth, not indeed in the sense of Protagoras, but in the opposite sense of Socrates. "Know thyself" becomes the ultimate categorical imperative. This self is not, however, a transcendental ego serving as a starting-point for metaphysical speculation, as in Fichte; it is, very simply, the concrete personality that constitutes for each one his appropriate ethical task. Realistically, the above definition of Truth involves the consequence that the only reality accessible to any existing individual is his own ethical reality. To every reality outside the individual, even his own *external* reality, his highest valid relation is cognitive; but knowledge is a grasp of the possible, and not a realization of the actual;

---

[13]*Unscientific Postscript,* 182.
[14]Either/Or II, 294.

the knowledge of actualities transmutes them into possibilities, and the highest intellectual validity of knowledge is attained in an even balancing of alternate possibilities with an absolutely open mind.[15]

Each of the brief characterizing phrases used in the above schematic outline stands for an entire section or volume in Kierkegaard's comprehensive literature of the personality; and he has himself given the content of these treatises an abstract categorical formulation, conceived with almost algebraic exactness. This is indeed a brilliant double achievement, by the recognition of which Kierkegaard's permanent fame as a thinker will be historically assured.

II

We now pass to a more detailed consideration of Kierkegaard's estimate of logic, formally taking up the reasons which constitute his critique of intellectualism. These reasons may be summarized under four principal heads. 1. Logic cannot, from its own resources, provide for transitions from one quality to another; in the world of fact, such transitions take place by a leap. 2. Logic cannot acknowledge, within its own sphere, the contingent; but the contingent is an essential constituent of the actual. 3. Logic deals only with universals; the particular, however, is absolutely inseparable from the actual. 4. Logic deals only with essences, whose being consists in their conceivability; factual existence is not an essence, and it involves a kind of being which cannot be logically conceived. Let us consider each of these points in turn.

A. *A logical transition from one quality to another is impossible.* The static character of the concept has often been contrasted with the dynamic character of temporal

---

[15]*Unscientific Postscript,* 280.

experience, sometimes with the intent of proving the concept, and sometimes temporal experience, unfit for knowledge. Of course, we may define knowledge in different ways; but in the generally accepted meaning, it would seem to be this static characteristic of the concept which makes knowledge of a changing experience possible.[16] Kierkegaard succeeds, perhaps, in obviating much superficial misunderstanding of the doctrine of the static concept, by formulating the distinction between a logical and an actual transition, and in calling attention to the fact that the change from one concept to another, whether in the revision of judgment or in the course of history, is not *logical,* but *actual.* A concept does not change itself, either into its opposite or into a mere other, but reality makes the transition from one concept to another by means of a *leap.* In logic, everything is and nothing comes into being—a truth which the Eleatic philosophy transferred to the realm of factual existence in consequence of a misunderstanding.[17] In a logical system of concepts, every movement is immanent, since the relations by which the system is constituted are, by the existence of the system, rendered internal relations; the whole is therefore presupposed in every part, and that which emerges from the logical development of such a system is exactly the same as that which was there at the beginning.[18] Movement, transition, mediation, are all transcendent concepts, and have no legitimate place in logic. To ignore this is to confuse both logic and the historical

---

[16]It is one of the many merits of Hüsserl's *Logische Untersuchungen* to have abundantly set forth and illustrated this point.

[17]*The Concept of Dread,* 12 n.

[18]Hence when logic rejoices in the orderly beauty of its ballet of the categories, it is pledged not to forget that this ballet is devoid of all actual motion; reason enough for its "unearthly" character!

sciences, where these concepts belong, and it makes ethics impossible; for it leads to the misunderstanding that the actual, whether past or future, may be viewed as necessary. By this interpretation all real movement is taken away from history and from the individual life, and the illusory introduction of movement into logic is a very poor substitute for such an irreparable loss.

In the realm of the actual, transitions come to pass. This is the essential nature of existence; its salient characteristic is change and striving, which is the source of all its pathos. All actual transition involves a breach of continuity, a *leap*. The leap is present in manifold forms, and it is one of the most important of philosophical problems to distinguish between transitions of different orders.[19] The most significant and decisive are those which take place in the ethico-religious life of the individual; this is the sphere of the essentially qualitative distinctions. But every leap possesses the logically negative character that it cannot be construed, except out of an immanence which has first included it, and the gap between

---

[19]For the sake of greater clearness, I append a few examples, culled mostly from material in Kierkegaard's journal. H_2 plus O becomes water, and water becomes ice, by a leap. The change from motion to rest, or *vice versa*, is a transition which cannot be logically construed; this is the basic principle of Zeno's dialectic, and is also expressed in Newton's laws of motion, since the external force by which such change is effected is not a consequence of the law, but is premised as external to the system with which we start. It is therefore transcendent and non-rational, and its coming into existence can only be apprehended as a leap. In the same manner, every causal system presupposes an external environment as the condition of change. Every transition from the detail of an empirical induction to the ideality and universality of law, is a leap. In the actual process of thinking, we have the leap by which we arrive at the understanding of an idea or an author. Kierkegaard finds a pardonable pleasure in noting the inconsistency of certain followers of Hegel, who have tried to invest with romantic glamour the experience by which they awoke to an understanding of his philosophy; as if a man were to boast of the miracle by which he became an adherent of the philosophy which denies all miracles. The change from scepticism to belief is a leap of fundamental importance; a radical doubt cannot work itself out into belief by an

two qualities can never be bridged by a demonstration; it must either be given or be achieved.

The historical actuality is thus marked by a transition to the new as a leap, whence is derived the sense of wonder. Wonder is the philosopher's receptivity for the historically new. Under a logical construction of history, wonder would be abolished; "for who could possibly wonder at a necessary construction?"[20] But such a construction of history is illusory, as everyone would easily understand if he attempted to construe the life of a single individual, say his own. Kierkegaard pithily remarks that the Hegelian interpretation of history helps us understand the past, by apprehending it as if it had never been present or future; it interprets the heroes of the past as if they had never been alive; and it seeks to aid us to an understanding of ourselves by treating us as if we were dead.[21] The futility of this kind of explanation of life, and the need of replacing it by an interpretation more human, is expressed in the following epigram from one of his journals: "The motto of all philosophy hitherto

---

immanent development of its presuppositions, in spite of the fact, exploited by a too facile idealism, that scepticism always posits an abstract certainty in the background. Doubt consists in falsely interpreting this certainty; hence it cannot be overcome except by the assumption of a new point of departure, reached in a decision of the will. In the inner life, the radical transitions are not merely given, but must be achieved as an expression of freedom. They are therefore both non-logical and pathetic; the breach of continuity which they involve necessitates an experience surcharged with pathos. Thus the transition from esthetic Eudemonism to ethics, or from the contemplation of nature to the idea of God, or from an intellectual knowledge of the good to its ethical realization, is in each case a pathetic transition. Cf. Søren Kierkegaard's *Papirer*, V, pp. 371-375.

[20]*Philosophical Fragments*, 66. Cf. Aristotle's remark that science tends to abolish wonder, by exhibiting as necessary that which at first appears to be contingent; citing the example of the geometrician who has demonstrated the incommensurability subsisting between the circumference of the circle and its diameter.

[21]"Misled by the constant reference to a continued process in which opposites come together in a higher unity, and so again in a higher unity, etc., a parallel has been drawn between Hegel's doctrine and that of Heraclitus,

has been, *There is nothing new under the sun;* the motto of the new Danish philosophy will be, *There are more things in heaven and earth than are dreamt of in your philosophy."*

B. *Logic cannot assimilate or acknowledge the contingent aspect of the actual, within its own realm of truth.* This is an immediate consequence of the fact that change transcends the sphere of logic, since change is a contingency. In a logical system all relations are necessary, precisely because in such a system no changes actually take place. Hence the logical as the necessary cannot exist, for everything that exists has come into being, *i.e.,* has suffered the change involved in passing from potentiality to actuality (κίνησις). This change the necessary cannot undergo; the necessary is, and never comes to be; its being is *sub specie aeternitatis,* in the realm which is the essential medium of thought. In logic, every movement is in consequence of a logical ground, and is hence both necessary and immanent; in reality, nothing happens in consequence of a ground, but everything takes place by virtue of a cause. The apparent necessity of a natural law,

---

that everything is in a state of flux. But this is a misunderstanding, since everything that Hegel says about process and becoming is illusory. Hence the System lacks an ethic, and hence the System knows nothing when it is asked, in real earnest, by the living generation and the living individual, to explain becoming, in order, namely, that the individual may learn how to act and live. In spite of all that is said about process, Hegel does not understand the world-process from the point of view of becoming, but understands it, by help of the illusion incident to pastness, from the point of view of finality, where all becoming is excluded. Hence it is impossible for a Hegelian to understand himself by means of his philosophy, for he can only understand that which is past and finished; but a living person is surely not yet deceased. Possibly he finds consolation in the thought that when one can understand China and Persia and six thousand years of the world's history, the understanding of a particular individual matters very little, even if that individual happens to be one's self. To me it does not seem so, and I understand it better conversely: that he who is unable to understand himself must have a somewhat peculiar understanding of China and Persia, etc." *Unscientific Postscript,* 272 n. Cf. also James: *A Pluralistic Universe,* 243-244, where Kierkegaard is quoted.

binding cause to effect, is no real or unconditional necessity; the appearance of necessity arises through an abstraction from the fact that the causes (the secondary causes) have themselves come into being, and by a forgetfulness of the fact that their becoming is not explained, but only presupposed, by the law; "should such forgetfulness perhaps also be necessary?" The past is indeed unchangeable but it does not share the unchangeableness of the necessary, for when the past came to be, it did not exclude the change by which it came to be; but the necessary excludes every change. The possibility of a systematic apprehension of the past, *ex post facto,* cannot alter the fact that the past is not more necessary than the future. Just as the optical illusion of seeing the square tower round is one which is induced by distance in space, so the intellectual illusion of apprehending the past as necessary is induced by distance in time.[22]

C. *The incommensurability between the universal and the particular reveals the impotence of logic in its attempt to define the actual.* The logical concept is always a universal, and even the so-called concrete universal is not concrete in the same sense that the actual is concrete, for the particular *qua* particular is essential to the actual, and repels every attempt to conceive it logically.[23] When abstract thought tries to conceive the particular, it transforms it into a universal. To ask what reality is in general, is one thing; to ask what it means to call this particular thing or situation a reality, by bringing the ideality of thought to bear upon its concrete particularity, is an absolutely different thing. The former question is perhaps not even legitimate; in any case the question

---

[22]Cf. *Philosophical Fragments,* 59-73.
[23]*The Concept of Dread,* 70 n.

and answer remain within the sphere of the abstract, and do not reach reality as actual. The latter question is a concrete question, and cannot be put in a logical or metaphysical system, or in any science; it can only be answered by the individual as an individual, who finds in the definiteness of time and space the particularization of his experience and his thought. Abstract thought solves all the difficulties of life by abstracting from them, whence arises its complacent disinterestedness; the concrete thinker, who faces the concrete problem of reality as above specified, discovers that this problem brings his subjective interest to a climax, since it reveals a future presenting a critical and decisive alternative. For abstract thought there is no "either-or," no absolute disjunction; "why in the world should there be, since abstract thought abstracts from existence, where the absolute disjunction belongs?" But for the thinker who faces the future with the subjective passion inherent in voluntary action *sensu eminenti*, there exists an absolute disjunction, a valid contradictory opposition; "whoever attempts to take this away, takes existence away, and does not therefore take it away in existence."[24]

On the universality of the universal rests the possibility of communication, and on its validity rests the acknowledgment of the existence of other selves. The universal is that which is common to different thinkers, or to the same thinker at different times.[25] But the incommensurability between the universal and the particular makes

---

[24]*Unscientific Postscript,* 270-271.

[25]The "ego-centric predicament" is an imperfect expression for the more fundamental "present-moment" predicament; it is just as impossible to know one's own past, or conceive one's own future, or realize the full significance of one's own present, without assuming the validity of universals, as it is to conceive the possibility or acknowledge the reality of another person without making the same assumption. To characterize the universal as indeterminate-

doubt and belief, truth and error, possible. When I interpret a particular sense impression as a star, I give it a place in a conceptual order; and when I interpret it as the same star which I saw yesterday or a year ago, or as a star which my neighbor means or sees, or as a star which once came into existence, whether an instant or ages ago makes no essential difference—I am in these interpretations or judgments identifying a present immediacy of sense with some conceptuality of the memory or the imagination. Scepticism is a protest of the will against every such identification, on the ground that it involves an inference transcending the immediately given, and because it is impossible to prove that such inferences may not turn out to be erroneous. Belief is a contrary movement of the will, an affirmation which recognizes that another interpretation is possible, but nevertheless risks the assertion of this interpretation as real. That alternative interpretations are always possible, is most frequently a latent consciousness; stupid and passionate people ignore it; and the immediate suggestions of sense, together with the familiarity of the habitual, not to speak of the partiality of the will, tend to lull this consciousness to sleep. On the other hand, the experience of error tends to rouse the mind from its dogmatic slumbers, thus positing the choice between belief and belief, or between belief and doubt.[26]

---

ness of meaning is confusing, since it needlessly breaks with traditional terminology, and necessitates distinguishing between two kinds of indeterminateness, one of which is *sui generis*. To call universals dead dictionary definitions, verbal forms without content, is likewise confusing, and is excusable only as a sort of vehement *argumentum ad hominem* relevant to a particular misuse of the universal, but not tending to clarify logical terminology.

[26]The philosophers who confidently appeal to Experience, spelled, like the Absolute, with a capital, as the adequate immanent guarantee for the security of judgment, seem not to have learned from experience that the consequences always come last, and cannot therefore be appealed to in the moment of judgment; their utility for the shaping of future judgments never reaches the

In the inner life of the self, the contrast between the universal and the particular finds its highest significance. The self is a synthesis of the universal and the particular. The ethical individual has the task of realizing the universal man in a concrete particular embodiment, and the individual is both himself and the race. The ethical solution of this contradiction constitutes the history of the individual, by which he also participates in the history of the race, and is essentially interested in the history of every other individual. Here lie all the ethical and religious problems of the individual life.[27]

D. *The heterogeneity of the logical and the actual is revealed, finally, in the fact that logic deals only with essences or qualities.* Factual existence, which is the mark of actuality, is not an essence or a quality; and the difference between the possible and the actual is logically nondeterminable, because the change from the one to the other is not a change of essence, but a change of being.[28] From this follow two important consequences: it becomes evident that demonstration or proof with reference to existence is a misunderstanding, and that to speak of degrees of reality without clearly distinguishing between

---

point where it abolishes the risk of error, or the incommensurability between the given and the inferred. On the other hand, the idealists seek to heal the open wound of this situation by reference to an Absolute Knower, failing to realize the power of the actual uncertainty and risk of error involved to depress the ideal certainty which the Absolute Knower possesses, to the status of an abstract possibility; other motives than those derivable from the realm of epistemology are necessary, in order to transmute this abstract conception into a concrete faith in a real actuality. But by this transference of the problem from the logical to the ethico-esthetic sphere, the content of the conception is radically altered, and we pass from the Absolute of metaphysics to the God of religion.

[27] *The Concept of Dread,* 26.

[28] *Philosophical Fragments,* 29-44; 59-73. It is this transition which, as Bergson teaches, offers a problem that no intellectual knowledge succeeds in solving; Kierkegaard insists that the problem is irrelevant to knowledge as such, and that the attempt to find a new form of knowledge that solves the problem (intuition) is illusory.

ideal reality and factual existence, involves a similar mis-understanding.

It is impossible to reach existence by means of a demonstration. All demonstration operates by essences or quales, and their existence is either assumed or irrelevant. (The objective existence of the essences postulated by logic is simply their reality for thought, but is not their factual existence.) Hence I can never demonstrate the existence of a stone or a star, but only that some existing thing is a stone or a star. The testimony offered in a court of justice is not for the purpose of proving that a criminal exists, but in order to show that the accused, whose existence is given, is a criminal. It cannot be proved that God exists; every such attempt inevitably reduces itself to a development of the consequences which flow from having assumed His existence, *i.e.,* to a making explicit the logical content of the conception of God. If God does not exist, of course it is impossible to prove His existence; but if He does exist, it would be the height of folly to attempt it. The procedure has esthetically the form of an insult, as if one were to assume to demonstrate, in the presence of someone, that he exists; for existence is higher than demonstration, and requires a more adequate form of acknowledgment. The only adequate expression for the existence of God is worship, and the attempt to demonstrate it, is consciously or unconsciously to ignore His existence, *i.e.,* His presence. All reasoning is *from* existence, and no reasoning is *toward* existence.

Factual existence not being a quality, is not subject to distinctions of degree. A fly, if it exists, has precisely as much existence as a God. The dialectic of existence is the dialectic of Hamlet, "to be or not to be." Ideally, it is not improper to speak of degrees of reality, but when we deal

with reality from the ideal point of view, we do not deal
with factual existence, but with ideal essence. Spinoza's
proof for the existence of God is thus a profound tautol-
ogy, resting on the identification of reality with perfection. It avoids the real difficulty, which is to bring God's
ideal essence into relation with factual existence.

The category which relates the ideal to the actual is
the possible, and knowledge is always a system of possibilities; intellectually and esthetically, though not ethically, the possible is higher than the actual, just as Aristotle says that poetry is more philosophical than history.[29]
Belief is the application of knowledge to the determination of the actual, and constitutes our point of contact
with the historical as such. The historical comes into being by setting aside the antecedent alternative possibilities; in precisely analogous fashion, belief comes into
existence by setting aside as invalid the alternative possibilities of knowledge. And just as the former transition
is a leap which cannot be logically construed, so the latter
transition, the transition from the many possibilities of
knowledge to the one reality of belief, is not necessitated
by knowledge, but is an act of the will.[30] The choice of
the will in believing is the means whereby the personality
constitutes, expresses, and reveals itself, on the different
levels of its subjectivity. Every deeper ethico-religious
conviction, as an interpretation of the universe and of
life, is an expression of the inner depths of the personality, rather than a necessary consequence of knowledge.
Faith is never grounded in the objective necessities of
logic or of metaphysics, and its firm conviction is incom-

---

[29] *Unscientific Postscript*, 283-322.

[30] The reader will note the identity of what is here called belief, with what
modern logic calls judgment, as something distinct from the ideal content of
propositions.

mensurable with the approximations and probabilities of history or of natural science; it is forever transcendent of every positive external objectivity, and its object exists only for the infinite subjective interest in which and through which it lives and works.[31]

Such is, in brief outline, and largely in free paraphrase, Kierkegaard's anti-intellectualism, viewed from the standpoint of logic. The reader may wish to compare these views with current attacks upon formal logic, and with the radical evolutionism of Bergson. The attacks upon logic charge that this discipline or no-discipline, as the impetuosity of its critics leads them to stamp it, does not describe actual thinking, does not reveal the actual motives of thought, and does not explain the actual progress of knowledge. This is evidently the same contrast between the formal and the actual which Kierkegaard has attempted to illuminate and to interpret. When compared with Bergson, Kierkegaard's position shows both essential resemblances and essential differences; but the comparison raises so many problems that the present paper cannot undertake even to mention them. Current controversy is almost wholly preoccupied with the problem of knowledge, leaving the problem of action far in the background. It is here, however, that the distinction between intellectualism and its antithesis is most sharply defined, for the mere knower is not as such the concretely real subject; as knower he makes an effort, the better to realize the function of science, to abstract from his real exist-

---

[31]For Kierkegaard, faith is by no means objectless; but its object is not given positively, outside the individual, but only negatively, within the individual; there is an absolute correspondence between the nature of this object and the individual's subjective mode of apprehending it. Kierkegaard's achievement is, so to have defined this subjective mode as uniquely to determine the object to which it corresponds.

ence. It is by such an abstraction that he seeks to become disinterested and objective, and to identify himself, as far as may be, with the objectivity that he knows. It is true that this undertaking is but an approximation, and is never completely successful; but it is folly to ignore the reality of the effort, and futile to deny that it may and does meet with a relatively adequate degree of success. On the other hand, it is surely necessary for every thinker to understand what relation his abstract thought and objective knowledge bear to life; if he seeks to forget life in a complete absorption in the tasks of objective thought, or assumes that the latter is the highest and noblest human pursuit, then he becomes, as Kierkegaard has shown in a style and manner worthy to be ranked as classic, personally insignificant and fundamentally a comic figure, a type of the absent-minded professor whose real life is lived in distraction, "and who even marries—in distraction." This species of abstract thinker Kierkegaard has immortalized in the figure of the "privat-docent." With greater objectivity than Schopenhauer, but with a point of view akin to his, he has drawn the picture of the "professor of philosophy, in the German sense, who is bound, *à tout prix*, to explain everything"; over against this picture he has set the ideal of "thinker, in the Greek sense, whose life is an attempt artistically to realize his thought," and who does not, therefore, need "many thoughts, all valid to a certain extent," but is satisfied with "one thought, which is absolute."

VI. KIERKEGAARD'S DOCTRINE OF THE THREE STAGES ON THE WAY OF LIFE

KIERKEGAARD'S abiding significance may be calculated from different points of view. From the purely literary standpoint it is connected with the depth and compass of his pathos; from the moralist's point of view it is bound up with the vigor and intensity of his insistence upon the central importance of the individual personality; while from the purely formal point of view of intellectual workmanship, it is dependent upon the clarity, definiteness, categorical precision, and universal applicability of his doctrine of the three stages or spheres of life—esthetic, ethical, and religious. Kierkegaard's concrete criticism of life, with all the changes undergone during the dozen years of his literary activity, nevertheless falls from first to last within the conceptional framework of these fundamental categories. *Either-Or* is a study in contrasting esthetic and ethical valuations; *Stages on the Way of Life* resumes this study and adds a specific religious system of valuations in the "Story of Suffering"[1] which constitutes the greater part of its bulk; while one of the last products of his pen, the theological essay on the difference between a Genius and an Apostle[2] makes use of the contrast between the esthetic and the religious to point the moral of a modern confusion in theological thought.

---

[1] *Stages on Life's Way*, 179-363.
[2] *The Point of View*, 146 n.

The theory of the three spheres or stages constitutes a philosophy of life in the form of a philosophy of evaluation. That life is rooted in valuation, and that there is no such thing as living in, or by the purely impersonal and non-emotional categories of metaphysics or science, is a view which Kierkegaard everywhere assumes and frequently asserts. In this respect he has found support in a modern thinker who otherwise represents a contradictory philosophy of life, namely, Nietzsche. The latter never wearies of asserting that life is valuing, and that the true creator is the creator of values. Whatever may be thought of Nietzsche's drastic criticism of Christianity, he shows at any rate a clear consciousness of what the question is about, by concentrating attention upon the life valuations involved, rather than upon questions of metaphysical or scientific or historical fact. There are many points of contact between Kierkegaard and Nietzsche; this particular point consists of a common view as to the essential formal character of a philosophy of life, an identical opinion about the nature of the problems which are fundamental to such a philosophy.

Kierkegaard would doubtless himself have characterized the studies offered by him in what we have described as a comparative philosophy of values, as psychological studies. The psychology, however, which is here offered us, is not identical with modern naturalistic psychology. The problem of description in terms of meaning and significance everywhere engulfs, in Kierkegaard, the problem of description in terms of structure; and the problem of explanation in terms of cause and effect, the mechanico-dynamical structure of psychological happenings in terms of natural law, is not even sighted. If the Kierkegaardian studies are psychological, they doubtless belong to that literary psychology which Santayana places in such sharp contrast to scientific psychology. Nevertheless, no one can deny that Kierkegaard succeeds in revealing and communicating a profound insight into the human heart, which is something that can scarcely be said as yet of modern scientific psychology, whose worshippers themselves frequently complain that the offerings at the altar make a fast rather than a feast; so that whether psychological or not, it would seem the part of wisdom to make the most of what Kierkegaard's insight so generously offers.

In this doctrine Kierkegaard has set himself the task of making a map of the emotional cosmos. This is an ambitious undertaking, and in the history of thought it has been the case that other problems have absorbed the best intellectual energies, with the result that the objective and the impersonal aspects of existence have been charted much more frequently and more accurately than the emotions. The popular consciousness identifies the emotional with the indefinite and the vague; and intellect and emotion are almost held to be mutually destructive of one another. In this field Kierkegaard is in many respects a pioneer, and no one has surpassed him in the compass and range of emotional command, or in the precision of intellectual characterization. He has shown that the life of feeling has inherent structure and system, that valuations fall into coherent systematic groups, that emotions are not merely a structureless mush, like the "skin and squash" of Kingsley's caterpillar; and he has also shown that it is possible to retain a deeper passion while thinking objectively about it; in other words, that we can be objective with respect to our own subjectivity without losing it.

The occasional application to these "ways of life" of the term *stages,* particularly in the title of one of Kierkegaard's chief works,[3] has given rise to some misunderstanding. In one sense they are represented as rival views of life, which present themselves as alternative for the individual's deliberate choice. In this sense the notion of a stage, as a step or period in a continuous process of development, is of course irrelevant and inapplicable. It is one thing to describe modern civilized life, for example in contrast with the simpler life of the ancient Orient, in order to elicit the judgment—"better fifty years of Europe than a cycle of Cathay";[4] it is quite another thing to trace a process by which oriental life gradually begins to move forward into a likeness with western civilization. It is one thing to describe California and Florida as rival winter resorts, and another to tell a story about a man who started for California and finally landed in Florida, he hardly knew how it happened. It is this latter kind of story that Høffding wants Kierkegaard to tell about the different stages of life, and he consequently objects because Kierkegaard does not offer a motivation for the transition from one stage to the other in a natural manner, but describes the transitions always as crises, as breaches of continuity.

The breach of continuity between the stages means for Kierkegaard three things: 1) The values in each stage are determined by specific passions or enthusiasms, qualitatively different. 2) A personality whose life is in the one sphere cannot by a mere process of reflection transport himself into the other; for this a passionate resolution of the will is necessary. 3) The change from one

---

[3]*Stages on Life's Way.*
[4]Tennyson: "Locksley Hall."

sphere to the other is never necessary, but always contingent; if it presents itself as possible, it also presents itself as possible of non-realization. Besides these general determinations of the "leap," there is also the leap *par excellence* by which the religious passion which in Christianity is called faith, emerges. This transition requires a divine assistance, and is a true creative act of God, within the framework of a pre-existent creation.

Why then does Kierkegaard use the apparently inexplicable concept of a stage or stadium for his theory? First, because he holds that each higher stage is constituted, not by abolishing the lower, but by subordinating it. The ethical individual has esthetic passion precisely as the non-ethical individual; the religious individual has esthetic passion and ethical enthusiasm; but in the ethical and the religious individuals the lower systems of feeling are subordinated, dominated by a higher passion which sets them limits. A second reason may be found in the fact that he seeks to enroll the different spheres, including the transition stages of irony and humor, on a scale of values, each marking the attainment of a certain depth or intensity in living, the paradoxical-religious sphere being marked by the highest possible tension, and the deepest possible passion capable of being elicited from human nature. On this single scale of values, the different spheres mark stages of attainment, from which point of view one may note the relative naturalness of the transitions.

In Høffding's sense of a motivated transition, namely, a transition seen as the necessary consequence of the preceding development, and uniquely determined thereby, a transition as likely to be unconscious as it is likely to be conscious, and most likely to be both, having the character of something that has happened to one, one scarcely knows how or why, but somehow one has come to act and feel differently—in this sense Kierkegaard neither does nor can motivate the transition from one sphere to another. He could not even attempt to do this without destroying both the ethical and the religious attitudes as he conceives them, and reducing all spheres to modifications and variations within the compass of the esthetic. In Kierkegaard's own sense, however, of a motivated transition—viz., a description of the crises in experience which give significance to the passionate choice of one of the alternate views of life, in this sense a major part of the literature may be said to present the problem of a psychological motivation. The second part of *Either-Or* attempts to motivate a transition from the esthetic sphere as represented by the Young Man, to the ethical, by eliciting and making explicit the immanent despair of the esthetic standpoint; *Repetition* seeks to motivate a transition to the religious through the experience of a poet who finds himself in collision with the ethical, unable to fulfill it because he is as poet, an exception, and therefore needs a religious explanation to bring him back to the ethical again. The third part of *Stages on the Way of Life* is a description of how an individual who begins with an esthetic-ethico view of life, finds himself in conflict with the ethical, and thus comes to need a religious explanation and a religious motivation. And so forth. Indeed the whole art of Kierkegaard may be said to have been expended in an attempt to motivate the transition, in his sense, from the esthetic and ethical to the ethico-religious, and the paradoxical form of the religious.

The peculiar feature of Kierkegaard's presentation of

this theory is of course its combination of abstract algebraic formulation with imagination and emotional expression. Not since Plato has the history of thought seen
so intimate a fusion of the poetic and the dialectic. Both
tasks were achieved by Kierkegaard with apparently
equal distinction, the intellectual formulation has epigrammatic brevity and categorical precision, while the
poetic incarnations of the standpoints presented have the
eloquence of passion and the sureness of definitive pathos.
But Kierkegaard's art is nevertheless not that of the novelist. His delineation gives us types; these types are consistent, to the verge of despair, they portray their standpoints in an incarnation of supernatural, wholly ideal
proportions. The novelist is, by modern canons of his
art, required to present human beings as they are, incon-
sistent, actuated by a variety of principles, mingling
strength with weakness, always as mixtures of this or
that, never as 100 per cent pure. If we admit that from
the standpoint of the novel this demand is justified, I am
of the opinion that there will nevertheless always be a
legitimate place for an exposition of the type of character and feeling having the ideal consistency with which
Kierkegaard invests his characters. All understanding is
in terms of ideal concepts. There are in nature no straight
lines, no perfect circles, no smooth planes, no rigid bars,
no points identifiable as absolutely at rest. And yet we
do not describe mixtures and relativities by reference to
concepts which are themselves mixtures and relativities,
but rather by reference to the approximate realization of
ideally pure categories. Impure water is described in
terms of pure water, crooked lines in terms of straight
lines, and so forth. There is no other way to make description precise. Kierkegaard's method of incarnating

pure standpoints in supernaturally consistent personalities as types, has the merit of frankly accepting the general method of intelligence, and of vivifying the emotional grasp of the reader.

The esthetic sphere receives its chief abstract formulation in the second part of *Either-Or,* at the hands of ethicist B, in the comment of Frater Taciturnus upon the third part of *Stages on the Way of Life,* and in the *Concluding Unscientific Postscript.* Kierkegaard's method consists in setting the ethical and the esthetic categories in contrast with one another, dealing with both simultaneously. It must be remembered that the ethical categories are purely ideal, and are presented by Kierkegaard with the *reservatio mentalis* that without a religious intervention and background, the realization of the ethical ideal is in point of fact impossible. It then becomes the function of ethics to develop a receptivity for religion, a sense of need for it, while religion is for its part a means of restoring to the personality the integrity of its ethical consciousness, essentially marked, however, by the consciousness that such restoration was needed, and hence essentially ethico-religious rather than ethical pure and simple.

The most concrete general expression for the esthetic is that it finds the significance of life in the extraction from it of the maximum amount of enjoyment, thus identifying human happiness with enjoyment. This formula covers a wide variety of attitudes, differentiated from one another by varying views about how to attain the maximum varying skill in reaching it, and varying selections of concrete forms of life in connection with which it is sought. The ethicist, on the contrary, identifies human happiness with the realization of an obligatory task, so essentially related to the personality as to be immanent within it, being nothing more nor less than the realization of his true and given self—given, that is, in the form of a task and a possibility, dependent for its realization upon the individual's own free co-operation.

This more concrete contrast between the esthetic and the ethical is made to rest upon a more abstract formulation of the contrast, in terms of what might be called metaphysical categories. In the first place, it is said that he who lives esthetically, i. e., he who posits life as enjoyment, in the search for enjoyment, lives statically. That is, he lives in and by that in his personality which is already given and completed, essentially speaking. He lives on the basis of that which he already is, taken immediately. He is, in other words, the natural man. Enjoyment is the accompaniment of a functioning whose organ is already adequate to its task; any immediate expression of the personality as immediate, apart from external hindrances, should yield enjoyment. He who lives ethically, on the contrary, lives dynamically. That is, he lives in and by the enthusiasm, but also by the effort and strain of an essential and profound becoming. That whereby the individual becomes what he becomes—that is, will in the profoundest sense, is the ethical in the personality; that by which the individual merely is statically, what he is, is the esthetic.

In the second place, we have, as equivalent to the above, still another abstract formulation of the contrast. Whoever finds the meaning of life in the esthetic, is bound to postulate an external or uncertain condition, as for example, prosperity or good fortune, success, etc., a condition which is in principle, whatever may be the appearances created by the accidental facts, always beyond his own control. Or if he seeks the meaning of life in something within the personality, as in the unfoldment of a talent, then he still posits a condition which is relatively external, since the condition is not given in and through his own will merely. It is *in* the personality, but has not been placed there *by* the personality. The ethical man, on the contrary, concentrates the meaning of life in that which he himself gives to life, and postulates no external condition for happiness, no condition over which he does not himself exercise full control. Thus the ethicist is, formally speaking, though not concretely, the stoic personality, whose essential happiness is always in his own power.

With this broad outline of the esthetic sphere, it is comprehensible that it includes much more than these particular esthetic attitudes to which Kierkegaard gives specific literary expression. Høffding has overlooked this, and thus comes to identify the esthetic too narrowly with the theory presented in the Rotation Method in the first part of *Either-Or*. This theory and the variants of it found in connection with the participating estheticists of *Stages on the Way of Life,* constitute merely a super-sophisticated, extraordinarily reflective attempt to formulate an esthetic view of life. But the esthetic sphere also includes those who live for their health, or in the conscious enjoyment of beauty and the distinction of fine physical appearance, those who seek the meaning of life in the successful development of a business talent, a poetic talent, a philosophical talent, etc., those few who concentrate upon a life of pleasure in the most abstract sense of that word, a pleasure which abstracts from everything but the enjoyment of the moment; it includes also those cynics who seek to enjoy the power to dispense with enjoyment, who throw away the opportunities for pleasure in order to enjoy this freedom. It also includes the reflective talent who succeeds in enjoying himself in the pleasures, rather than the pleasures directly; the epicurean, who chooses the plain and simple pleasure of the plain and simple life, as offering the greatest promise of security; and it includes the highly complicated personality who perceives the vanity of life, and enjoys a reflection upon his own despair. And of course it includes all mediocrities, in so far as their lives are determined essentially by the contrast between the agreeable and the disagreeable.

There are five chief incarnations of the esthetic type which Kierkegaard has pictured for us with especial interest and enthusiasm. All are sophisticated and reflective, and thus represent very highly specialized forms of the esthetic. I cannot of course characterize them concretely within the limits of this paper, but must restrict myself to a brief mention. The first is the Young Person, author of the first part of *Either-Or,* creator of the demoniac figure of John the Seducer, absorbed in the psychological study of the many various forms of the unhappy consciousness—but deceptively, says Kierkegaard of him, not from sympathy but autopathically and egotistically. He has an intelligence which has compassed the world in reflection, but he lacks the experience of a decisive personal commitment to anything in life. He seeks to grasp life without plunging into it, to swim without entering the water, to get experience at second hand, through the medium of reflection alone. In the *Stages,* he therefore finds love a riddle and marriage a mystery, because his thought cannot explain such an experience beforehand, but finds it ridiculous and contradictory. He is a possibility who has so far postponed a decisive action that all his thought merely plunges him into melancholy. His formula is *reflective melancholy*.

The second figure is Constantin Constantius. He is the author of *Repetition*, the arranger of the banquet in *Stages on the Way of Life*. He represents a *cold and superior intelligence*, who has despaired of the possibility of a successful repetition of life's happiest moments; he expresses himself contemptuously about woman as the weaker sex, to be dealt with as a sort of jest of the gods.

The third is Victor Eremita, publisher of A's and B's papers in *Either-Or*, and author of a speech about Woman in the *Stages*. His formula is *sympathetic irony*, a variant of the esthetic standpoint which is very close to the ethical, since it is cognizant of the ethical categories, but uses them only to recall them again as inapplicable.

The fourth is John the Seducer, whose diary is published in *Either-Or*, and who expounds his view of life in the *Stages*. Woman has for him only one moment, is a lure of the gods, whom only the Seducer knows how to enjoy without being caught and imprisoned in the illusion and drudgery of life. He is morally dead, and the ruin of his personality is evident the moment he opens his mouth to speak.

The fifth is the Dressmaker—that fanatic figure who devotes his life to making woman appear as ridiculous as she is. His method is to entice her to a worship of fashion—the crazier the better. This fanaticism is the expression of *esthetic despair*.

The Young Person furnishes us a theory of the esthetic life, whose essence is the use of memory or forgetfulness to tamper with and contest these emotional experiences; the chief requisite being freedom from every deeper

enthusiasm, detachment from every intense hope and
aspiration, a refusal to enter into any permanent or binding commitment, as marriage, friendship, a career, etc.
With the use of extraordinary skill, and with the aid of
freedom from economic cares, it may thus be possible to
stave off boredom for a while.

There are many who would call Kierkegaard's ethical
sphere religion, since it everywhere presupposes in the
background the existence of a divine being. The ethicist
receives an ideal self, embedded in concrete historical
situations, from the hand of God, the human self is always
recognized as a derivative self, and the obligation of realizing in the concrete this true or ideal self is recognized
as an obligation which places a man in contact with the
divine. But for Kierkegaard the subjective mode of constituting the relationship to God is decisive for the religious sphere, and he does not recognize the attitude described above as religious. The ethicist has no other
relation to God than that which comes through accepting
his duty as from Him, he has no other relation to God
than that which is universal to all men, and universal as
a common public tie which binds them together. His
relation to God is never private; it is not really to be
distinguished from his relations with other men; the
ethical life is an overt life, without secrets, without mysteries, and without privacies. God is the universal background for the ethical life, but He does not in any special
sense break into it; His position is the position of the
point which determines the perspective of the picture,
but which does not form a part of the picture itself.

The common presupposition behind all of Kierkegaard's delineations of the ethical life which thus rounds
itself out by excluding the religious in the stricter sense,

is, that the personality is given as essentially sound, its integrity is assured, the self is capable of realizing the ethical ideal. The ethical attitude is therefore one of self-expression, I had almost said, self-assertion. The ethical individual makes real the ideal possibility latent within him, and in the strength of a fundamental integral personality realizes a concrete integral personality, declining the paradigmatic human self in all the cases of life. The mood is therefore the mood of action, action with victory assured. Ethical faith is the resolute faith in the victory, and is the direct expression of ethical enthusiasm. Ethical enthusiasm is specifically distinct from all forms of esthetic enthusiasm. Esthetic pathos receives its adequate expression in words or in other forms of art, ethical pathos has no other expression than in the transformation of existence, in the transition from potentiality to actuality. Esthetic pathos leads a man to forget himself and to lose himself in or fuse with the object or idea; ethical pathos leads a man to forget the whole world in order solely to attend to himself and his own ethical transformation. Esthetic pathos is essentially imaginative, the pathos of distance; for ethical pathos the imagination and its products are irrelevant. From the standpoint of the personality, all esthetic pathos is immaturity, ethical pathos is maturity. Esthetic pathos is also differential pathos, aristocratic pathos, varying in depth and quality with the esthetic endowment of the personality; ethical pathos is equally accessible to all human beings, it is the poor man's pathos. Esthetic pathos is essentially determined by the accidental; ethical pathos has liberated itself from the accidental and the uncertain, and bases itself securely on the essential and the eternal in the personality.

If the ethical ideal were possible of realization, no

scope would be found for the religious life. This means that the religious life begins with a discovery that there is something wrong with the personality, that it is not yet ready to essay the ethical task, but needs a period of preparation, of preliminary transformation, before the ethical task can be begun. The more deeply this discovery is made, the more profound and decisive the religious life.

The ethical task requires of the individual an absolute devotion; the ethical personality presents itself for the individual as an absolute end. But the individual is endowed with esthetic passion, as well; hence the problem arises of correlating the esthetic and the ethical. The formula for a harmonious and successful correlation is realized when the individual commits himself absolutely to the absolute goal—the personality in its eternal validity, and relativity, i.e., with the possibility of resignation and control always open, and with the decision in the hands of the sthenia to the relative ends. If the personality is in every instant ready to do this, if no lower end is ever encouraged in a rebellion, no merely esthetic passion ever allowed to obscure the horizon—then the ethical task is realized, and the religious remains a king without a country.

But experience teaches that this is not so; and the individual begins by finding himself absolutely committed to relative ends, thus interfering with his absolute commitment to the absolute end. In this situation the individual must first be changed, and the change must come from the eternal and the divine, toward which the actual and the imperfect self assumes a passive attitude. I submit myself passively to the divine, in order that the imperfect in me may be rooted out. The first expression for the process is suffering, and suffering is a decisive category for the religious life, just as enjoyment is the decisive category for the esthetic life. Kierkegaard does not teach that all suffering is religious although all suffering may become religious by being incorporated into a God-relation of the significance just described; but all religious life involves suffering, so that if the suffering is taken away, the religious life is also abolished.

This suffering arises from the necessity of a reformation of the individual, from an incommensurability between the individual and his task, not that the task is therefore relinquished, but with the holding fast of the task. Pleasure is the sign of successful exercise on the part of an organ completely adequate to its mode of functioning; religious suffering is the sign of a transformation in the personality by which its inadequacy is in process of being changed to adequacy. When the question is raised as to why the personality is inadequate and needs the transforming discipline of suffering, the answer is one which deepens the suffering and intensifies the inadequacy. For the only answer which the individual can find, or can accept without trivializing life or making it meaningless, is that the imperfection is at bottom guilt. So the religious life advances to a higher stage, the personality now has to relate himself to his ideal through the never-suspended consciousness, the everlasting memory, of the sense of guilt. The sense of guilt is not the memory of an individual wrongful act, although such a memory may play a part in it; but it is the consciousness of a quality affecting the whole personality, a total and all pervasive coloring, which does not admit of differences of degree when viewed essentially and from within, although externally, as between man and man, the quantitative conception of more or less guilt has its appropriate use. But between man and God, guilt is guilt, and that is the end of it, the quality being essential and the degree being irrelevant; its intrusion in the relation between God and man means that God disappears, or ceases to be God, and becomes a fellow Pharisee.

Kierkegaard's most original contribution to the characterization of religion consists in the distinction between two forms of it, the immanent and the transcendent, Religion A and Religion B, as he terms them in the *Unscientific Postscript*. Religion A is the form we have hitherto described, characterized essentially by a passive relation to the divine, with the accompanying suffering and sense of guilt. But it is distinguished from Religion B, or transcendent religion, in that the tie which binds the individual to the divine is still, in spite of all tension, essentially intact. The individual's eternal destiny is indeed placed in jeopardy, but it is not forfeited. The extremes of the eternal and the temporal still hold together, though it is at each moment as if the breaking point had been reached. Such a form of religion is independent of Christianity, and indeed of any historical situation, and could have been found, whether actually so found or not—only in paganism. The Socratic ignorance, and the Socratic gazing into space as a form of communion with the divine, seemed to Kierkegaard to be the best example of this kind of religion.

The distinctive feature of transcendent religion can be briefly stated. It consists of a transformation or modification of the sense of guilt into the sense of sin, by which all continuity is broken off between the actual self and the ideal self, the temporal self and the eternal. The personality is invalidated, and thus made free from the law of God, because unable to comply with its demands.

There is no fundamental point of contact left between the individual and the divine; man has become absolutely different from God.

This is the situation of Christianity. It is marked by an absolute transcendence, by the introduction of a new immediacy or passion, namely the passion of faith; a new point of departure for the individual's consciousness, namely conversion; and a new point of contact with the divine, namely through God manifesting Himself in time, outside the individual, since He cannot manifest Himself *in* the individual. All these conceptions are, from the standpoint of the invalidated personality, paradoxical and absurd, and every essential Christian category, the doctrine of sin, the doctrine of the forgiveness of sin, the doctrine of the God-man, etc., is marked by the sign of the absurd. Reason and Faith are not allies, but contrary passions, Reason being the self-assertion of the personality, its sense of fundamental integrity, while Faith is a new passion which embraces a re-integration of the personality as a divine gift, and makes everything new. In it Reason is subjected and made subservient, just as self-love is subjected in love, and in a sense constitutes its necessary background. It need perhaps scarcely be said that Kierkegaard does not mean by reason any abstract logical faculty, but the systematized common sense of the personality in its fundamental self-confidence and self-assertiveness.

The difference between the various stages may be described briefly in terms of their relation to time. For the esthetic life, time has no fundamental significance, enjoyment culminates in the moment, and for the esthetic view the happy moment is everything. The ethical life accentuates time as the necessary medium of a history and a solution for the permanent.

Religion A emphasizes time still more strongly, by intensifying the significance of the transformation that may occur in it but not decisively, while Religion B emphasizes time paradoxically by making the temporal commensurable for an eternal decision.[5]

---

[5]*Unscientific Postscript,* 493-498.

VII. KIERKEGAARD'S TREATMENT OF THE DOCTRINE OF SIN

KIERKEGAARD'S writings cover the whole range of philosophical-theological problems, and his interpretation of Christianity is both original and profound. But of all his work, perhaps none goes deeper into the mystery of life, or reveals a more profound psychological insight, than his treatment of the doctrine of sin.

The psychological material which Kierkegaard offers in connection with this subject is found mainly in two works: *The Concept of Dread* and *The Sickness Unto Death*. But the whole voluminous Kierkegaardian literature bears a more or less direct relation to the problem of sin, which Kierkegaard regards as central for every religious view of life, and as the starting point for the Christian consciousness.

The consciousness of sin is the most concrete expression of the subjective self, its most intimate apprehension and evaluation of itself. It is the deepest self-consciousness of which the human mind is capable. Hence it is important that it should be distinguished from less concrete and decisive self-judgments, and isolated as far as possible from confusions and compromises, from half-hearted and imperfect movements of the soul, in order that it may stand out in its ideality, its true inner significance. This task Kierkegaard sets himself in several works, but chiefly in the last two or three hundred pages of the *Concluding Unscientific Postscript,* where he discusses the question of what inner experiences the personality must command in order that Christianity may have reality for it, or in order that the problem of Christianity may reveal itself in its pathetic validity.

First, the individual's self-consciousness must be so far developed, so profoundly stirred, that it confronts the ideal of an absolute good, an eternal *telos*, which is identical with its own immortality. Otherwise no consciousness of sin in the Christian sense can ever arise. The existence of such an ideal for the individual is not determined by the possession of a more or less adequate intellectual conception of what this good may be, in the sense of logical content, but depends solely on whether the individual acknowledges something which is absolutely the transformation of his personal existence, so that all other ends become by comparison relative. This is existential pathos, which expresses itself, not as esthetic pathos is satisfied to express itself, namely in words, but in deeds, or rather in an inner transformation and direction of the subject's existence with respect to the absolute good. The development of this attitude is tantamount to the development of the personality to its highest potentiality.

But such an attitude cannot be held fast in the concrete circumstances of life without suffering. For the individual at once discovers that he is already, before he has begun his high task, absolutely in the power of relative ends, and that he must first free himself from these, in order to yield an absolute devotion to the absolute good, and a relative recognition to the relative goods. The relativity of the latter consists in the fact that they are subject to renunciation just in so far as they may conflict with the demand of the highest good. The process of thus training oneself loose from the relative is what produces suffering. This suffering is then the more concrete expression for the consciousness of immortality, and is essential to the religious life, a mark of the religious spirit, so that if this suffering is absent, it means that the relation to one's own immortality has ceased. But this is not all; for a still more concrete expression now appears: namely, the sense of guilt.

The sense of guilt is the most decisive expression for "existential" pathos, and seems to be the farthest possible removed from the vital task of an absolute loyalty to the absolute good, and a relative attachment to the relative goods. And yet it is the only way in which a human being can concretely sustain a relation to an absolute good. Nor can this guilt be shifted, for example, to life itself, or to whatever power has set the individual in the midst of life. An innocent person has nothing to do with guilt, does not understand what is meant by the term. Hence for him the question of shifting blame cannot arise. But for one who is guilty *in toto,* the question of innocence or guilt in a particular situation has reality. He may then justify himself with respect to a particular case, but in so doing he accuses himself and reveals his guilt *in toto.* This is the dialectic of guilt, it is absolutely imprisoning; no other concept is so ensnaring. It is the total priority of guilt which makes possible justification or blame in the particular case.

But childish and comparative conceptions of guilt forget the totality, and apprehend only the quantitative and numerical aspects of the guilt-consciousness. But when the idea of God is present to the individual, the least fault, even the smallest (that it is the least or the smallest, the individual will not however know, since the consciousness of God excludes comparison with other human beings) is sufficient to posit the *quality* of guilt; this is the substantial element in the guilt-consciousness.

Nevertheless, the personality, despite the sense of guilt, retains its continuity with itself, remains the same identical person, still maintains its relation to the highest good. As eternal, the highest good can never lose its point of contact with the individual, though the sense of guilt becomes concretely the painful, torturing expression for this relation.

But if the eternal reveals itself at a particular point in time, then there is a breach effected between it and the individual of such a radical nature that the individual is now cut off from the highest good, has forfeited his highest self, has become another, is now heterogeneous with the good, has become incapable of fulfilling the ethical requirements. This is the Christian sense of sin. It is the consequence of a revelation from God, and is impossible except in connection with such a revelation.

VIII. AN EXPOSITION OF *FEAR AND TREMBLING*

HAVING in an earlier work *(Either-Or)* delineated the ethical consciousness with a universal religious background, Kierkegaard is in this volume concerned with some of the distinctive traits of the religious concept of faith, taken in the more specific sense in which it is fundamental to the Christian consciousness. It is here depicted as a major human passion, affecting daily life at every point, its content being the entire essential reality of the individual's existence. By virtue of its transcendence of the calculations of worldly wisdom and of the naive illusions of immediacy, in consequence of the firmness of its grasp of the finite life as distinct from the withdrawal from it which ensues when resignation is the final word, and in view of its struggle with and victory over that fear and trembling which its sense of responsibility makes it feel, faith becomes the highest of human passions. It is here presented as heroic, and is poetically apprehended with an authentic esthetic pathos, deriving from the realities of Kierkegaard's personal life. The pseudonym places himself admiringly outside, assigning to himself the lower plane of infinite resignation.

The chief categorical determinants assigned to faith and developed in the essay are: (1) the *particularity* of its relationship to God, dispensing with every form of universal intermediary: community, state, humanity, tradition, so that the believer sustains *qua* individual an absolute relation to the Absolute; (2) the infinite *resig-*

nation with respect to finite goods which it psychologically presupposes, thus dissociating itself *toto coelo* from those dreams of wish-fulfilment with which the inexperienced confuse it; (3) the *double movement* of the spirit, by which after the infinite resignation it again lives in the finite, but only in virtue of a God-relationship which has no dependence upon the calculations of the understanding; (4) the fearful *teleological suspension of the ethical* as exemplified in Abraham, whom the poetic imagination of the author makes to live vividly in the present.

This suspension of the ethical consciousness finds a more essential and universal expression in the Christian consciousness of sin and its forgiveness, though the treatment of this *motif* is here withheld, and given a place in the later volume, *The Concept of Dread.* Other aspects of faith are dealt with in a companion volume, *The Repetition.*

The various determinants of faith are by Kierkegaard concentrated in the single category of the *absurd,* since the movement of faith seems paradoxical to the ordinary consciousness from which faith emerges. The paradoxical is Kierkegaard's careful and precise development of a thought which the Greeks dimly shadowed forth as the divine madness (Plato's *Phaedrus).* Since even thoughtful readers may misunderstand this category through approaching it too exclusively through the traditional and imperfect contrast between faith and reason, I may perhaps be pardoned a word of comment. This category has nothing whatever to do with a supposed antithesis between intellect and will. Kierkegaard did indeed hold that any individual who permits his life to culminate in unutilized thought, speculation or knowledge, is to be apprehended as esthetically comical in his absentmindedness, and to be condemned ethically as attempting to evade the essential task of human existence, which in his view consists in realizing a *decisiveness of spirit* that forms and establishes the personality. But this involves no positing of an antithesis between intellect and will; on the contrary, it protests against the leaving incomplete a movement in which intellect, feeling, and will normally play their several and proper roles.

The paradoxical is rooted in an entirely different antithesis, an antithesis, namely, between God and man, between God's understanding of what human life ought to be, and man's. It makes its appearance only when the individual has become ethically mature, when he has been developed ethically and religiously to the point where there can be some question of his submitting himself to the divine in order to be radically transformed by the discipline of the relationship. In this conflict the individual's strength consists in his weakness, his victory in his defeat. The human, all-too-human understanding of life which he thus comes to renounce is no abstract intellectual function, but a concrete consciousness involving intellect, feeling, and will. In other words, it is his *reason* as concrete expression for what he initially *is*, in contradistinction to what he strives in faith to *become*. Hence there exists indeed no paradox for faith in its perfection, but for the human individual who is in process of becoming, the paradoxical cannot be avoided without arbitrarily limiting the spiritual process. Kierkegaard's insistence upon the paradoxical is a consequence of his deep-seated predilection for apprehending the spiritual life in process, and hence ethically, rather than esthetically, in a foreshortened perspective, or altogether in static terms.

Most writers on the philosophy of religion display no inkling of the existence of such a conflict, and much less do they reveal any sympathetic apprehension of its significance. Their description of spiritual attitudes is much like those naive paintings which depict a landscape in general, fitting everything and nothing. Thus to describe religious faith as devotion to an ideal, without distinguishing differences between ideals, and without expending a word upon the all-important question of the "how" of this devotion, is about as illuminating and intellectually satisfying as it would be to describe man as an animal, foregoing all specific determination. Kierkegaard offers to those whose experience has been concrete enough to demand a more precise intellectual orientation in this field an exceedingly rich and concrete psychology of the varied aspects of the life of the spirit. And his categories have a sharpness of definition not even approximately realized in the more recent literature of the subject.

IX. A DANISH THINKER'S ESTIMATE OF JOURNALISM

BUT why misuse the limited space of a philosophical quarterly to discuss the newspaper? The press is a recognized triviality which infests modern life; every man of sense knows that it prints an inordinate quantity of slush, which he does his best to avoid, seeing that he cannot dispense altogether with the newspaper. But philosophy at least deals with high and important matters, and the philosopher only demeans himself when he condescends to treat seriously the trivialities of everyday life—so I imagine some reader reacting to the title of the present article. My answer is twofold. In the first place, a triviality which occupies the major part of the unmortgaged time and attention of millions of men, and which is in fact almost their only mental pabulum, constitutes for this very reason, namely, because it is a triviality which thus engrosses them, a most important matter for the reflection of the ethical thinker. And as for philosophy's being too lofty to deal with everyday matters, this was also the view of Callicles, which he expressed in criticism of Socrates;[1] but it is not my opinion, and I shall ask the reader's indulgence while I unfold, in an introductory paragraph or two, a view of the nature of philosophy which I think can properly be called Socratic.

Real thinking is like real charity, in that it begins at home. It does not everlastingly stand on tiptoe to catch

[1] Plato: *Gorgias*, 490c, 497a.

a glimpse of the glories of the world; for it knows that the interpenetration of ordinary and everyday matters by the power of thought is both more difficult and more profitable than adventurous speculations in the realm of the extraordinary and astounding. It is not always scanning the distant horizon for something that is new; for it knows enough to suspect that the new will probably turn out to be something old, since it has learned by a thousand experiences that what men call the new differs from the old only by an unimportant change of form. Genuine thinking is not indeed incompatible with an insatiable curiosity for factual detail. But it is not identical with such curiosity; it springs from a deeper source, and its satisfactions are of a higher order. Real thinking does not imagine that a new continent of fact must first be discovered before the enterprise of thought can prosper; it is a suspicious circumstance when a philosophy announces that its own essential content (not its accidental stimulation) depends for its existence absolutely upon "modern" discoveries and "modern" inventions. A suspicious circumstance; for it suggests that such a philosophy has consciously or unconsciously raised some relativity to the rank of an absolute, and confounded a difference of degree with a distinction of kind.

Genuine thinking is content to know only what everybody knows. It is even content to know much less, if only it may know what it knows with categorical precision, making its *corpus* of fact luminous with an intellectual clarity, and significant as the focus of precise relations. It is indeed true that Greece had thinkers of eminence who deemed it profitable to make extensive journeys in order to gather materials for philosophizing. But the greatest of all Greek thinkers, the man aptly described as "equally great both as character and as thinker," never willingly left his native city, but found in the daily life of his immediate surroundings an infinite abundance of food for thought. And it is a well-known fact that he was content, after extraordinary and strenuous dialectical exertions, to arrive at the goal of "ignorance," so that he was conscious of knowing less than the humblest of his contemporaries; without however being on that account an ordinary ignoramus.

But if real thinking begins at home, it necessarily concentrates upon the thinker himself, and the situation that confronts him. When the thinker turns his thought in this direction he finds himself standing in a multitude of relationships, acting and acted upon. He is in part dependent upon an immediate physical environment, and his mental furniture is, generally speaking, of the same pattern as that which serves for his contemporaries. All of these relationships make demands upon him; they require determination and clarification, interpretation and valuation. If his intellectual impulse is at all profound, he will become aware of a systematic scheme of possible and actual knowledge, the tentatively organized answers to the questions which his environment forces from him; and he will in his reflection become increasingly conscious of a technology of thought. He will note that the solution of the problems of thought involves both the acquisition of factual detail and the utilization of logical categories; he will observe that the latter, as instrumentalities, in their turn demand clarification and testing, reflection and inquiry.

It is at this point that there arises what might be called the thinker's temptation. If the vital impulse in him is permitted to become weak in proportion to the abstract-intellectual impulse, if in consequence he slips into the role of a semi-detached talent, instead of assuming the full responsibilities of a deeply rooted individual, he will lose himself in the exploration and organization of the data or the instrumentalities of thought for their own sake. He will heap up what constitutes for him an unmanageable load of factual detail, of historical knowledge or natural science; or he will perhaps develop the necessary abstractions of thought into an imposing edifice whose home is in the clouds. In forgetting to think all these things in relation to himself, he will cut the umbilical cord which alone can convey life and meaning into the mass of brute fact, or into the otherwise ghostly "ballet of the categories." He will be like a man who takes a running start in order to jump a stream, but who runs so far that he arrives at the bank breathless and spent, unable to jump because of an unreasonably thorough preparation; or perhaps he will even have forgotten his purpose, thus devoting himself to preparation for preparation's sake.[2]

In order to be vital, thought must be concrete, not only in relation to its object, but also in relation to the thinker whose thought it is. But in order to be intellectually significant, it must be sufficiently abstract to justify the claim of universality. Thinking therefore involves a mutual and untrammeled intercourse between the abstract and the concrete, the concrete being apprehended through

---

[2]It seems to me highly probable that this is what Socrates meant by his abandonment of the scientific speculations of his early manhood, having determined, in the beautiful and simple words of Diogenes Laertius, that "physics was not man's proper business"; and thereafter began to "philosophize about moral matters" wherever men were gathered together (Diogenes Laertius' *Lives*, II, 5, 21). And I take it that this is also what the first of living American teachers and writers of philosophy means when he says that all philosophy is "in some sense a branch of morals" (Dewey, *Experience and Nature*, p. 33).

the abstract, and the abstract being exemplified in the concrete. A well-balanced thinker is therefore as abstract as he is concrete, and as concrete as he is abstract.

Philosophy is thus in its ideal form only that most intimate and thorough penetration of reality by thought, which the thinker finds humanly possible. And this reality is no esoteric realm of mystery, but is that daily reality of human life which the philosopher shares with all his fellow-men. A modern thinker who understands himself after this fashion will necessarily have his attention attracted to the modern newspaper, with its complementary correlate, public opinion. Public opinion existed also in the Greek state, and exercised its influence upon the individual mind; it had, then as now, its servants and its instrumentalities. But the immense comparative size of modern states, together with the development of means of communication undreamed of by the ancients, gives to this concept an extraordinary special significance for the modern thinker. Where as many as three human beings are gathered together, the potentiality exists for the formation of something that might be called public opinion.[3] With so limited a scope, however, the abstraction inevitably involved in the recognition of a "public," as well as the degree of impersonality fostered thereby, is at least subject to a ready and immediate control. But when millions of human beings are brought together in a multitude of essential or accidental forms of contact, the force of "public opinion" becomes at once more inescapable and irresponsible.

Of this public opinion, the modern press is both serv-

---

[3]Perhaps it was for this reason that Socrates always demanded that the issues raised by his questions should be confined to himself and his interlocutor; any human being might play the latter role, but only one at a time.

ant and master, both creature and creator. It gives a
tongue to the impersonal impulses generated by the multitude, and so intensifies their power and extends their
scope. Press and public are thus a mutual fit, and the
essential faults of the one are also the essential faults of
the other. The press mirrors life; but this does not mean
that it clearly reveals the nature of life's underlying realities, so that he who runs may read. The mirror of the
press reflects a mere surface, a confusing phantasmagoria
of appearances more or less distorted in the reflection; the
depths underneath these appearances are never reliably
revealed in the light of life's meaning and value. In fact,
"journalism" and "journalistic" are words that have come
to stand for the treatment of any subject in terms which
neither make nor fulfil any claim to the communication
of such deeper insight. He who cannot understand life
without the newspaper will be still more unable to understand it *with* the newspaper, since the latter will in that
case serve only to intensify and vary his misunderstandings.

This tendency to smother the dawning consciousness
of life's meaning under the agglomerate mass called the
"news of the day" is one which presses upon the modern
man with so steadfast an insistence that, if it be true that
education is the process of arriving at an understanding
of life, then no modern man can be called educated
unless he is able to read his newspaper between the lines.
For this reason, if for no other, it is a vital necessity for
every modern thinker to have a theory of the newspaper,
and to have a theory of the newspaper which corresponds
in its intellectual significance to the significance of his
thought in other fields. In the absence of such a theory
he may doubtless exhibit extraordinary talent, and make

contributions of weight to the more abstract fields of philosophic science; but he is not an ethical thinker. And of one malady he must stand convicted: the malady, namely, of "professorial absent-mindedness," which has other forms than those exhibited in forgetting one's umbrella when it rains, or holding the egg in the hand while the timepiece boils.

More than one nineteenth-century person of eminence found himself prompted to reflection upon the phenomenon of the press. Of these, Balzac has perhaps been the most explicit in public appraisal. What he has said on this subject in *Illusions perdues,* the second part of *Un grand homme de province à Paris,* seems to me in very large measure invested with a permanent significance. It is true, as the book itself suggests, that the universality of the comment is to a certain degree impaired by a too particular application to a condition in the journalism of Paris which was already past when the novel was published. It must also be confessed that sometimes the violence of the expressions bears testimony to a certain thinness of the thought; so that criticism is carried to the borders of vituperation. Nevertheless, this novel of Balzac's would doubtless make wholesome reading for students in our schools of journalism, if in their haste to learn the petty tricks of the trade, and eagerness to enjoy the artificial stimulations of the "newspaper game," they permitted themselves time to think deeply on any fundamental problem of life. It would be tempting to quote Balzac at length. But the material is readily accessible, and I shall cite merely a phrase that sounds like a summary conclusion: "If the press did not exist, it ought never to have been invented."

Nietzsche has permitted to Zarathustra an expression of

disgust: "They vomit their bile and call it a newspaper."[4] In several other passages this writer comments upon the insincerity *(Unredlichkeit)* of the press, ascribing its power, among other things, to the fact that each individual who serves it feels himself only fractionally responsible.[5] And elsewhere he makes the shrewd remark that no one who wishes to become a thinker can afford to read a newspaper every day.

Emerson has also evaluated the press. What he says on the subject is quantitatively insignificant, but the sureness of touch by which he lays hold of the essentials gives proof also in this field of his significance as a thinker. I shall quote two pasages, the first from his little pen portrait of the *London Times* in *English Traits:*

The parts are kept in concert, all the articles appear to proceed from a single will. The *Times* never disapproves of what itself has said, or cripples itself by apology for the absence of its editors, or the indiscretion of him who holds the pen. It speaks out bluff and bold, and sticks to what it says. It draws from any number of learned and skilful contributors; but a more learned and skilful person supervises, corrects, and co-ordinates. Of this closet, the secret does not transpire. No writer is suffered to claim the authorship of any paper; everything good, from whatever quarter, comes out editorially; and thus, by making the paper everything and those who write it nothing, the character and awe of the journal gain.

The morality and patriotism of the *Times* claim only to be representative, and by no means ideal. It gives the argument, not of the majority, but of the commanding class. . . . The editors give a voice to the class who at the moment take the lead; and they have an instinct for finding where the power now lies, which is eternally shifting its banks. Sympathizing with, and speaking for the class that rules the hour, yet being apprised of every ground-swell, every Chartist resolution, every Church

---

[4]Nietzsche:*Also sprach Zarathustra,* XI, "The New Idol."
[5]Nietzsche: *Menschliches, Allzumenschliches,* I, §447.

squabble, every strike in the mills, they detect the first tremblings of change. They watch the hard and bitter struggles of the authors of each liberal movement, year by year; watching them only to taunt and obstruct them—until, at last, when they see that these have established their fact, that power is on the point of passing to them, they strike in with the voice of a monarch, astonish those whom they succor as much as those whom they desert, and make the victory sure. Of course the aspirants see that the *Times* is one of the goods of fortune, not to be won but by winning their cause.

Here we have two fundamental attributions. First, the creation of a fantastic quasi-unlimited institutional authority to replace a real but limited personal authority, achieved by the clever use of anonymity. This characteristic will be enlarged upon in the quotations which follow, and which lend a title to this article. Second, the specious creation of the appearance of leadership, by a calculation a little in advance of the apparent fact, of the direction in which the cat of public opinion is about to jump. This latter analysis reminds me vividly of what an energetic and zealous missionary spirit once said to a friend of mine, who had attempted real leadership and consequently found himself in difficulties: "I'll tell you the secret of leadership, *Follow!*" Writing for the press is, generally speaking, commercialization of talent, and publishing a newspaper is today a branch of Big Business. It is therefore evident that what Emerson says of the *Times* when it was surnamed the "Thunderer," could in his spirit be applied *a fortiori* to the press of today, and especially to the great majority of daily newspapers. To expect moral or intellectual leadership from this quarter is as absurd as to expect figs from thistles.

The second passage is found in Emerson's "Lecture on the Times," delivered in Boston in 1841, and embodied in the volume published as *Nature: Addresses and Lectures.* He speaks of the scholar as existing for the sake of furnishing hospitality to every new thought and every untried project, in so far as it "proceeds out of good will and honest seeking." Then he adds: *"All the newspapers, all the tongues of today, will of course at first defame what is noble;* but you, who hold not of today, not of the times, but of the Everlasting, are to stand for it; and the highest compliment man ever receives from heaven is the sending to him its disguised and discredited angels" (italics mine). And is not this the very truth? Even at its best, the newspaper is of the moment, for the moment, and by the moment; and no man who has the least inkling of the eternal in his breast can cease to wage everlasting war against the perspectives and points of view of the moment, which are the perspectives and points of view that dominate the daily press.

By these quotations from well-known men I have sought to gain relief for the passages that follow, containing an estimate of journalism by a writer relatively unknown to the English reader, though he is doubtless the greatest thinker yet produced in the Scandinavian north. The translation is made from entries in Søren Kierkegaard's diaries of the years 1849 and 1850. The reader will not need to be reminded that in their present form the passages cited were not intended for publication. In the works published during the author's lifetime, most of which appeared before the date of these jottings, no closely parallel passages, explicitly dealing with journalism, are to be found. But the view of life reflected in them is identical with that which gradually emerged as underlying the varied and abundant Kierkegaardian literature. I have thought that what this thinker has to say about the press might have its significance for the readers of a philosophical journal devoted to ethics, as capable of arresting the attention and giving a challenge to thought.[6]

I

In every profession, and in relation to every subject, it is the minority that knows; the multitude is ignorant. The truth of this is as clear as daylight, for if it were not so, everybody would know everything. But just because this is not so, it follows that every human being ought to have his own particular field, of greater or less scope, and more or less involved and difficult, in which he knows more than the rest; so that he is the teacher, and the others, the crowd, the plurality of men, are learners. And so on all the way around, every man having his own special sphere of knowledge and authority.

But now the press, what are its tactics? Everything that the press has to say, whether the subject be politics or criticism or what not, it says in such a manner as to suggest that knowledge is the possession of the many, of the majority. It is this which makes the press the most profoundly demoralizing of all the forms of sophistry. People complain that a newspaper occasionally publishes a lying article. How trivial a fault, when set over against the fundamental fact that the whole form and spirit of this means of communication is essentially a lie!

In ancient times they flattered the multitude by material means: bread, money, and the circus. In modern times the press flatters the middle classes intellectually and spiritually. To meet this situation we have need of a species of Pythagorean silence. We need total abstinence societies with respect to the reading of newspapers much more than with respect to the drinking of intoxicants. How ridiculous for a newspaper to assume an aristocratic pose! No indeed; if the publisher wants to be an aristocrat, let him first cease to publish a newspaper. To be an aristocrat among journalists is like being an aristocrat among *lazzaroni.*

---

[6]When these jottings were made in his diary, Kierkegaard had a decade of extraordinary literary productivity behind him, during which time he had produced, as Brandes says, "a literature within a literature."

II

After much hard work, an intensive self-cultivation, and a long period of development, the most gifted talents in a country at last become authors, and authors of books. But the reading of books is confined to a comparatively small number. The daily press has, on the other hand, a practical monopoly of circulation; it is read by all. Here we find busily engaged these spiritually bow-legged, knock-kneed, club-footed, flat-footed, *item* long-fingered creatures, the half-witted and yet cunning derelicts who go by the name of journalists; here they keep themselves busy, and their *raisonnement* is read by all. *Pro dii immortales!*

If there were only one speaking trumpet on board a ship, and this was in the possession of the pantry-boy, and if everybody looked upon this as a perfectly natural and proper state of affairs: what then? Everything that the pantry-boy had to say: "mouse in the larder," "fine weather today," "Lord only knows what's wrong in the ship's hold," etc., etc., would be published abroad through the speaking trumpet. The captain, on the contrary, would be limited to the use of his own natural voice, for what he had to say was of course not so important. At times he would be reduced to begging the assistance of the pantry-boy, in order that his commands might be made audible. At such times the pantry-boy would feel at liberty to revise the words of command; so that in passing through him and his trumpet they would become nonsensical and misleading. The captain would then be compelled to strain his voice in competition, but without success. At last the pantry-boy would become the master of the ship, because he had the speaking trumpet.

Pro dii immortales!

III

As soon as the truth is defined in terms of what the majority can understand, it is *eo ipso* betrayed. For most men are precisely in the position of needing a very long period of discipline and preparation before they can even begin to understand the truth. So that what most men can understand is galimatias. We should therefore speak as follows: What most men are ready at once to understand, without further preparation, is unequivocally nonsense. Then comes the next thought: What most people regard as nonsense may really be nonsense; but it may also be the truth. The truth is always in the minority, although it does not follow that the minority always has the truth.

IV

The following is the relation that exists between literature and the press. An author writes a clear, consistent, connected, fully matured presentation of some thought, perhaps the fruit of many years' labor. Nobody reads it. But a journalist reviews the book; in the course of half an hour or so, he writes something that is neither more nor less than pure nonsense. This is then supposed to be the purport of the author's book; moreover, everybody reads it. The significance of an author's existence thus becomes evident: he exists for the sake of affording some journalist an opportunity to write nonsense for everybody to read. Had there been no author the journalist would not have had this opportunity; *ergo,* it is of the utmost importance that the supply of authors should not fail.

V

The daily press is the evil principle of the modern world, and time will only serve to disclose this fact with greater and greater clearness. The capacity of the newspaper for degeneration is sophistically without limit, since it can always sink lower and lower in its choice of readers. At last it will stir up all those dregs of humanity which no state or government can control.

Only a very few people will ever understand the fundamental falsity of the daily press. And of these few only a very small number will have the courage to speak out, since it will involve a species of martyrdom to break with the majority, and with the power of the press and its enormous circulation. The press will always mistreat and persecute such a man.

VI

The ruinous and demoralizing influence of the press does not consist so much in the fact that it prints what is false, as in the demoralizing security it affords in connection with every opinion that it presents, namely, that there are a lot of people who say and think the same. The mere fact that an opinion is printed in a newspaper is a sufficient guaranty that this is the case. And sad to say, what most concerns the majority of men is not whether a given opinion be true or false, but whether it will appear that they do or do not stand alone in their opinion. The guaranty of security which the press affords is therefore a demoralizing leading-string, dragging men down to ever lower and lower levels; and this calamity is far greater than the mere communication of something that happens not to be true.

VII

Complete publicity makes it impossible to "govern." All government is rooted in the thought that there are a certain few who have superior insight, who see so much farther into the future that they are able to govern. Complete publicity, on the other hand, is rooted in the thought that *all* should rule.

There are none who understand this better than the gentlemen of the press. No institution has been more anxious to set the seal of secrecy upon its entire domestic economy: the identity of its contributors, the nature of its purposes, etc., all the while insisting that the processes of government ought to be public. And quite consistently. For the underlying idea of the press has been to do away with "government"—in order to secure the powers of government for itself; and for this reason it has also attempted to secure to itself the secrecy without which it is impossible to "govern."

VIII

The fact that in modern times almost all communication is through the medium of the press has given rise to universal confusion. There has been collected in modern states a huge inorganic precipitate: the multitude. No one ever really comes to grips with this huge mass. Those who teach are not personalities who make their appearance in character; they are authors who have found for themselves a hiding-place from the world, and now and then from the place of their concealment send out a few thoughts.

The only conflicts we have hitherto had in modern life have been the conflicts with the governments; for the governments have had it in their power to inflict penalties upon the press. But the real conflict, truth's conflict, the conflict with multitude and public, these abstractions which furnish an evil refuge for every lie—this conflict has been utterly lost from sight.

IX

The cause of this terrible evil (the evil of the press) lies among other things in the following facts of human nature. The world is once for all ruled more by the fear of man than the fear of God. Hence the fear of becoming an individual, and hence also the tendency to conceal one's self behind some abstraction; hence anonymity, calling oneself "we," and the like.

On the other hand, every outstanding individual is always an object of envy. Human envy cannot endure the thought that a mere individual should amount to anything, let alone that he should be pre-eminent, and exercise genuine leadership. Envy therefore favors the creation of abstractions; and over against an abstraction even the most eminent individual is lost in insignificance. This holds even when it is a notorious fact that the abstraction in question was created simply through some individual calling himself "we." Envy cannot stand the sight of superiority; hence it promotes the growth of abstractions, which are invisible.

And lastly, an abstraction is always *en rapport* with the fantastic element in human nature, and the fantastic has a tremendous power. Even the most gifted individual is only an actuality, and as such finite; but "we, the editors"—God only knows what capacities conceal themselves behind this sign.

Summa summarum: The human race ceased to fear God. Then came its punishment: it began to fear itself, began to cultivate the fantastic, and now it trembles before this creature of its own imagination.

X

Public life has become permeated with consciencelessness from beginning to end.

There exists a huge monster—whether bloodthirsty or not I shall not attempt to decide, though the history of the last few years shows how readily the thirst for blood can be aroused—in any case a hungry monster. This monster is the "public." With desperate passion it hungers for "something to talk about." And the journalists are its obedient servants; they see to it that the public is provided with something to talk about. In ancient times men were thrown before wild beasts; in modern times it is the public that devours men, after they have been prepared by the journalists in the form which the public finds most palatable, namely, in the form of idle gossip. Every public man is as such a victim. If he happens to be an egoist, and has made up his mind to endure this exploitation because he knows that it is unavoidable if he is to attain worldly success, he will suffer less. He will not in that case be a martyr; he will not suffer sympathetically, and he will be more nearly understood by his contemporaries. But he will be devoured by the public just the same, and the dish will be prepared by the journalists as idle gossip.

XI

As long as the daily press flourishes, Christianity is an absolute impossibility. For if Christianity is to enter into daily life as a real factor, it is *ipso facto* inevitable that its representative will attract considerable attention to his own person. Not protected by any illusion (and this is an absolute necessity for anyone who desires to preach Christianity in truth), he must direct attention to himself. But the moment he does this, the press will lay hold of him. It need not say a single malicious word, a continuous stream of idle gossip will be quite enough. Let a widely circulated newspaper publish his picture twice a day for two weeks, simultaneously exploiting the most trivial details concerning his person: it will be enough to undermine him. To endure such treatment he will have to possess a considerable degree of heroism. But this we must assume him to have, and in so far he is not enfeebled. But then it will require an almost equal degree of heroism on the part of his contemporaries, in order that they should not lose, under this treatment, all ideality in their conception of him; and there exist in each generation very, very few who in such circumstances are capable of holding fast to an ideal conception of a man. The constant reiteration of the nonsense will exercise its power over them—and so he is undermined.

XII

The world's deepest misfortune is the unhappy objectivity (in the sense of the absence of personality) characteristic of all speech and teaching, and that the one great mechanical discovery after the other has made it possible to expound doctrines impersonally in constantly increasing measure. There no longer exist human beings: there are no lovers, no thinkers, etc. By means of the press the human race has enveloped itself in an atmospheric what-not of thoughts, feelings, moods; even of resolutions and purposes, all of which are no one's property, since they belong to all and none. It is a torture to the soul to note the callous incorrigibility with which a human being can resort to wherever he thinks there is some truth to be had, for the sole purpose of learning to expound it, so that his music-box may add this piece to its repertoire; but as for doing anything of it, the thing never even occurs to him.

XIII

Jesuitism was in its degenerate days a shameless attempt to control the consciences of men. The press is the basest conceivable attempt to make want of conscience the chief ruling principle of the state, and of the human race.

XIV

Woe, woe, woe, unto the daily press! If Christ now came to earth, as sure as I live, He would not attack the high priests and the like; He would focus His attention upon the journalists.

XV

God really intended man to talk with his neighbor, and at the most with several neighbors. Man is not greater than that. In every generation there are a few men sufficiently gifted and mature to make it reasonable for them to use such a tremendous means of communication as the press. But that almost everyone, and particularly all muddle heads should use such a means of communication—with nothing or rubbish to communicate: what a lack of proportion.

XVI

I have long been convinced that the daily press is a form of evil. But what a prospect that opens out! And now we have reached the point where even revolutionary governments suppress newspapers. It is enough to make one long to be an author, now that all one has to say about the press would be understood.

XVII

The lowest depth to which people can sink before God is defined by the word "Journalist." It is an impious attempt to make an abstraction into an absolute power; and anonymity was the fulfilment of the triumph of lies.

If I were a father and had a daughter who was seduced I should not despair over her; I would hope for her salvation. But if I had a son who became a journalist, and continued to be one for five years I would give him up. Possibly I should have been wrong in this particular case, possibly the daughter would have been lost and the son won back again; but ideally speaking my observations are correct: to serve politics through the daily press is too much for a man. Who would dare disclaim having sometimes, and perhaps often, made use of a little lie: but a little lie used every day—and in print, so that as a result one is appealing to thousands and thousands—that is frightful. One is appalled at the way a butcher uses a knife: but that is absolutely nothing to the terribly irresponsible and hardened way in which a journalist uses lies.

Thus far Kierkegaard on the Press. I refrain from extended comment, preferring to leave the reader to his own impressions. Perhaps I ought at once to say, however, that my own experience of and reflection upon the contemporary American press would not justify me in using this absolute and sweeping language with which to clothe my own personal impressions in words. Not that I intend to criticize this language as wholly inapplicable to the contemporary scene; a few modest essays of mine into the public life of my home community have enriched me with an experience of the press which enables me to understand, at least, the criticism I have here presented, even though the experience in question does not permit me to adopt as my own, in all respects, the language I have quoted. I do not claim the right to look down from the heights of a superior moderation upon the "extreme and paradoxical exaggerations" of the Kierkegaardian polemic, as I imagine that some doughty champion of mediocrity in both life and thought might speak; I can respect the insight of genius even when I cannot assimilate all its expressions to my own more limited experience.

It scarcely needs to be pointed out that one cannot very well compromise with the criticism here offered, by endowing it with a real but limited applicability to the Danish or Parisian press, say of the years between 1830 and 1850 (which were the years falling within the scope of Kierkegaard's personal experience), but denying to it any relevancy with respect to the American press of the first half of the twentieth century, for example. The intelligent reader will readily perceive that the criticism claims *philosophical,* and not merely historical, validity; that the press is here conceived as constituting a category, namely, *the sophistical exploitation of the moment for the sake of livelihood, profit, or power.* It is the immanent dialectic of the press that Kierkegaard purports to lay bare, not merely some transitory phase of its external embodiment; and it is on this basis that the criticism must stand or fall.

I believe it to be of major importance clearly to apprehend the point of view from which Kierkegaard's polemic proceeds. The evaluations which appear in it and which motivate it are the evaluations of an ethico-religious individualism. It is apparent that these severe judgments upon the press presuppose a powerful ethical passion which supports them and urges them to expression. The ethico-religious view of life here disclosed is *democratic* in the best and truest sense of that much-used word; for it assumes the existence of an essentially human problem, in the attempted solution of which every individual human life becomes significant, not merely for an external observer, but for itself. It dignifies every human being by assigning to him, and to him alone, the realization of his own proper human task. It refuses to puff the individual out romantically into fantastic proportions, by pretending to endow him with the capacity to solve another's problem in his stead, or assuming to saddle him with the doubtful duty of saving another's soul; to say nothing of dooming him like an Atlas to bear the world on his shoulders, and requiring of him an advance solution of the problems of future generations.

There exist certain contemporary criticisms of the press that achieve a considerable degree of significance, but none of them proceed from the foregoing point of view. Mr. H. L. Mencken has expressed himself upon the newspaper with his customary frankness and vigor; it is hard to see how anyone could carry adverse criticism to farther lengths. But the point of view is that of an *esthetico-aristocratic* individualism, an individualism which looks down upon the "booboisie" from the lofty heights of cultural superiority, and which knows of no ethical principle of life powerful and profound enough to constitute a common bond between privileged and unprivileged. Mr. Mencken's criticism, however, has the very great advantage of perceiving that the public shares essentially in the sins of the press; though it must not be forgotten that the press has the greater responsibility of catering to the weaknesses of the public in order to make money. Mr. Mencken sees that it is nonsense to paint the newspapers as the chief or sole corruptors of an otherwise immaculate people. Mr. Upton Sinclair, on the other hand, scarcely perceives this truth; his merit is that he has salvaged from the almost universal bankruptcy of modern culture in this respect, the capacity for moral indignation. At least this is a point which I, if no one else, shall always count in his favor; believing as I do that even the cleverest man, if he lacks moral passion, is only a cleverly constructed automaton. When Mr. Sinclair speaks of the press he sermonizes upon the theme that the love of money is the root of all evil. But he tends to identify the love of money narrowly with a desire, and sometimes still more narrowly with a successfully realized desire, to share in the prizes of a capitalistic society. Consequently he dreams that some more or less radical change in society's form of organization, political or economic, but chiefly the latter, would make it positively easy for us all to be good and happy. In other words, Mr. Sinclair is essentially an externally-minded politician, who looks to the forms of society for the principles of life; he is not essentially an ethical thinker, despite his strong moral bias.[7]

Finally, I shall mention Mr. Walter Lippmann, who is a competent analyst of newspaper technique, and of the physics and psychology of public opinion. His social psychology is concrete and intelligent, in close touch with the facts of contemporary society. But he is too abstractly intellectual, and also too oversophisticated, to approach the phenomena with any considerable degree of moral passion; and, in my opinion, at least, there does not emerge from his criticism any clear or distinctive ethical view of human life. The reader of these pages who has felt the lack of such a view, adequately expressed, in contemporary philosophy and literature, may perhaps find his need satisfied by a study of the writings of Søren Kierkegaard.

---

[7]Mr. Sinclair also displays a truly journalistic overconfidence in the illuminating power of a wealth of factual detail, leading him to stress the faults of particular individuals and institutions, at the risk of his reputation for accuracy, and the detriment of his capacity to understand and portray what is universal.

CORRESPONDENCE

Letter to Dr. Lowrie, March 12, 1935. Comments on suggested translations for "Philosofiske Smuler."

I hesitate to add complexity to the problem here, by throwing out a new suggestion. However, I shall state my preference and some reasons. It is "Philosophical Chips" either with omission of the sub-title or with the variation, "A Bit of Philosophy." This choice rests upon the relation it bears to the quotation from Hippias Major which introduces the *Postscript* (back of title-page). Fowler translates: "But now, Socrates, what do you think all this amounts to? It is mere scrapings and shavings of discourse, divided into bits." I agree that reference to the "Bits" is simply impossible; "Fragments" is correct enough, but is not colorful enough, so it seems to me, to reflect the temper of the original. What I object to in both "Crumbs" and "Morsels" is the too close association with the thought of food, not necessarily present at all in the original. None of the words suggested lend themselves well to repetition in a sub-title, since the contrast between the plural of the main title and the singular of the sub-title lacks meaning, though quite appropriate in the Danish. For the sub-title, "A Bit of Philosophy" comes nearer the intent of the original than any of the others, though it seems impossible for the main title.

Letter to Dr. Lowrie, March 26, 1935.

I hasten to say that I am not by any means committed, and that I see force in what you say. My earlier preference for "Chips" had a varied motivation. My ear objects a little to the sound of "Crumbs," which is otherwise the most obvious and literal rendering. In modification of this, it may be said that though "Crumbs" is a literal rendering, the word in English does not have the very generalized connotation which "Smuler" has in Danish; for which reason I cast about for a word of similar general significance, but without the close association with food that "Crumbs" has in English. I must admit that Max Müller's use of "Chips" [*Chips from a German Work-Shop,* Ed.] for the same sort of a literary idea, since it gave a parallel though not identical "figure of speech" base for Kierkegaard's meaning, encouraged me to think that the term would do. But I do not wish to be guilty of insisting on an idiosyncracy, and shall be glad to accept majority opinion, if I ever publish a translation of "Smuler." I could wish that your correspondents and associates might think a little of "Fragments" as a compromise. It lacks the virtue of being colorful and metaphorical, being simply a straightforward rendering of the underlying idea in literal terms; but the difficulty is that there is no support in English usage, unless I am mistaken, for the image that "Crumbs" sets up in the mind in connection with the thought to be communicated. When S. K. wrote "Smuler" he had such support in Danish (of course I do not mean in connection with a philosophical book, but in connection with all sorts of things in daily life) ; a translator, however, who writes "Crumbs" in English is in the position of importing a new usage into the language, and hence of encountering an instinctive sense of awkwardness and strangeness. Perhaps I exaggerate this difficulty; but if it is at all real, there is some reason for the choice of a word that is free of any such initial resistance in the mind of the reader. "Fragments" is such a word; it lends itself readily to reduplication for the purpose of the sub-title, and it conveys the thought with precision. The one thing it lacks is the colorfulness that comes from being metaphorical, which the original of course has.

P. S.: It has just occurred to me that we do use "crumbs" in the required metaphorical sense in the phrase "crumbs of comfort"; and perhaps in others I do not now think of; this speaks in favor of this translation. As for the sub-title, it should be noticed that the Danish uses "en Smule this or that" as an almost literal equivalent of the English "a little of this or that," "En Smule Filosofi" makes the same impression on a Danish ear and mind as "A Little Philosophy" would make on an English ear and mind. However, the greater dignity of "A Fragment of Philosophy" doubtless is a point in its favor.

D.F.S.

Letter to Dr. Lowrie, April 24, 1935.

I am prompted to say a word about "Momentet." This word is not generally identical with the English "Moment" but rather means phase, part, factor, aspect, or the like. To live "i Momentet" is to live submerged in some partial phase of a whole, to the exclusion of the rest, or of the control of the whole, i.e., to live anarchically. This can also be applied to the case of Time and its moments, but this would be merely a special application, not a general equivalent. In some contexts, I think "instant" is exactly equivalent to "Øieblik," but not in all, and particularly not in the context of the rubrics for the pamphlets of the agitation. Here the stress is not upon the instantaneous, but upon the *present* as filled with significance, e.g., Christianity brought to bear upon the contemporary situation, and through the medium of the pamphlet or newspaper, that "tongue of the day," as

Emerson says. It is in this way "Øieblikket" is used in the *Smuler* also: a *"moment"* which is also the *"fulness of time."*

Letter to Dr. Lowrie, June 21, 24, 1935. Comments on translation of various passages.

I have been driven . . . . to seeking a certain freedom from the idiosyncracies of Kierkegaard's Danish style, by the results of my previous efforts to reproduce it more literally. I found that I did not succeed in producing a natural and flowing English by this method; although the result satisfied me while still hypnotically under the influence of the original, because I read my own satisfaction with the original into my reproduction; as soon as I had laid it aside for a while, and come back to it with the spirit of the English language dominating my imagination, I found it unpleasant reading because of a sense of foreignness. One thing is certain, unless one can give to the English reader who does not know Kierkegaard at least the negative pleasure of not giving him a disagreeable sense of something strange and awkward in the style, he had better not be translated at all. . . . . There will of course be a loss in stylistic distinction, for only a writer as great as Kierkegaard himself could really reproduce his style in satisfactory English. . . . .

In working on the *Postscript,* I am more and more impressed by the fact that each of Kierkegaard's works, especially the esthetic pseudonymous writings, has a distinctive and unified style of its own. Even the *Postscript* differs from the *Smuler* very characteristically throughout in spite of the close relationship in subject-matter. There are passages in the *Postscript* which I have not as yet been able to come within hailing distance of solving,

not as far as meaning is concerned, but as far as a satisfactory English style in the translation is an absolute
desideratum.

My intention is to use *learner*[1] when the connotation
is general, and to use *disciple* only when the connotation
specifically involves having "received the condition,"
which I believe also to have been Kierkegaard's general
practice. . . .

The meaning, in my understanding, of the cry in the
desert[2] is as follows: A cry (in the desert or anywhere
else, the specification being for the sake of a more concrete imagery, and the echo of the New Testament reference to John the Baptist merely accidental and associa-
tional and stylistic) meets with its own suitable response
in its own environment, so that there is nothing incommensurable, the relativities all having been preserved.
This is not the case when God's eternal purpose enters
into a temporal context; God's appearance in the world
is not the natural answer of the environment to the
human cry. In objecting to *learner's love* for the reason
assigned, namely that Socrates is praised for not seeking
love (and embraces), it is forgotten that it is Kierkegaard's point, not to decry the seeking of love as such, but
to make a distinction between such love as is a true expression for human relationships (Socrates' love lay in
seeking the learner's independence), and the love between
man and the divine, which is impregnated with the
thought that man owes God everything. Besides, Kierkegaard is saying that God's love seeks an end corresponding to itself; what else can this be but the love with which
the learner responds? This is also made explicit in a
later passage. . . .

---

[1] *Fragments*, 9-14.
[2] *Fragments*, 18.

The matter of capitalizing and underscoring common nouns which are used as categories, has been the subject of some thought. My principle is (whether I have succeeded in making my practice consistent, I am not sure) to say "moment" when the meaning is generic, moment in general, and to say "Moment" when the meaning is specific, a moment of time filled with the Eternal[3]; while I underscore only upon a first introduction, when it is intended to emphasize that we have here a category. But when "moment" is subject in a sentence whose predicate qualifies it as decisive, i.e., qualifies it as a Moment, then we have a ticklish and subtle point of logic. I have assumed that the still unqualified subject, moment, is moment in general, and hence not entitled to capitalization.

May I make a comment on your interpretation.[4] First, a word about the question raised as to the extravagance of the eulogy of Mozart, and the reality of Kierkegaard's admiration. I confess I do not think the raising of the latter question quite apt. The extravagance of the eulogy is a matter of style, a portrayal of romanticism as characteristic of the ideal author, an imaginary character who is consciously depicted as losing himself in complete rapturous admiration. Kierkegaard has within him a consciousness which would not permit him to go to such extremes in his own person, in spite of the fact that the material for the feeling expressed undoubtedly comes from his own experience. (It is not so easy to interpret the underscoring in K.'s copy; this may have reference to another meaning underlying the apparent meaning, or may indicate some association. In any case it is necessary to understand what K. means by "losing the reason" in

---

[3]*Fragments*, 17-18, 21, 23.
[4]Lowrie, *Kierkegaard*, 249-51; *Either-Or* I, 38, 47-48.

this case.) The question for Kierkegaard is whether the expression of adulation is imaginatively or poetically true for the imagined ideal personality who writes it; this is the only kind of sincerity we can demand of him here. Compare the "Explanation" at the end of the *Post-script.*[5]

Now for the "farewell to Eros." I see in this passage a vivid portrayal, generalized in expression (your "what" as a translation of "hvad" means anything that has been so-and-so admired) but particularized in its occasion, which is this matter of trying to understand Mozart's music after having admired it so long—a vivid portrayal of the relation always obtaining between enthusiastic admiration and analytic thought, the latter always carrying with it the danger that what seemed wonderful to immediate enthusiasm may prove illusory in whole or in part when reflected upon. And it seems to me clear that it is not *Eros or the erotic,* but Mozart's expression of it in music, which is the immediate subject-matter, first for admiration and then for thought. The very notion of expressing *admiration* for the erotic in the personality seems both awkward in itself and foreign to S.K. The idea is clearly expressed that the excellencies of the music will endure the trial of thought and come out unimpaired. Could he have said this if it had been his intention to express a farewell to the immediate-erotic as a factor in his personal existence? And how could this have been made consistent with the avowed purpose of letting an esthete express himself? I am forced to the conclusion that your interpretation is over-ingenious; and this seems especially true of your remarks about personification or the lack of it. There is no mystery about the "hvad"; it means "whatever" or "anything."

---

[5] *Unscientific Postscript,* 551-554.

Letter to Dr. Lowrie, July 6, 1935.

I feel, as a matter of principle, two considerations quite keenly. First, that the thought should be reproduced with the most meticulous fidelity. Second, that style in the strictest sense is not transferable from one language to another, the best achievement possible being the production of a close analogy. Where it seems, either because of the genius of the language, or because of the limited linguistic resources of the translator, that a choice must be made between an idiosyncracy of style in the original, however valuable and beautiful in its own linguistic atmosphere, but stilted and foreign in the second language if literally transferred, and a mere paraphrase, I would choose a paraphrase if one could be found, just as I prefer to break up many of Kierkegaard's long sentences into shorter units, as a concession to the spirit of modern English.

Letter to Dr. Lowrie, July 30, 1935.

I have made an effort not to depart from literalness, even in sentence structure, except where I was forced to do so by my inability otherwise to attain smooth and readable English. My thought is that an English translation of Kierkegaard should be directed to the "general reader" of "general culture," who reads for his own sake, and for the sake of the thought, and not in order to write a doctor's thesis or a book out of it. Hence readability and naturalness of style and diction seem to me a prime *desideratum.* You should note what a relief it is to my college students to be permitted to read Plato in Jowett's somewhat free translation, after they have been for some time obliged to read him in one of the more literal translations. His ability to create an English rendering in real

English with some dignity of style, is a service to English readers of Plato, which in my opinion far outweighs the presence here and there of the inaccuracies that pedants make so much of. Of course I hold no brief for errors or howlers anywhere; but it is possible to lose sight of the chief purpose of literature in an anxious worship of the letter. Kierkegaard himself speaks somewhere in a very deprecating tone of over-anxious translators who copy every word. And Hegel remarks of the writing of epitomes, that the Spirit is the best epitomator, which remark might also be applied to translation. One must learn by trial and error to steer between the Scylla of a slavish following of the original, with a consequent woodenness of style in the new language on the one hand, and a paraphrase so free as to give more of the spirit and style of the translator than the author. I must confess that my earlier translation [of the *Fragments*] sinned in this direction.

Letter to Dr. Lowrie, August 12, 1935.

Kierkegaard uses the word "Spekulation" in three different senses. First, as a designation for Hegel's philosophy and the Hegelizing tendency as the outstanding philosophical contemporary tendency. Second, as a name for Philosophy generally, considered as man's intellectual formulation of the content of his own Reason or Understanding (which includes his sense of values), and which could therefore also be rendered by the English: Common Sense, provided we insist on some intellectually significant degree of conceptualization or systematization. When J. C. [Johannes Climacus] poses the problem of the relation between Philosophy and Christianity as the underlying problem of the "Smuler" [Fragments], this is what he means by Philosophy, and he frequently uses

"Spekulation" as identical therewith. Third, he uses the word for a neutral dialectical formulation of the problems of life and reality, such as that which J.C. himself in the first instance represents. Thus the "Smuler" and the "Efterskrift" [Postscript], while also having a deeper significance if we raise the question of their purpose in connection with the pseudonymous literature, and if we take into account the indirect communication which characterizes them, are nevertheless by virtue of their stress upon conceptual formulation and categorical exactness, a contribution to Philosophy or Speculation in this, for Kierkegaard, wholly clear and legitimate sense. In this aspect they are objective, as all intellectual apprehension must be in the first instance, and thereby also neutral; K. himself says that J.C. can be interpreted just as much from the standpoint of an attack on Christianity as from the standpoint of a defense.[6] That is, the dialectical formulations will stand whether we decide to reject or to accept Christianity. So it cannot be argued that "Speculative Hypothesis" contravenes any *teaching* of Kierkegaard; and it must also be remembered that it was contrary to Kierkegaard's spirit to imagine that his thought could be guaranteed consistency and clarity by a meticulous use of words as formulas.

The other important point raised in your letter is the question of blessedness versus happiness as a translation of "Salighed." I am well aware of all that you say, and know that the English Bible uses blessedness for the precise concept of an ethico-religious happiness. I may still reconsider my choice; but here I can only tell you the reasons that have motivated my earlier preference for happiness. Blessedness has never, so far as I know, become

---

[6]Dru, *The Journals,* paragraph 994.

a generally used philosophical term in English. Berkeley and Bishop Butler use "happiness" for this concept, and thereby preserve a point of contact with ethical speculation generally. The word blessedness, as it seems to me (as is not the case with its equivalent "bliss"), savors of the narrowly theological, even the sanctimonious. On the other hand, "happiness" is a fair English equivalent, and it does not seem to me to be true at all that it carries in English an exclusively esthetic connotation, as does "Lykke" in Danish, which includes an element of luck or lucky chance. This is not true, i.e., not necessarily true, of the English "happiness" which as frequently as not has in it the element of a justified happiness, not merely a chance feeling of happiness. This is expressed in the phrase among others, of the "organic conception of happiness," and it is not unusual to draw a distinction between happiness and pleasure on this basis. My reason is then that the term "happiness" interprets K.'s meaning better than "blessedness" to a philosophically-trained English reader, in that it is without disturbing, narrowly-technical, theological coloring, and because with the accompanying adjective "eternal" conveys the meaning with precision. I do not think there is the slightest chance of confusion with what K. regards as the purely esthetic interpretation of happiness. An English philosopher treating this concept would have to begin by pointing out its dialectical character, i.e., the possibility of a number of different conceptions of "happiness," and that it is by no means an ultimate datum for consciousness, but a critical concept, involving the difference between true and false happiness; but I do not think that any English thinker would be tempted to use the word blessedness as his category for true happiness. And in that case why should K. be translated so as to make him use a term not philosophically acclimatized? Especially when the "Smuler" is precisely intended for philosophically-trained minds?

Letter to Dr. Lowrie, Sept. 14, 1935, regarding the translation of the Danish word, "Forstand," in Chapter III of the FRAGMENTS.

One very fundamental question of translation raised in your letter I must comment on here, not that I am not keeping the issue open, but because I would like to have your further reaction, after you have been apprised of my reasons for translating as I did. I refer of course to the choice of "Reason" as equivalent to "Forstand." This matter has caused me much anxious reflection; I must admit that I rather anticipated the objection you have urged.

Let me state briefly the considerations actuating me in choosing "Reason" as the main term, though I can use understanding also in less decisive contexts, and for the derivatives.

First: The Kantian distinction between the Reason and the Understanding is entirely foreign to Kierkegaard's circle of thoughts, in the sense that it is irrelevant to his problem, and is never officially referred to.

Second: The Hegelian distinction, which is different from the Kantian, is formally repudiated by Kierkegaard in and with his insistence upon the validity of the principle of contradiction. Hegel regards this principle as valid for the lower "Understanding," but not for the higher "Reason." As you know, Kierkegaard regards this as an important and fundamental issue for the dialectical formulation of Christianity, and his repudiation of the Hegelian view here is absolutely uncompromising.

Third: Unless I am entirely mistaken, the Scandinavian languages, like the English, do not in daily use make any distinction in principle between *Fornuft* and *Forstand*. In English, whenever I want to subjectify, and make reference to my own private grasp of some matter, I generally speak of my understanding, of its being understandable (this is on the way to becoming universal); but when I claim human universality for some view, I speak of its being rational, or, on the contrary, irrational. But this distinction between the more subjective and the more objective, has nothing to do with Kierkegaard's thoughts centering about the "Paradox" category. A paradox which merely offends my private understanding is subject to being resolved through a better understanding within the limits of what it is possible for me to understand as a human being; such a paradox is relatively and transitorily a paradox, a paradox for a limited and imperfect understanding, a paradox for some particular individual, but not a paradox for the race. Hence it is not the Absolute Paradox in Kierkegaard's sense.

Fourth: Your own argument furnishes me with the most powerful and urgent reason for translating as I did, precisely in order to forestall what I must regard as a fundamental misunderstanding of Kierkegaard's view of Christianity. If I use the word *Understanding* in Chapter III, I am aware that I will evoke the suggestion that human nature contains a higher principle, the Reason, which does not need to be set aside, and for which the Absolute Paradox is not paradoxical. I am convinced that such a thought is flatly contradictory of the entire spirit, purpose, and letter of Kierkegaard's work. If there is such a principle in me, then there is no Absolute Paradox, then the Teacher is not God, then the entire virile Christian terminology of the new birth, of the believer being a new creature, etc., falls down like a house of cards, and becomes mere rhetorical exaggeration, an immature and irrelevant adornment of what is essentially the Socratic position. So Kierkegaard would say, and so he would have to say, unless he were to consent to the destruction, by means of insidious or unmeaning compromise, of his entire dialectical position.

Fifth: It must of course be remembered, and this would have to be noted equally whether we translate by Understanding or by Reason, that the concept of *Forstand* is concrete and not abstract. It does not stand for an abstract human faculty, like the function of thinking in categories (Kant), or the power of general ideas (the soul, in Plato), and so forth. It stands for the entire rational self-consciousness of man as man, and includes of course a sense of values. If it did not, it could have no bearing upon the apprehension of the divine. Thus the Reason as I use it, and I am convinced that this is also in accordance with the main body of English tradition, stands for the essential and reflective common sense of mankind, in which each individual participates, though of course, with respect to his actual as opposed to his ideally potential grasp, at any one time, only imperfectly. Here is where Socrates' "maieutic" operates, in the attempt to bring the individual's actual understanding more closely in line with the universal Reason of mankind. This is nevertheless a process within an immanence. When Kierkegaard says that the "Smuler" [*Fragments*] treats of the relation between Philosophy and Christianity, he might also have said that it treats of the relation between the Reason and

Christianity. In lecturing upon Philosophy I myself define it as the organized and reflective common sense of mankind; this I have learned from Kierkegaard. Logic, on the other hand, is abstract; it is too abstract in fact to come into any sort of conflict with religion in general, or with Christianity in particular. To define Christianity as paradoxical is precisely to assert the validity of logic within its own abstract sphere. But logic does not decide what exists or what does not exist.

It may be of importance to mention that both Bohlin and Geismar indirectly support my interpretation of the Paradox-idea as given above in connection with the fourth consideration. You know, of course, that Bohlin distinguishes between an empirical-religious strain in Kierkegaard, side by side with another, the intellectualistic-speculative-dogmatic strain; to the former he ascribes the edifying and the Lutheran element in Kierkegaard's writing; to the latter he ascribes the insistence on the Paradox, and so forth. Geismar, while not in every point agreeing with Bohlin, is nevertheless impressed by his imputation of "intellectualism" to Kierkegaard, and sympathizes with it. He connects this intellectualism with what he calls his negative attitude toward life's cultural values, toward marriage, etc. Now this so-called "intellectualism" is nothing but a circumlocution for the absoluteness of the Paradox, or for what I see you refer to as the Athanasian dogma. If the Paradox were made relative by some such distinction as you suggest drawing, between the Reason and the Understanding, or as Kierkegaard himself expressly says, between a higher and a lower understanding, then Bohlin's objections would disappear, and we would have Socrates' pagan position dressed up as Lutheran orthodoxy; the traditional Christian terminology in popular dress for the people, a private interpretation for the cultured and the philosophical among the theologians *unter uns*. Bohlin and Geismar both keenly feel the divergence of their own standpoint from Kierkegaard's, though they are not quite willing to make it so central as I have made it.

Letter to Dr. Lowrie, Oct. 3, 1935.

The vexed question of Reason and Understanding[7] again. I am not quite willing to say that there is no difference of meaning in Danish between *Forstand* and *Fornuft*, but merely that I know of none that is consistently and clearly a matter of accepted usage. And this is also true of English. My chief positive reason for translating "Reason" is that the matters involved in the usual and well-known antithesis between Reason and Revelation are precisely the matters dealt with by Kierkegaard's theory in the "Smuler." Where the English has Reason and Revelation, the Scandinavian languages have as often as not "Forstandet och Uppenbarelse," but also alternatively, but without any real change in meaning, "Fornuftet och Uppenbarelse." On the other hand, we English never, or as good as never, say: The Understanding and Revelation. Now a word about your remark in the last letter before this one, to which I am replying. In that remark you take an example from the word reason in an abstract use, as when we say 2 times 2 equals 4, a truth of the reason. Of course there can be no contradiction or opposition between Revelation (namely, a revelation of God and His true nature, which *ipso facto* is a revelation of the nature of man and the true meaning of human life, of what genuine love is, etc.) and on the

[7]As used in Chapter III of the *Fragments*.

other hand, an abstract mathematical or logical truth or consideration. There is in such a case no commensurability. But Reason is also the name for man's concrete and rationalized consciousness of himself, of God, and of his own relationship to God. If there is any meaning or truth in Kierkegaard's doctrine of the Absolute Paradox, it is just this "Reason" which must be set aside in order that the "Paradox" may bestow itself. If by the Understanding we mean some subordinate function of human nature, something for example that has to do only with the finite but not with the infinite, then the Understanding would be not only an inept, but a starkly false translation of *Forstand*. I think that in these words I have expressed the full strength of the motives which have guided me to choose "Reason," though I am not indifferent to any further considerations.

Letter to Dr. Lowrie, May 16, 1936.

I have finally plumped for "Fragments" after all. I assure you that this last was not done lightly; the matter has been on my mind for many years, off and on for at least twenty of them, and now intensively for the last year; I could not seem to come to rest in a choice. However, since I finally settled down to "Fragments" after all, it now seems to me that this straightforward choice (a literal rendering) is the best, and that my former objections were somewhat fanciful and supersensitive. The sub-title, "A Fragment of Philosophy," will also be used, so that the complete title-page at any rate will not be misleading.

Letter to Dr. Lowrie, October 19, 1936.

It has belatedly occurred to me that there is one feature of my choice of title which may have been open to misunderstanding. The office in N. Y. preferred "Fragments" from the beginning, but in view of my indecision we decided to leave the matter open to the very last. When you wrote to me no notice of my final preference had been given the publishers; what you had heard was simply an echo of the preliminary title used by the N. Y. office. But I had gradually accustomed myself to the idea of using "Fragments," as, all things considered, the most innocuous of the various alternatives; and I was on the verge of conceding the matter of title without yet formally acknowledging my state of mind. In view of our previous correspondence, I can now see, what I was too pre-occupied to notice on the occasion of my last letter to you, that it might look as if I were intentionally concealing from you the title which I had already arrived at, and of which I had formally notified the publishers. . . . Only when the page proofs were set up, several weeks later, was the die definitely cast. . . . This is a full statement of the whole matter, and I must leave it to you to judge whether there was in this sequence of events a "betrayal" on my part.

Letter to Dr. Lowrie, March 23, 1937.

I have restored the little bit of psycho-analysis to the manuscript[8]; it contains no reference, near or remote, to onanism; it is merely a hypothesis that the erotic in Kierkegaard was in a separate water-tight compartment from the sensuous, purely psychical, etc. I do not think that there is anything in this as a matter of fact; the article on Mozart's music in *Either-Or*[9] proves to my mind the

---

[8]The manuscript of Dr. Eduard Geismar's book, *Lectures on the Religious Thought of Søren Kierkegaard*, which Professor Swenson rewrote for American publication. Augsburg Publishing House, 1937.

[9]*Either-Or*, I, 47-48.

contrary; it seems to me to be a simple-minded misunderstanding of the predominance of the intellectual in the linguistic expression that Kierkegaard permits himself; something similar would be true of every decent and clean-minded man. The sensuous-erotic does elude direct expression whenever the intellectual and the spiritual is strongly present. But the theory is bound to be expressed anyway by somebody before long, and it is characteristic of Geismar's view of the last agitation[10]; so I think he ought to be allowed to say it.

Letter to Dr. Lowrie, April 26, 1937.

When I write my Introduction to Geismar's lectures I am going to stress Kierkegaard's unique moral power, his distinction as an ethical force. And I am going to ascribe this moral force to his full-blooded and aggressive other-worldliness, defining the latter term more carefully than is usually done. My purpose in doing this is to offer by indirection and without frontal attack, a criticism of Professor Hirsch's trivialization of Kierkegaard's attack on the worldliness of contemporary Protestantism; and also to attempt for our clergy a clarification of the concept. I note that when Dewey in *A Common Faith*[11] indulges in polemics against what he calls supernaturalism, he is really protesting against the conception that there is anything eternal in man. Only, the term "supernaturalism" has irrelevant and misleading and prejudicial associations for the modern mind.

Letter to Dr. Lowrie, Dec. 22, 1937.

The proper place of the esthetic in the religious life is a difficult problem, as is the whole question of the reli-

---

[10]Søren Kierkegaard's conflict with the church.
[11]Chapter 3.

gious use of the cultural and economic. Your sermon
touched upon a particular expression of a general principle about which I have had some correspondence lately
with Professor Geismar. I like Geismar's sincerity and
simplicity very much, and hence I felt bound to tell him
that I could not agree with certain principles involved
and implied in his reservations over against what he calls
the Kierkegaardian asceticism. He came back at me with
a request for help in clarifying the problem, which em-
barrassed me terribly, partly because I was in no fit intellectual condition to make an adequate reply. I have
been thinking about it off and on, and think now that
his main difficulties are two: first, an attempt to settle, at
wholesale and by a rule, for the Church and its conduct,
what can only be settled at retail by each individual for
himself; second, that he operates too much with collective categories.

The relativities cannot be expunged from life, so much
is certain. An asceticism which makes this attempt always
ends up in emphasizing one set of relativities as over
against another set. This principle you will recognize as
the doctrine of the *Postscript*. Geismar thinks that he
agrees with the formula of the *Postscript:* an absolute
relation to the absolute end, and a relative one to the
relative ends. But he does not think that Kierkegaard later
remains on this standpoint. In particular he says that being relative or being made relative does not mean a lowering of value. The rest follows automatically.

My own understanding is about as follows. To say that
an end is relative is to say that it is subject to renunciation when it becomes necessary for the realization of a
higher purpose. Whether a given individual is called
upon to renounce some cultural or economic relativity,

money, marriage, love, cultural activities, depends on what his moral insight proposes to him as a task, and how far he needs to throw off weight in order to be able to realize this task. In an imperfect world opportunities for renunciation must necessarily occur; but what God asks of each one had best be left to God Himself, working through the conscience of the individual. But, as I wrote to Geismar, I would rather cut off my right hand than so to validate the relative by a principle as to foreclose in advance the possibility and religious validity of any particular form of renunciation, or any particular degree of renunciation. To do that would be to make the life of Christ an immoral exaggeration instead of an ideal pattern; it would be to "clip the claws of Christianity," as Geismar admits he seems to himself to have done, which makes him uneasy in his mind.

My explanation to myself of how Geismar has involved himself in this difficulty, is that he has not thoroughly assimilated the individualism of Kierkegaard. He talks as if the problem were to lay down rules for the teaching or conduct of Church and State. The individual is the point of attack, however, both for God and the religious man; what happens in Church and State is a reflex of what happens first in the individuals. Cardinal Newman put his question wrongly: Which is the right Church? When you put the question that way, Roman Catholicism is an almost inevitable outcome. The religious question is: How shall I live and be constituted, in order that where two or three or more of those like-minded with me are gathered together, there Christ will also be? And where Christ is, there the Church is. Newman should have heeded the reply received by the woman at the well:

Neither here nor there, but everywhere—in spirit and in truth.

If in any given situation the purely external activities of a religious organization have become an empty shell, if the spirit does not rule and interpenetrate, then the reformer will have the task of condemning the whole as a fraud. I am no reformer, but I do think it obvious that the Churches of the modern world are pretty feeble, and that it is often the case that the higher the spire the lower the inspiration. Under such circumstances to condemn the artistic and institutional is by no means asceticism in the ordinary sense, but is to call attention to the fact that the religious is a higher life, and that it cannot be reached directly by means of an elaboration of the cultural, but stands on a footing of its own, being in such wise independent of the cultural that the latter is a matter of indifference as a relativity, and a fraud if forced to play the role of something absolute.

Letter to Dr. Lowrie, May 19, 1938, commenting on certain features of Dr. Lowrie's KIERKEGAARD.

You will not expect here any extended commentary, but I wish to particularize enough to say that I have not seen a better handling of the conflict with the Church. It was a master stroke of handling to give so much space to the reflections in the Journals preceding the explosion; for it makes it evident how fundamentally important the attack was from the point of view of Kierkegaard's entire understanding of Christianity, how integrally it was a part of his life-work, and how much a carrying out to the full of the implications present as early as the writing of the *Postscript*. Indeed, there are not many of the ideas involved in it which are not foreshadowed in that work, though they are there treated more lightly and with less of sledge-hammer earnestness.

I think the engagement and its breaking is also exceedingly well done, as well as the affair with the *Corsair*. I am glad that you do not say what so many have said, that the passages in the Journals about the matter show sickliness and a humiliating weakness of character. Kierkegaard's business was reflection, and sensitiveness was his stock in trade. A man who could feel his own faults and errors so profoundly, and extract from them so much wisdom, had a right also to extract wisdom from the wrongs done to him by others. The objection referred to comes from people who have the professorial habit of never reflecting about themselves, but about such large matters as do not concern them.

I think you are prompted by a sure and happy instinct in treating the dialectician and philosopher that was in Kierkegaard as lightly as you have done. You have seized upon the substantial core in Kierkegaard; another writer may some time supplement your work by a treatment of the less basically significant abstract-dialectical form in which his thought was cast.

Letter to Dr. Lowrie May 31, 1938.

I cannot quite agree with your antithesis between a "literal" and a "literary" translation. The translation of a stylist like Kierkegaard is not faithful if it is not literary in the good sense. One of the most striking features of his style, even when he handles abstractions, is its ease and naturalness, almost like a man talking at your elbow; this naturalness and ease cannot be reproduced in English if one slavishly follows the structure of the originals. Your translations strike me for the most part as very happy;

but every once in a while I strike a locution which, in the quality of the English reader, makes a sharp pain run through my mind. I know precisely how these things happen. One who reads him in the original with pleasure becomes hypnotically affected by the Danish style; when he puts this into English hé may get the same pleasure from it, not because the translation succeeds in reproducing the original effect, but because he is in a position to feel it in the terms of the original Danish. This hypnotic effect I have had a terrible time to emancipate myself from, and I know only too well how it blinds one to faulty and un-English locutions, which must be exceedingly distasteful to the cultivated reader who comes upon Kierkegaard for the first time.

Letter to Dr. Lowrie, May 12, 1939.

I have read Hirsch's *Studien* since I wrote you last. I am impressed with its solidity and perspicacity; it is a genuinely scholarly work, and the author has the needed presuppositions for understanding Kierkegaard in his main purpose and spirit. There is no question but that it is the best of all the German works, indeed the only one of them that will repay closer study. I still think his doctrine of a *differentia specifica* is a lapse, and I should imagine that the present situation in Germany and elsewhere should have made it evident to him. He should content himself with saying: As far as I am concerned, I do not have the insight or the call to emphasize the Christian heterogeneity so strongly as to bring about a collision with my environment that might lead to mistreatment or persecution.

I am sending you a reprint of my paper on the Existential Dialectic. It seems to me now very poor, although it was very well received at the meeting. Being written during my depression, there is no style. Besides it is entirely fragmentary, since it does not deal with the paradoxical. But I had to leave that out because of limitations of time.

From Review of Professor Hollander's SELECTIONS FROM THE WRITINGS OF KIERKEGAARD, *University of Texas, 1923.*

Professor Hollander thinks, as other critics have thought before him,[12] that a good dose of French and English empiricism would have been an antidote for the speculative tendency of Kierkegaard's mind, fostered by the "bloodless abstractions" of German metaphysics. Aside from the fact that the romantic movement in German philosophy was not exactly "bloodless," whatever other faults it may have had, I doubt very much whether this so-called empiricism would have had any message for Kierkegaard's mind. We must not forget that Kierkegaard was in reality a much more concrete thinker than either Comte, Mill or Spencer ever dreamed of being, in the same sense that Socrates was a more concrete thinker than the Greek representatives of the natural-scientific trend of thought who preceded him. Socrates, it is well known, studied natural science in his youth, and gave promise of entering upon a promising career as a philosopher of the conventional type; but he soon discovered that "physics was not man's proper business, and began to philosophize about moral matters in the streets and in the market-places" (Diogenes Laertius). The truth is that nineteenth century empiricism, with its absorption in the description and explanation of natural facts, and its ten-

---

[12]Brandes and Høffding.

dency to depend upon natural sciences almost exclusively
for the categories with which to interpret the life of the
human spirit, was so incorrigibly abstract and remote
from life as to fully deserve the characterization which
Kierkegaard applies to the speculative idealists, that they
suffer from an absent-mindedness that verges upon a
ridiculous distraction. In his rich imaginative and poetic
endowment, in his passion for sincerity and personal assimilation, and in the ethical, non-sentimental Christianity which he inherited from his father, Kierkegaard had
an "antidote" against speculative aloofness from life, if
one were needed, far superior to scientific studies, which
are always somewhat abstract in themselves, and which in
the case of the empiricists misled them into the formulation of a shallow, half-popular compromising philosophy
of life of exceedingly doubtful permanent value.

When Professor Hollander characterizes Kierkegaard's
individualism as aristocratic, he apprehends only one
side of it, the esthetic. Fundamentally, his individualism
was religious, and therefore democratic in the best if
not the only real sense of that much abused term. And
when he further says that its aim was, "not to transform,
but to transcend the existing social order," it tempts me
to propose an amplification of the formula to guard it
against the usual misunderstanding. It was the spirit of
Kierkegaard's individualism, not to seek a transformation
of the existing social order to make it possible for the
individual to transcend it and find his truest self; but
that the individual should be challenged to transcend the
existing social order and find himself, thus making it
possible for that order to be transformed. His individualism consists in conceiving the task as one which must be

attacked from within outward, instead of from the outside inward.

From review of Theodore Haecker's SØREN KIERKEGAARD, *1937.*

As a good Catholic, the author finds the source of most of Kierkegaard's errors in his lack of a relationship to the teaching authority of the Church, and to his having "no guide but his conscience which he followed faithfully." The criticisms are directed chiefly to the "exaggerations" of his dialectic, his bitter one-sidedness in applying a corrective to the decadence of his age and environment, his failure to understand marriage and the hope inspired by the sacrament of baptism, and his lack of appreciation for any other form of the Christian community than that which is represented in the Invisible Church, specifically his neglect of the institutional presence of the Church through its possession of the sacraments.

These points might be argued, but a brief review is not the place. I content myself with two remarks. There are indeed many who cannot breathe freely in an atmosphere of consistent pursuit of a thought to its last consequences; but Kierkegaard's passion for such dialectical fearlessness is precisely the ground for his greatness as a thinker. When Haecker says that Kierkegaard's ethical passion was so strong as to lead him to stress works at the expense of grace, I admit that I fail to understand him. I know of no author, ancient or modern, who so carefully seeks to guard against misunderstanding on just this point; works lay no basis for desert, but are an expression of the gratitude which the experience of the boundless love of God awakens in the mind that has found God in its own infinite humiliation.

Letter to Rev. C. Clare Oke, August 23, 1938, answering the following two questions:

1. Just what does Kierkegaard mean by the statement on page 60 in the Interlude in the *Fragments:* "The necessary cannot undergo any change, since it is always related to itself, and related to itself in the same manner"?

2. "Becoming is never necessary. It was not necessary before it came into being, for then" (as necessary, cf. topline of the page) "it could not come into being; nor after it came into being, for then it has not come into being." The last clause seems to be contradictory.

I think the difficulty in understanding Kierkegaard in such logical passages as are found in the Interlude of the *Fragments* lies partly in the greater degree of abstractness in terminology and phraseology which he permits himself, as over against the usual style of English philosophical writing.

I read the first statement as follows: Necessity is a concept which always arises out of a self-relation, and is rooted in the fact, as Aristotle also says, that a thing is what it is. Thus in thinking about some change, we see no necessity in it as long as we really think of it as change, in process of changing. But if we take the change as given, and raise a question about its structure, we find in it universal and particular elements. The universal factors, repeated in the same way in other changes, may be what we have been accustomed to call laws of nature. After analysis comes synthesis. So we ask, as a check upon our analysis, do these universals plus these particulars (circumstances, etc.) result in giving us the change as it was before analysis? and if the analysis is correct, we find that the elements analyzed out, when they are synthesized again, actually do and necessarily must make up the given change. Necessarily must; because a thing is necessarily what it is. The necessary is thus always related to itself, i.e., is always the expression for a self-relation. That it cannot undergo any change is an inevitable consequence; again, because a thing is what it is, and this is what is necessary about it. But all this reflection is based upon an analysis of the structure of a given change, and abstracts wholly from the coming into being of the change. In the latter aspect, no necessity arises; for becoming is a free transition.

The second statement thus becomes merely an application and expansion of the first. I do not think there is any contradiction in it: what seems to be a contradiction arises from assuming and denying two hypotheses contrary to fact. The first is: Suppose that something possible was necessary. Then it could not come into being, for its necessity would cause it to remain unchanged as a mere possibility; but a possibility cannot be a possibility if it is necessarily prevented from becoming an actuality. Hence, nothing can be necessary which is possible, since its necessity would make it impossible. If a possibility were necessary, or if a necessity were a possibility, i.e., if something were necessary before coming into being, the self-contradiction that its necessity prevents it from changing its status (from possibility to actuality) shows that the antecedent hypothesis is false. The second is completely analogous to the first: Suppose that something which had become actual were also necessary. This would deny that it could ever have changed its status, and so forth, precisely as above.

A general statement of the principle is, that necessity and change are mutually contradictory concepts. The special application of this in the Interlude is, that there is a contradiction between necessity and the particular kind of change or transition which Aristotle calls *kinesis,* the transition from possibility to actuality, which transition is in general what we mean by becoming, or coming into being. While everything, the expression of freedom and the consequences of natural laws plus conditions and circumstances (particulars) may be looked at under an aspect which makes them exemplify necessity, this can be done only in so far as we wholly abstract from the fact that they have come into being, or are coming into being, or may in the future come into being. Only when we look at the logical contents involved in their relations to themselves; or think of them twice, in terms of a reduplication (as when we first think of a change unanalyzed and then think of the same change analyzed, and find that the latter is inevitably identical with the former), only then do we get necessity. But then we must abstract from their becoming; for their becoming is itself a change, and cannot be necessary. There is no *logical* transition from one concept to another.

This is at any rate Kierkegaard's position. It has two aspects, or makes front in two directions. It seeks to explain what the necessity-category means, and from what reflection it arises; it asserts that it arises from a reduplicating reflection, and out of the self-identity which such a reflection discovers. Only self-identity is necessary. Then it also seeks to explain how it happens that changes, events, and so forth, may come to seem necessary. This is because we are confused, and do not notice that in order to find the necessity we abstract from the change, the becoming. It is only by abstracting from the change of becoming, the change from possibility to actuality, a change in status, in type of being, but not a change in content, that a reflection upon the content as given, and in its relation to itself, makes this content take on an aspect of necessity. Time may be involved in the content of a conception, without being involved in anything happening to the conception, as for example its transition from the status of a possibility to the status of an actuality.

I am very glad to hear of your interest in Kierkegaard. I am sure he has a contribution to make, both positive and negative (as a corrective) to our philosophical and religious thought; and that this contribution is not only highly original and couched in terms of a literature that is emotionally and intellectually exceedingly rich, but also of immense importance for every man who will take the time to understand and appropriate it. I have added the latter condition, in deference to his own principle of subjectivity; it is the subjective translation into personal assimilation which finally produces the truth in the pregnant sense. To know the truth merely, is to make it a lie; it really becomes a truth when it is the truth *for me,* that is, the truth is a being, a kind of personality, an incarnation of the true highest value.

Extracts from Discussions

I have never seen any passage in which Kierkegaard shows scorn for objective *validity*. His respect for workmanship in the objective sciences — logic, mathematics, the historical disciplines, the natural sciences — is frequently expressed. His scorn is not for objectivity as such, but for objectivity as a supreme spiritual attitude, affecting superiority over pathos and passion in the highest

concerns of the spiritual life; for complacency pretending to be higher than concern; for a cold disinterestedness presuming to rank higher than a passionate interest
in *re* the crucial issues of life. His problem is Christianity, and his point is that nothing can be known about
Christianity without subjectivity and passion, and that
spirit is an inward passionate self-concern.

The ideal of an impersonal objectivity in a critical historical study, intended to lay bare the thought-structure
in skeleton form, is of course one on which Kierkegaard also insists. But it is an entirely different question
whether some of these thoughts, those that express categories of the personal life as distinct from the abstract
logical sphere, can be really understood without a background of emotional-volitional experience.

Initially Kierkegaard's "irrationalism" consists in a
conviction that becoming is something more than knowing; ultimately it culminates in the doctrine of the Truth
as paradoxical to the Reason; but here the Reason concept is concrete, essentially identical with the passion of
self-assertion, self-justification, so that the conflict is between two passions, not between passion and abstract intelligence. The latter kind of a conflict is scarcely conceivable, since the two factors are incommensurable.

Primarily Kierkegaard's method of "indirect communication" is a challenge to the emotional will, and consists in trying to help the reader understand the personal
significance of the issues presented. It involves a two-fold
reflection: (1) the objective reflection by which the
thought gets an adequate verbal embodiment; (2) the
subjective reflection by which it is a) assimilated to the
personality, b) called to the attention of a reader so as
to elicit his self-activity. There are a host of secondary

considerations involved in the art, e.g., taking away the prestige of the writer, isolating the reader, etc. The entire method is not emotive as something other than intellectual, but the intellectual grasp of values in terms of the proper emotional mood, i.e., the intellectual invested with its own proper emotion versus the intellectual as emasculated in an inhuman abstract objectivity. The "emotive" function is a personal assimilation of the intellectual content.

Letter to O. C. Phillips, September 2, 1938, commenting on various passages in a paper written by Mr. Phillips.

I agree with what you say about A's book. Without having thoroughly assimilated Kierkegaard, without really having tried to learn from him anything fundamental, he proceeds to lecture him as a professor would talk to a hopeful student of brilliant gifts. But this attitude is of course nonsense, since A is a mediocrity correcting not only a genius, but also a man experienced in life, in a manner of which both extensively and still more intensively, A has not the slightest conception. "He fought valiantly for a cause he did not understand," says A of Kierkegaard. How infinitely comical an assumption of intellectual superiority! You see why the good God sometimes lets a genius be born. It is so that mediocrities may find a sort of gymnastic exercise in correcting their errors.

Karl Barth has of course in a certain sense understood Kierkegaard. But he is not the dialectician that Kierkegaard was, and consequently permits himself to formulate his thought in a phraseology which a careful and seasoned reader would find inadequate, if not sometimes misleading. In the commentary below, I shall have occasion perhaps to illustrate this point lightly once or twice. But it would take a reading of Kierkegaard himself in his entirety to give the proper evidence for this opinion.

1. The little phrase about "applied Christianity" might to my mind suggest a serious misunderstanding. As this phrase is sometimes used, well, in that sense you are, I think, quite right in finding in Kierkegaard a contrast and a correction. But it must not be forgotten that Kierkegaard's developed doctrine, in the *Unscientific Postscript,* about the subjective thinker, his double reflection, and his principle that subjectivity is truth, is precisely an insistence upon an applied Christianity. There is no objective truth; an objective Christianity without its subjective correlate in the mind and existence of the individual (the application) is precisely paganism; Christianity is spirit, spirit is subjectivity, subjectivity is inwardness, and inwardness is passion: these and many other similar expressions of Kierkegaard's show how fundamental was his insistence that Christianity exists only in its application. The difference between him and modern thought is that the latter tends to conceive the application extensively and externally, as an effort to change in this or that detail the external order, the social environment; while Kierkegaard conceives the application as a continuous inward transformation of the individual self and of his mode of existence, bringing in its train, it is true, also external changes as a by-product, for which the individual is not by any means wholly responsible, and which in any case, even in the maximum of their beneficence, are heterogeneous in value with the inward state of the personality.

2. You show that the divinity of Christ is and has been subject to grievous misunderstanding. And it is also true

enough that there is a contrast, in a sense, between starting with man and starting with God. But Kierkegaard's method of seeking to prevent such misunderstanding is quite different from that suggested by the Barthian formula. He concentrates, not upon the dogma, but upon the *relation of the individual* to the God-man. He asks how the subjectivity of the individual must be qualified merely in order to make it possible for the problem of Christianity to confront his consciousness, to exist for him at all, and then goes on farther to delineate the subjectivity of the individual in the happy relationship of faith, and in contrast with the unhappy relationship of offense. It is in this field that we have Kierkegaard's great and original contribution.

3. Here I wish to expand a little the point made in the preceding paragraph. Perhaps the most original contribution of Kierkegaard, from the abstract-intellectual point of view, is the principle that in the world of the spirit object and subject are so connected with one another as to create what the mathematician would call a one-to-one correspondence. He characterizes *Faith,* for example, in such definite subjective terms that it can correspond to only one object, the God-Man, as Absolute Paradox. He regards immortality, for example, as a personal eternal happiness, not as an abstract negative conception, getting its meaning not from apocalyptic visions or poetic imagination, but from the relationship of the individual to it: an infinite passionate personal interest as the primary possibility of having such a happiness, and a form of existence absolutely transformed by the conception as the developed potentiality of the primary potentiality. If the transformation of the life is not absolute, i.e., unconditional, then the individual has no relationship to

an eternal happiness as his absolute end. The question of the true nature of God is transformed by Kierkegaard into the question of what relationship of the individual, what state of his subjectivity, is such as to make his relationship a true God-relationship. And so everywhere. Thus it would be more in Kierkegaard's spirit to say that the essence of Christianity was faith as an infinite personal interest in the absolutely paradoxical, in the absurd; or more ethically, as the suffering Truth, than to speak of it as the dogma of the God-Man. At any rate, any divorce, however unintentional or slight, between this dogma and the corresponding subjective relationship to it, at once brings us out of harmony with Kierkegaard's thought.

4. A rejection of the Jesus of history must be carefully distinguished from a rejection of the historical Jesus. The latter would be a repudiation of the God-Man, by making the second half of the synthesis unreal. Kierkegaard's point is the synthesis. Otherwise the paradox disappears. The paradox is the unity of God and an individual man in distinction from other men; and the particular individual is the historical individual.

5. Perhaps the distinction between direct and indirect knowledge of God needs more elaboration, by the discussion of the intermediaries which make the latter indirect. A desperate sense of one's own individual moral bankruptcy, the consequent leap of the individual into the arms of the Paradox (utterly impossible without the preceding despair), an infinite interest in one's moral integrity, and so forth—these are the things that break the continuity of his life for the individual, and invalidate his direct knowledge. It is the tremendous and genial psychological, poetical, and dialectical elaboration of

these intermediaries which constitutes Kierkegaard's chief distinction. It may be summed up in one phrase: no naturalization of Christianity; when it comes into the life of the individual, it comes always as the result of a breach in continuity in his adult consciousness. The Christianity of children is not Christianity.

6. To say that faith starts with God is true enough, but not adequate as a dialectical determination of its nature. For this may be interpreted as if it meant that God is for faith an initial postulate for its thinking, the point of departure for conclusions (about miracles, in your example). But this is misleading; and on this point Karl Barth is much less carefully oriented than Kierkegaard. What I have said about points 2, 3, and 5 above, may serve as a further commentary.

7. The little polemic against Idealism, with its contrast between our idea of God and God Himself, perhaps needs certain distinctions as a supplement before it is wholly clear or valid. Kierkegaard is indeed a realist, but not in the sense that he supposes it possible to approach or set up a relationship to any object except through ideas, consciousness. The contrast between idea and object is, logically considered, simply the contrast between two poles of the same experience. The language of daily life does draw such a distinction as is drawn in your text, but the real meaning is to distinguish between a true and a false idea of a given object, or to distinguish the adequate idea from the inadequate one. What you here have in mind is doubtless the same as that which Kierkegaard expresses by the distinction between Immanent Religion on the one hand (Religion A of the *Postscript*), and Transcendental or Paradoxical Religion on the other (Religion B). Or, to use other words, between

one idea of God expressing the immediate human ideal
of the divine, and one expressing the ideal of the divine
that is developed out of the consciousness of sin in the
passion of faith.

8. Barth's distinction between faith and human experience or convictions seems to me undialectical, and
thus easily subject to misunderstanding. Of course faith
is a human experience; if not, it does not exist at all. The
Church even teaches that faith is abolished in eternity,
so that it is according to this teaching an essentially temporal human experience. It is true that it is not a primary
but a secondary human experience, coming after an experienced breach in the adult consciousness, and constitutes a new beginning; it comes after something historical, and in the fullness of time; but it is nevertheless
conviction and experience, and it is *in* the individual
even if it is not *of* the individual. This matter is fully
discussed in the *Philosophical Fragments,* in the last three
chapters; from the reading of which you may note how
much more careful Kierkegaard is here than Barth.

9. My impression is that the discussion about the role
and place of the Church is inadequate to represent Kierkegaard's thought on this subject. I cannot explain how
in any detail, but for one thing the exposition uses metaphysical categories too exclusively, where moral categories
would be better. And if the subject is to be dealt with
metaphysically, it should be in terms of the fundamental
distinction between becoming and being, the dynamic
and the static. Kierkegaard's doctrine is, that the Church
should ideally represent becoming, dynamic movement
in the moral sphere; and that the State ideally and actually always represents something established. His criticism is that the established Church has, as established,

missed its significance as a Church. And of course he does not refer merely to what the English called an "establishment," i.e., governmental protection. Our free sectarian Churches in America are for the most part quite as truly representative of an established social order as is a European state church, and hence not really churches.

10. I especially appreciate your estimate of the significance of the fact that Christianity threatens to become, in modern times, a minority religion. Kierkegaard would of course say that it always has been, and that its apparent supremacy in the world is an illusion. The tendency you mention is therefore from his point of view an advance, since it is a clearing away of illusions.

Comments on Professor John Wild's paper, "Kierkegaard and Classic Philosophy," October 9, 1938, which he was to present at the meeting of the American Philosophical Association. (As Professor Wild received it, this letter had been somewhat condensed and abbreviated.)

Your stress upon the substantial influence of the Greeks upon Kierkegaard's thought has my entire sympathy. From one side, his thought may be regarded as a reaction from Hegel, assisted in attaining form and clarity by the study and assimilation of Greek thought. However, this is one-sided unless it is remembered that the reaction from Hegel was by no means primarily produced by a study of the Greeks, but had its root in the intensive and passionate struggles of his personality in relation to the ideals that had their focal point in his breaking the engagement with Regina Olsen. So that the remarkable psychological fact emerges, that the motives for the decisive break with Hegel were being rooted in his life while he was writing the Hegelianizing dissertation on Socrates. He hoped to be able to marry, and to take his place in the totality pretty much in the Hegelian sense of "Sittlichkeit"; when he found this impossible for himself, he also began to recast his evaluation of Socrates radically.

You have doubtless noticed that the picture of Socrates in the *Fragments* and in the *Postscript* differs essentially from the picture in the dissertation. In a place in the Journals, written in 1850, there is a passage which puts this antithesis in the strongest possible form, though indications are also given in the two works mentioned, and in the entire spirit of later references in the "Literature." You may be interested in this brief passage, as it may not have been noted in the German literature on K.; hence I submit a translation:

"A Passage in My Dissertation

"Influenced as I was by Hegel and the whole modern spirit, without sufficient maturity really to apprehend the great, I have somewhere in my dissertation not been able to refrain from showing that it was an imperfection in Socrates not to have any eye for the totality, but merely to look upon the individual numerically.

"Oh, Hegelian fool that I was—precisely this is the outstanding proof which shows how great an ethicist Socrates was!"

As you will have noticed from a passage in the *Postscript,* Kierkegaard continues to view Socrates from the point of view of Irony, but alters the concept itself. His later view gives Socrates a positive inner content as ethico-religious inwardness, in place of the absolute negativity of the dissertation; and makes him a typical existential thinker, though equipped only with ethical presuppositions. In the passage in question, after having described Socrates as an ethicist with irony as his incognito, he adds: "What then is irony, if we wish to call Socrates an ironist, not like Magister Kierkegaard consciously or unconsciously presenting only one side of the matter? Irony is a synthesis of ethical passion, which in inwardness infinitely accentuates the personal self in relation to the ethical requirement—and of culture, which in external relations infinitely abstracts from the personal ego, treating it as one finitude among all the other finitudes and particularities."[13] This is of course a very different picture of Socrates from that in the dissertation, where Socrates does not possess the Idea, but destructively prepares the way for it, and finds his justification in the testimony of history, i.e., an instrument who does not know for what ends he is used. It is the later picture that becomes the object of Kierkegaard's unbounded admiration throughout the literature, and is most strongly expressed in the final agitation. The change is not motivated by a new empirical approach to the external facts, but almost wholly by a revolution in valuation on the part of Kierkegaard himself, a revolution which dates from the period of the engagement and is rooted in the spiritual struggles of that period. And the formula that "Subjectivity is Truth" is of course an expression of the altered standpoint. This may be quite familiar to you; but I thought I would call it to your attention if perchance it had in some way escaped you. The *Journals* throw a flood of light on the personal origin of these alterations in the scheme of valuations that form a framework for Kierkegaard's thought.

---

[13]*Postscript*, 449.

In describing how and in what forms the problem of truth arises for the "existing individual,"[14] I shall necessarily have to touch upon what you mention under the caption of "merging truth with value." Only I should prefer to describe this a little differently. Modern philosophy is one-sided in its approach to the problem of truth, emphasizing chiefly the truth of propositions, or of a system of propositions (objective truth), while neglecting what the Greeks did not forget, and what daily life still reminds us of in such expressions as, "true statesman, true love," etc. Kierkegaard's analysis points out that a question of truth arises wherever we have a relation between ideality and reality, either so that the ideality of a meaning reduplicates the ideality incorporated in a reality (objective truth), or so that the reality incorporates and reduplicates a certain ideality or value. The latter gives us, in relation to man, what Kierkegaard calls subjective truth. What both have in common is the reduplication necessarily involved as soon as we think ideality in relation to reality.

I am glad that you are going to stress the matter of "concern" as characteristic of the existential thinker, i.e., his subjectivity, his inwardness, his infinite personal passion. Of course I cannot avoid mentioning this also, in explaining what Kierkegaard means by subjectivity. Perhaps you have noticed how the description of the ethical task in the second volume of *Either-Or*,[15] as the realization of an immanent teleology within the personality, the choice of one's own self, becomes in the *Postscript*,[16]

---

[14] Referring to his paper on the "Existential Dialectic of Kierkegaard" that Mr. Swenson was to present at he same meeting of the American Philosophical Association. (See Chapter IV.)

[15] *Either-Or*, II, 229-30.

[16] *Postscript*, 115-117.

through the stressing of the category of imperfection characteristic of the religious, developed into the theme that the highest ethical task for every individual is to become subjective, with its corollary of the ironical distinction between being subjective as a matter of course, "also a sort of subject," and being subjective in truth.

I cannot avoid dealing with the emphasis upon change, motion, transition, in explaining the Kierkegaard category of existence as a process of movement, and therefore always including both positive and negative factors. It is possible that at this point, judging from your comment anent Kierkegaard and the Greeks, our views will clash. I see the doctrine of the "leap," of the "paradox," of the principle of immanence, as characteristic of the intellectual as such, and of transcendence as characteristic of existence as such, since it involves change, all as different sides of the same stress upon change or movement in Kierkegaard. Hence I also come to the conclusion that the category of change has never been applied so radically by any school of philosophy to the life of man, as it is in Kierkegaard. The humanists and pragmatists of our day are all, in spite of everything they say of change, by contrast with Kierkegaard, adherents of the point of view of immanence. It is, of course, his incorporation of Christianity in its most severely orthodox form into his thought which has given Kierkegaard this radical insistence upon change and transition in relation to human life; the interpretation of Christianity as the Absolute Paradox is the concrete expression for this. His view of the decisiveness of the moment in time is again an illustration of how he stresses change. Perhaps it is this radical stress that you propose to criticise.

What you say of his descriptive philosophical psychology interests me. I have often pondered this, and thought how the difference from so-called scientific psychology might be formulated. The *mechanism* of thought and experience, its conditions in the body and the environment is, of course, as you say, a problem of *control;* the study of it yields an explanation that ministers to a kind of external control. Why then does this psychology seem so poor and trivial beside the literary psychology (to use the current phrase) of thinkers like Aristotle and Kierkegaard? And what are the differentiating criteria? I have proposed to myself the following: Viewing human life as a striving for the realization of ideals, does not the latter sort of psychology have its strength in that it views the empirical psychological phenomena in the light of these ideals, and in relation to this striving (teleologically indeed, but not chiefly in the biological sense) ?

I am glad to see that you link Kierkegaard with Plato in the attack on sophistry. Plato gives us a category of the sophistic, the sophist in every man, that has a value wholly independent of the historical justice done to Protagoras or Gorgias or Hippias, so that the animadversions of Grote, for example, are trivial and irrelevant. Kierkegaard certainly follows in Plato's footsteps, and enriches the psychological delineation with a more varied phenomenology, and sharpens the terms of the indictment. I note also his development of an artistry in communication, *in re* the sophistical, which Plato at least did not dream of. He sees the modern world as everywhere dominated, much more completely than was the case in the ancient world, by a form of sophistry still more wretched and more corrupt. I remember an expression in a letter of William James[17] which would have found full ap-

---

[17]Perhaps refers to a letter to the *Boston Evening Transcript.* See *The Thought and Character of William James,* II, 311.

proval at the hands of Kierkegaard. James says in effect: In our modern democracies power has become sophistical, and safeguards itself by hiding behind lies and illusions. The truth of this can be seen in our modern dictatorships; for the control of all propaganda, and the willingness to make use of a propaganda of lies and deceptions, is precisely the tribute which modern dictatorships pay to democracy. In ancient times tyranny tended to be bolder and more truthful; power made its appearance as naked power, undisguised and unashamed. But now it works through newspapers and publicity agents.

I shall put an end to these reflections by a comment on your last point, the sense in which Kierkegaard believes himself to make protest against Philosophy itself. I have been much troubled to get clear ideas on this subject, and I am convinced that the matter is not simple, but very complicated. First, it cannot be denied that Kierkegaard frequently uses the terms, "Speculation," "Philosophy," "the philosopher" in an extensional sense, as applying to the major trend in contemporary thought, the Hegelian and the Hegelian school. But this does not exhaust the matter. He also attacks the notion that the ends of thought are as such the highest ends for human life, since he posits subjectivity, concern, passion, as an essential expression for human existence. Here the contrast is between objectivity as a culminating rather than a relatively-intermittent and instrumental attitude, and subjectivity as the only essential expression for personality and human existence. At the same time that he is doing this, he also professes his own respect for speculation, and confesses that his own life is devoted precisely to speculation, "as far as circumstances allow." Take the following from the *Postscript* (page 135):

"Only a very limited intelligence, or someone who cunningly wishes to guard himself against feeling impressed, could here assume that I am in this objection playing the role of a vandal, seeking to violate the sacred security of the precincts of science, and to have the cattle let loose; or that I am a lazzarone placing myself at the head of a herd of newspaper readers and balloting idlers, in order to rob the modest scholar of his lawful possessions, earned by the employment of his happy gifts in resigned toil. Verily there are many, many, who possess more than I do in the realm of the mind; but there is no one who more proudly and gratefully believes that in this realm there prevails an eternal security of property rights, that the idlers remain outside. But when a generation *en masse* proposes to dabble in universal history; when demoralized by this, as one is demoralized by playing the lottery, it rejects the highest of human tasks; when speculative philosophy is no longer disinterested, but creates a double confusion, first by overleaping the ethical, and then by proposing a world-historical something as the ethical task for the individuals—then it is due to science itself that something be said about it. No, all honor to the pursuits of science, and all honor to everyone who assists in driving the cattle away from the sacred precincts of scholarship. But the ethical is and remains the highest task for every human being."

Kierkegaard does not deny the possible propriety of an individual scholar here and there devoting himself to Logic, the natural sciences, etc., provided he first seeks and receives an ethical justification for his procedure, but he regards the most natural task for a born thinker to be a concentration upon the simply human, the ethical, and seeks to show that for the wise man (the philosopher) there are in this field such an infinity of tasks and problems, more complicated just because he is a wise man (a philosopher), that there need never be any necessity for him to pass over to the philosophy of history for want of matter for reflection. And here he makes Socrates' desertion of natural sciences and concentration upon the ethical his great example. That is to say: he regards a devotion of reflection to objective problems as relatively justifiable, as capable in this or that individual of an ethical expression; but an individual who is free to choose his field will normally choose the ethical. If he is a thinker, he will grasp the ethical in the form of concepts and categories which relate it to the whole of life; but he will not regard his thinking as anything more than a personal relativity; essentially he will have his life in the ethical, where even the simple man can have it, and essentially in the same way. His polemic is thus directed against assuming the tasks of objective thought to be the highest for human beings, thus introducing discord into humanity by setting wise men against the simple, instead of seeking a reconciliation with all men in the ethical. But I am gossiping at an inordinate length about things which must be familiar to you. I merely wished to warn against what seemed to me the danger of an over-simplification of Kierkegaard's polemic; perhaps also the assumption of a blind spot just where he was more than ordinarily clear-sighted.

CHRONOLOGICAL TABLE OF
KIERKEGAARD'S LIFE AND WRITINGS

1813 — 5 May — Born in Copenhagen, youngest of seven children.

1830 — Matriculated at the Unviersity of Copenhagen.

1838 — First book, *From the Papers of One Still Living*; a Critique of Hans Christian Andersen as a Novelist.

1840 — Candidate in Theology.

1840 — September — Engaged to Regina Olsen.

1841 — September — *On the Concept of Irony*; a doctoral dissertation.

1841 — November — Breaks off his engagement to Regina Olsen.

1843 — February — *Either-Or*; first work belonging to the "literature."

1843 — May — *Two Discourses of Edification*; first religious publication.

1843 — October — *Fear and Trembling*; *Repetition*; *Three Discourses of Edification*.

1843 — November — *Four Discourses of Edification*.

1844 — June — *Philosophical Fragments*; *The Concept of Dread*; *A Book of Prefaces*.

1844 — *Two Discourses of Edification*; *Three Discourses of Edification*; *Four Discourses of Edification*.

1845 — April — *Three Occasional Discourses*; *Stages on Life's Way*.

1845 — December — Attack on the *Corsair*.

1846 — February — *Unscientific Postscript*.

1846 — March — *A Literary Notice*; characterization of two generations.

1847 — March — *Edifying Discourses of Varying Tenor*.

1847 — September — *The Works of Love*.

1848 — April — *Christian Discourses*.

1848 — July — *A Crisis in the Life of an Actress*.

1849 — May — *The Lilies of the Field and the Birds of the Air. Two Ethico-Religious Essays*.

1849 — July — *The Sickness Unto Death*.

1850 — September — *Practical Introduction to Christianity*.

1850 — December — *One Discourse of Edification*.

1851 — August — *Two Discourses at the Friday Communion Service. A Note Concerning My Authorship*.

1851 — September — *For Self-Examination*; *Judge for Yourself*.

1854 — December — First article protesting Professor Martensen's canonization of Bishop Mynster, as a "witness for truth."

1855 — May — Beginning *The Moment*, a series of ten pamphlets.

1855 — 11 November — Died at Frederik's Hospital.

1859 — *The Point of View for My Authorship* (written 1848-1849).
1876 — *Judge for Yourselves* (written 1851-1852).
1869-1881 — *From Søren Kierkegaard's Papers*; 8 volumes.
1904 — *My Relationship to Her;* papers concerning the engagement.
1901-1906 — *Samlede Vaerker*, 14 volumes.
1920-1931 — *Samlede Vaerker*, second edition, 15 volumes.
1909-1934 — *Papirer*, 18 volumes.

KIERKEGAARD IN ENGLISH

Selections from the Writings of Kierkegaard, trans. L. M. Hollander, 1923 (University of Texas bulletin 1226). The first English translation of Kierkegaard, but little known. In the foreword to the first edition of the present volume, Swenson's 1936 translation was cited as "first" (p. ix, above), yet an excerpt from Swenson's own review of Hollander appears on pp. 231-33.

Philosophical Fragments, trans. D. F. Swenson, 1936.

Purify Your Hearts, trans. Aldsworth and Ferrie, 1937.

The Journals, selections, trans. A. Dru, 1938.

Purity of Heart, trans. D. V. Steere, 1938.

Christian Discourses, and *The Lilies of the Field and the Birds of the Air,* trans. W. Lowrie, 1939.

The Point of View, Two Notes About the Individual, and *On My Work As an Author,* trans. W. Lowrie, 1939.

Fear and Trembling, trans. R. Payne, 1939; trans. W. Lowrie, 1941.

Stages on Life's Way, trans. W. Lowrie, 1940.

Training in Christianity, An Edifying Discourse, and *Two Discourses at the Communion on Friday,* trans. W. Lowrie, 1940.

For Self-Examination, and *Judge for Yourself,* trans. W. Lowrie, 1940.

For Self-Examination, trans. E. and H. Hong, 1940.

The Present Age, trans. A. Dru and W. Lowrie, 1940.

Concluding Unscientific Postscript, trans. D. F. Swenson and W. Lowrie, 1941.

Three Discourses on Imagined Occasions, trans. D. F. Swenson, 1941.

Either/Or, vol. 1 trans. D. F. and L. M. Swenson, 1941; vol. 2 trans. W. Lowrie, 1944.

Repetition: An Essay in Experimental Psychology, trans. W. Lowrie, 1941.

The Sickness Unto Death, trans. W. Lowrie, 1941.

The Concept of Dread, trans. W. Lowrie, 1944.

The Attack Upon "Christendom", trans. W. Lowrie, 1944.

Works of Love, trans. D. F. Swenson, 1946.

On Authority and Revelation: The Book of Adler, trans. W. Lowrie, 1955.

Kierkegaard's Writings, ed. and trans. H. V. and E. H. Hong, 1978-
   A projected 25-volume scholarly edition of Kierkegaard's works, in process of
   publication by Princeton University Press.

ABOUT KIERKEGAARD

T. J. McCormack's review of H. Höffding's *Sören Kierkegaard als Philosoph*
   (1896 German translation of 1892 Danish original) in *The Monist* 7 (October
   1896): 137. The first-known reference to Kierkegaard in English.
D. F. Swenson, "The Anti-Intellectualism of Kierkegaard," *Philosophical
   Review* (July 1916). Reprinted as ch. 5 in the present volume, the article that
   introduced Kierkegaard to English readers.
E. O. Geismar, *Lectures on the Religious Thought of S. Kierkegaard,* with an
   introduction by Swenson, 1937.
T. Haecker, trans. A. Dru, *Søren Kierkegaard,* 1937.
W. Lowrie, *Kierkegaard,* 1938.
J. Wahl, *Etudes Kierkegaardiennes,* 1938.
D. F. Swenson, *Something About Kierkegaard,* 1941, 1945, 1983.
W. Lowrie, *A Short Life of Kierkegaard,* 1942.
R. Bretall, *A Kierkegaard Anthology,* 1946.
J. Collins, *The Mind of Kierkegaard,* 1953.
W. Hamilton, *The Promise of Kierkegaard,* 1969.
International Kierkegaard Commentary, ed. R. L. Perkins, 1983-
   A projected 25-volume commentary on the works of Kierkegaard, in process
   of publication by Mercer University Press. (Vol. 1, *Two Ages,* 1983.)

INDEX